Imagining Architects

Imagining Architects

Creativity in the Religious Monuments of India

Ajay J. Sinha

Newark: University of Delaware Press
London: Associated University Presses

Associated University Presses
440 Forsgate Drive
Cranbury, NJ 08512

Associated University Presses
16 Barter Street
London WC1A 2AH, England

Associated University Presses
P.O. Box 338, Port Credit
Mississauga, Ontario
Canada L5G 4L8

The paper used in this publication meets the requirements of the American National Standard for Permanence of Paper for Printed Library Materials Z39.48–1984.

Library of Congress Cataloging-in-Publication Data

Sinha, Ajay J., 1956–
Imagining architects : creativity in the religious monuments of India / Ajay J. Sinha.
p. cm.
Includes bibliographical references and index.
ISBN 0-87413-684-9 (alk. paper)
1. Vesara style (Architecture) 2. Architecture, Hindu—India—Karnataka. 3. Temples—India—Karnataka. 4. Creation (Literary, artistic, etc.) I. Title.
NA6007.K27 S56 2000
726'.145'095487—dc21 99-26852
CIP

PRINTED IN THE UNITED STATES OF AMERICA

Contents

List of Figures

Note: Except for map, all figures are from Henry Cousens, *The Chālukyan Architecture of the Kanarese Districts,* Archaeological Survey of India, New Imperial Series, vol. 42, Calcutta, Government of India, Central Publication Branch, 1926.

List of Plates

Note: All photographs are by the author except where they are otherwise indicated.

Preface and Acknowledgments

At UJJINI, A PILGRIMAGE CENTER IN THE SOUTHwestern region of India well known to the local population, a large stone temple built probably in the twelfth century lives today as a shrine to the Hindu god, Shiva (pl. 1). A three-inch layer of oil and soot covers the carvings of the stone, giving evidence of decades or perhaps centuries of active worship at the site. Amidst brightly painted gateways and subshrines, as well as well-kept apartments of the trustees and priests, the blistered, blackened mass of the large shrine has the brooding quality of ancient geological forms or aging banyan trees often seen in the center of village squares, except that Ujjini's visual effect is a result of an ongoing cycle of rituals. The sedimentation not only gives testimony of heavy use, but also effectively contributes to the potency of the sacred site. Erasing evidence that the structure underneath is man-made, the layers of crust, left deliberately to grow, activate the monument as a visible sign of Shiva's mysterious and eternal power manifesting itself at Ujjini.

Research for the book began with an interest in the visual means by which religious structures in India acquire their sacred potency. Its challenge has been to recover that potency in a historical period from which only stone temples remain. Michael Meister has recently written, "In India, an object's aesthetic value is as much a consequence of use and reception as of its making."[1] The study is based on a belief that making and use of monuments are not divorced from each other in India's religious culture as the disciplines of art history and anthropology often seem to make them. Rather, I suggest that the making of shrines in a given historical period absorbs and extends previous use. The book turns its attention from traces of subsequent use at shrines such as Ujjini to a study of the visual means employed in stone temples in the region of Ujjini, the modern state of Karnataka in southern India. These temples were built in the eleventh and twelfth centuries, when Ujjini's original shrine was also created. Ujjini conceals the original stone with a saturated crust. I peel away the layers of subsequent use to analyze a slow sedimentation of day-to-day work on the original stone designs of Karnataka temples.

Meister writes, "[W]e must recognize that use of an object . . . materializes thought."[2] A historical explanation of the relationship between thought and its materialization also requires an explanation of agency. A close look at the design of Karnataka's temples reveals in piecemeal, seemingly idiosyncratic, visual details a systematic synthesis of making and use, leading to the evolution of a new potency for the region's sacred structures. The designers of Karnataka's stone monuments, like the community of users at Ujjini, are anonymous for the most part. In analyzing temples as a slowly accumulating residue of their artistic labor and thought, the book offers a close up of their active and creative role in making monuments whereby they adapt their local architectural tradition to contemporary systems of use and meaning.

The book results from two field trips in Karnataka, first in 1988–89 and then in spring 1997. In these years, it has benefited from the generosity of many institutions and individuals. I thank the American Institute of Indian Studies for granting me a Junior Fellowship for the initial research, which took the shape of a Ph.D. dissertation in the History of Art Department at the University of Pennsylvania in 1993. In spring 1997, a research fellowship from the American Philosophical Soci-

Plate 1. Ujjini, Siddheśvara temple, south, twelfth century

ety as well as a faculty grant from Mount Holyoke College helped me with the work in India necessary for the completion of the book.

I was first inspired to study temples in Karnataka by M. A. Dhaky's ground-breaking book, *Indian Temple Forms in Karṇāṭa Architecture and Inscriptions* (1977). I extend my deepest gratitude to Dhaky for his generosity as the associate director for research at the Center for Art and Archaeology of the American Institute of Indian Studies in Varanasi and thank Geetaben Dhaky for her hospitality at their residence both in Varanasi and Ahmedabad. I thank the Archaeological Survey of India for permission to visit and photograph archaeological sites in Karnataka and the Department of History and Archaeology at Karnatak University, Dharwar, for giving me a regional base for research. In Mysore, I am indebted to Dr. K. V. Ramesh of the Epigraphic Department of the Archaeological Survey of India and Dr. C. S. Patil in the office of the Mysore Archaeological Department. In Dharwar, I thank Professors S. Settar, A. Sundara, and S. Rajasekhar for sharing with me their knowledge of the archaeology of the region. I also thank Dr. Sadaksharayya for letting me use the resources of the Karnatak Research Institute in 1997, B. V. Mallapur for patiently illuminating me on Karnataka's religious traditions, and S. B. Hiremath for translating old Kannaḍa inscriptions for me. In Dharwar, intellectual stimulation also often came from outside the field of art and archaeology. In particular, I fondly remember the challenges of the late K. J. Shah, an intellectual giant who taught philosophy at the university, as well as B. S. Bendigeri, my music guru who often informed me of unknown temple sites and living religious practices.

I am indebted to Michael Meister at Penn for the numerous challenges of studying stones he placed before me in my years as a graduate student. Now, I also thank him for a wonderful, mildly nudging, alert friendship and also for his comments on chapter 7 of the book. I am grateful to Dede Ruggles for reading a draft of chapter 1. I thank Irene Winter, Renata Holod, David Brownlee, and Holly Pittman for their critical comments on a paper I presented at Penn in the initial, and admittedly crude, phase of my work. I am flattered by the generosity of the anonymous reader of my manuscript at the University of Delaware Press. At Penn, I gratefully acknowledge the invaluable resource of the photographic archive for temple sculpture and architecture and also thank the South Asia Regional Studies Department for a unique, interdisciplinary environment from which this study draws its initial conceptual frame. Over the years, Darielle Mason, Katherine Hacker, John Mosteller, Philip Wagoner, Michael Rabe, and Andrew Cohen have shared my enthusiasm for Indian temples. From Dennis Hudson, Richard Davis, and Indira Peterson, I have learned much about the complex religious and aesthetic traditions in India. At Mount Holyoke College, I thank all my colleagues in the Art Department for their support and encouragement; in particular, the book has benefited from discussions with Michael Davis, my medievalist colleague, who offered me a comparative perspective from a Western tradition of religious architecture.

I want to especially acknowledge Gulammohammed Sheikh for letting me use his painting in the book. I also thank Dr. B. N. Goswamy for valuable suggestions on the proposal for the book, as well as an insistence on the Indian artist as a "thinking man," which I have attempted to reflect in my study of Karnataka temples. I am grateful to Dr. Kapila Vatsyayan of the Indira Gandhi National Centre for the Arts in New Delhi, India, for explaining matters pertaining to architecture in religious texts. I also thank Adam Hardy for allowing me to see his dissertation on Karnataka monuments, on which his masterful publication (1995) is based. Ratan Parimoo, Dipak Kannal, and Shivaji Panikkar generously invited me to test my ideas in talks at the College of Fine Arts in Baroda. Gerard Foekema shared his observations on Karnataka temples with me, along with a taxi fare, while traveling together in northern Karnataka in spring 1997. Rajeev Lochan's assistance in developing my photographic films in Delhi was invaluable. Gail Glanville at Mount Holyoke College was most generous in her help with office services.

I warmly acknowledge the many debts of my family, which in India can add up to a whole village. I thank Mati (my mother), my parents-in-law, Bhaisaheb (who read the whole manuscript), Bhabhi, Aruna, Yash, Anup, and Anju, for the direct and indirect ways in which they have supported my project, ranging from a gentle scorn when my writing kept me away from a family event to financial assistance when we needed it the most. Malini has been a valuable companion; I cannot thank her enough for the critical attention with which she read an entire draft of the manuscript. To Kanha, who complained that his dad was "never" around, I can only assure that now I will be. He, Rohit, and Mona also embody the intelligence I envied when I deleted incomprehensible passages from my drafts. Finally, I remember my brother J. P. (1949–1992), whose untimely death when this project was under way leaves me with a sobering lesson that some traces of human struggle are more fragile than what history is capable of retrieving; that lesson has been a guiding metaphor in this book.

Imagining Architects

1
An Architectural Mule

> I believe that my originality (if that is the right word) is an originality belonging to the soil rather than to the seed. (Perhaps I have no seed of my own.) Sow a seed in my soil and it will grow differently than it would in any other soil.
> —Ludwig Wittgenstein, *Culture and Value*.

Term and Form

Artistic terms often have a seductive quality; as condensed verbal equivalents, they seem to hold the key to artistic practice. In the history of Indian art, where so little by way of historical or interpretative record is available to throw light on unfamiliar objects, a temptation to seize terms and to create etymology for them has always existed, also perhaps as a legacy of the Indology of the nineteenth century and its linguistic ways of understanding cultural phenomena.

Vesara is a name commonly used in art historical literature for a group of stone temples built in the eleventh and later centuries in the Karnataka region of southern India. Scholars have generally defined Vesara as a hybrid form of temple architecture created in Karnataka by mixing typical features of South Indian and North Indian forms. This definition of Karnataka monuments is partly influenced by a regional bias and partly by the Sanskrit word, Vesara, found in twelfth-century southern religious texts such as the *Kāmikāgama,* which scholars have usually taken to mean "mule" or "hybrid."[1] The identity of the mixed type hardens through a discursive practice.[2] Vesara emerged in the eleventh century and distinguished Karnataka and neighboring regions of greater South India for more than two hundred years. Some scholars have described Vesara's hybridization as the natural result of Karnataka's location, sandwiched geographically between North and South India.[3] Others have taken Vesara's intermediary place to mean its derivative status within a modern system of classifying Indian temples, at least once arguing for the removal of Vesara from the historical narrative altogether on that basis.[4] The linguistic term, Vesara, thus has proved to be what E. H. Gombrich in a different context has called a critic's "term of exclusion," producing historical interpretations to establish the marginality of Karnataka within a framework of geographical determinism.[5]

The history of Vesara architecture proves to be far more complex than the distinctions between pure and hybrid styles in current scholarly literature allows. In particular, Karnataka shows a wide variety of unusual architectural experiments in the eleventh century, which are puzzling because they are all concentrated in a relatively small area north of the river Tuṅgabhadrā (fig. 1). Because current definitions of Vesara do not reflect the complexity of these monuments, I have reversed the direction of interpretation, beginning with the monuments themselves. The question of defining Vesara architecture has been treated in this book as a problem of negotiating the process by which these monuments were made. The analysis emphasizes the role of the makers and their perception about their architectural innovations as far as they can be demonstrated in the archaeological and epigraphic evidence available from this period. For, whether or not these eleventh-century architects called their creation Vesara, their experiments reflect an evolving self-consciousness

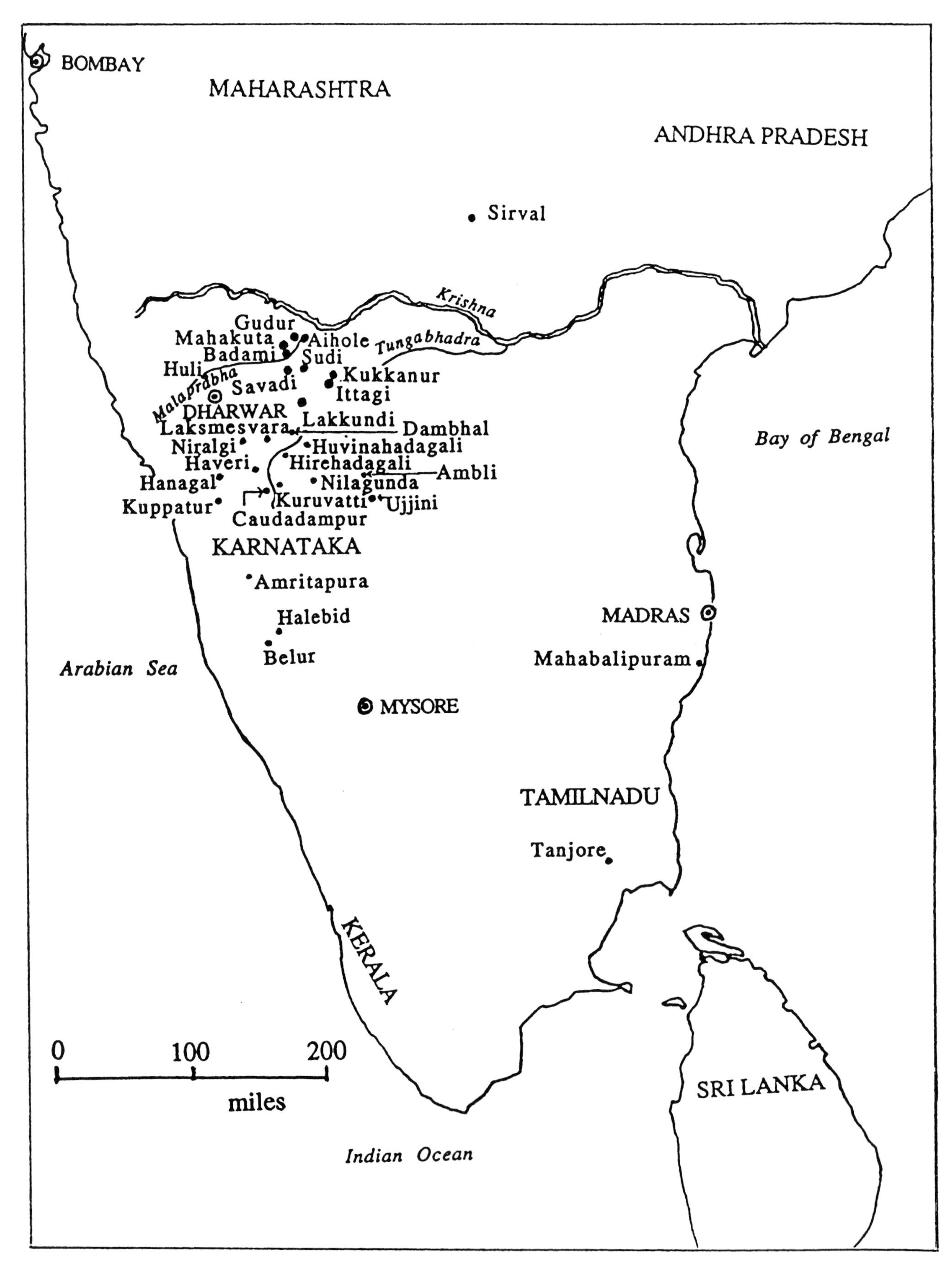

Figure 1. Map of southern India showing Vesara sites in Karnataka

about a distinctive temple form in the region. Perhaps the Kāmikāgama, the ritual text that first used Vesara to suggest a hybrid style of architecture, records a twelfth-century viewer's perception of this new form. Unfortunately, neither the text nor the term sufficiently explains the diversity and intent of the monuments.

It is not known whether the architects who designed temples in eleventh-century Karnataka would have called their design Vesara.[6] But the term also cannot be dismissed as purely a construct of modern scholars since it is used in religious texts of southern India at least since the twelfth century; Vesara is also mentioned in stone inscriptions connected with monuments belonging to the twelfth century. Assured of its validity in these—even if somewhat later—sources, the book uses the term to underscore the architectural experiments of the eleventh century that led eventually to the new regional form, whatever their makers would have called Vesara in its formative period. But in turning from the text and the term to the makers and their making, the book's primary aim is to explore the nature of architectural innovation, which has not been adequately studied in traditional accounts of India's religious art and architecture.

Beyond the terminological issue, current scholarly explanations of Vesara architecture revolve primarily around questions of its stylistic definition and developments. James Fergusson, a pioneer of Indian temple architecture in the nineteenth century, grouped Vesara monuments under "Chālukyan style," giving them the name of a major dynasty of Karnataka.[7] For Fergusson, Chālukyan represented one of the "three styles into which Hindu architecture naturally divides itself."[8] Henry Cousens, the archaeologist who published the first monographic report on Karnataka monuments, traced the history of Vesara within a development of South Indian temples, extending and modifying Fergusson's stylistic framework. He described Vesara primarily as "an outgrowth" of the South Indian temple style called Dravidian, reflected in Vesara temples by a tower having a stack of horizontal stories above the shrine wall. Cousens downplayed Vesara's hybridity as an occasional tendency to mix North Indian features, which he only explained as an aberration and an excess resulting from Vesara's prolongation of the southern tradition.[9] Cousens's characterization of Vesara as an overgrown southern form has been passed on through survey books.[10]

Historical explanation often depends on a historian's vision of how things are or should be, even if the written narrative itself is a combination of objective reasoning and observation.[11] My criticism of Vesara's current explanations, thus, is not that they lack empirical observation but that Vesara is too diverse to be explained within an essentializing linearity and uniformity of such approaches. Vesara critiques the modern systems of stylistic classification that have tended to reflect the history and regional distribution of Indian temple architecture in images of biological mutation, implied here in words such as "hybrid" and "outgrowth." If one does seek the natural world for analogy, perhaps an image of forest with a confusing array of trees, plants, and underbrush may be more appropriate for Vesara's history than the cellular growth of a single organism.[12] Wittgenstein's aphorism about "originality belonging to the soil" quoted in the beginning of the chapter guides my study of Vesara, shifting attention from notions of internal growth to a reflection on the conditions in which Vesara architecture might have developed, adding to this geographical and ecological image the particular history of Vesara architecture, in which the chief agents are its makers.

My argument fundamentally is that Vesara cannot be recorded as if it were a fossil of a natural object available to be typologized, compared, and analyzed within pre-existing scientific patterns. I am uneasy with these methods that examine material culture in a way that separates it from the particular conditions of its human makers.[13] The biological metaphor has been handy so far because the makers of much of ancient Indian art, including Vesara architecture, have been anonymous. But a close examination of Vesara temples in the eleventh century demonstrates a deliberate attempt on the part of their makers to modify regional traditions.[14] Geographically close to each other, these temples are so diverse in their design that we must posit the intervention of their designers, drawing upon local traditions and yet creating works that cannot be fully predicted by previous monuments in those traditions. To explain the diversity of these monuments and the intentions behind them has been the particular challenge of this book.

In a 1977 monographic study, M. A. Dhaky, a major scholar of Indian temple architecture, grappled with the issue of Vesara's classification.[15] He examined the current perceptions of Vesara architecture against one that the Karnataka architects themselves might have had of it, analyzing two rare stone inscriptions, some South and North Indian ritual texts on architectural styles, as well as various forms of miniature shrine models carved on the walls of these Karnataka temples. The enormous value of this study is that it provided ground for a basic methodological shift: instead of treating Vesara architecture from the perspective of style—as art historians generally do—he proposed to look at it as a production dependent on the knowledge and perception of its makers. Dhaky showed convincingly that Karnataka architects created Vesara as their own indigenous temple form and that they consciously distinguished it from other regional temple forms in India. Observing miniature models of Vesara on temples, he concluded that although Vesara was based on the typical southern temple form called Drāviḍa, it was no longer Drāviḍa in the sense that earlier buildings were. Responding to the scholarly notion of Vesara as a mixture of South Indian and North Indian architecture, he also pointed that there was in Vesara only "a vague similarity, a faint but unmistakable flavour that distantly remind[ed] one of Nāgara (the typical North Indian temple form)," but that there was nothing in it that could be directly called "a genuine and typical Nāgara" feature.[16] Dhaky's analysis substantially modifies the traditional explanation of Vesara as a stylistic mixture.

Dhaky's observation that the architects distinguished Vesara as their own morphological temple type is especially important because it calls into question the notion of Vesara as a mixture of Nāgara and Drāviḍa architecture. The two temple forms, Nāgara and Drāviḍa, are easily distinguished by towers above their sanctum. A Drāviḍa temple's tower appears like a stack of distinct, horizontal stories leading the viewer's eye up to a cupola, which is usually square, octagonal or circular (pl. 5). A Nāgara temple's tower is integrated by an arrangement of webbed, vertical bands curving up to a finial marked by a flat, circular, ribbed stone called *āmalaka* (pl. 4). All Vesara temples maintain a Drāviḍa profile. A vertical chain of pediments created in the center of each face of their tower, however, suggests a "vague similarity" (Dhaky's phrase) with the webbed band of a Nāgara temple, assuring scholars of Vesara's tendency to mix up forms (pl. 36). I am driven by Dhaky's tentativeness about this mixture to argue against the merely formal explanation of Vesara in current scholarship. In particular, Dhaky's observation implies that architects who distinguished between regional architectural types in the eleventh century also made a distinction between their own temples and the typical southern form, namely Drāviḍa, that had prevailed in the Karnataka region previously. In defining the scope of their new regional form, thus, they had also broken away from the premise of southern architecture to which they had belonged. A detailed documentation of the formal shifts in the eleventh century will demonstrate a far more complex, conceptual change within the framework of the region's sacred structures.

The history of Vesara architecture must be related to a break in the chronology of previous Drāviḍa architecture of Karnataka. While it would be incorrect to argue that Vesara architecture developed in the eleventh century on entirely new grounds, in an isolationist way, it is also wrong to explain the evolution of monuments in Karnataka as a smooth, systematic flow of forms and ideas, as scholars since Cousens have tended to do. Piecemeal innovations in a wide range of temples show a rupture in the tradition of southern forms these architects had inherited, as well as the creation of a new conceptual logic within the formal means of Drāviḍa architecture. Drāviḍa architecture was by no means static, but its evolution only partly explains the formal inventions of Vesara temples. I have described the chronology of Vesara architecture partly as the serialization of its difference from Drāviḍa.

The book was initially titled "the Originality of a Hybrid," intending to focus on these discontinuities in Karnataka, and to examine the manipulation of available regional forms and ideas by Vesara architects. It continues to question the prevailing theses of a formal continuity between Drāviḍa and Vesara as well as Vesara's definition as a mixed style, and pushes beyond the description and documentation of these monuments within those frameworks. The question of originality becomes important in the context of the traditional definition of Vesara as a derivative architecture, which many studies have assumed as their natural framework. This assumption and an uncritical documentation of monuments perpetuate each other. If Vesara is derivative, it might seem that it is only necessary to document its excesses and ramifications, or ways that it derives or indulges in technical or artistic elaboration. And in any case, the fundamental question of what Vesara does that is different and separate from anything attempted before or in other regions, and why, is quickly inundated by descriptive information.[17] From the vast variety of temples in the region of northern Karnataka, I have isolated monuments that help me focus on the question of Vesara's originality, and have tried to avoid the equally valid task of being comprehensive.

Approach

The history of Vesara monuments is discontinuous and devious. Some aspects of its movements are clear, others are not. Thus challenged, my approach to Vesara architecture has been conceptually archaeological; I have collected and pieced together fragments of ideas and visual details available from Karnataka and explained Vesara's coherence in a way that is reasonably defendable and certainly open to test.

The origins of Vesara architecture in Karnataka are multiple and cumulative, for its break with the Drāvida tradition did not occur at an instant. Early evidence of the rupture is located in small, usually overlooked, tenth-century temples at Aihole, a temple site in northern Karnataka otherwise well known for seventh and eighth century monuments. Bold experiments and breakthroughs in the eleventh century suggest a departure from Drāviḍa and an exploration of new, foreign ideas, making the question of Vesara's origins a complex one. It might be more appropriate to speak of Vesara's originations rather than origins, shifting the emphasis from a fixed point of beginning to the process of emerging, in which many different monuments demonstrate self-conscious questioning and creative efforts at formulating a new architecture. The unsteady process of formation continued at least for the major part of the eleventh century and is typified by the monuments discussed in chapters 4 and 5. The chronology of events maintained here is an essential part of my argument, distinguishing Vesara's origination in this century from the evolutionary scheme imposed on it by previous scholars.

My view of Vesara's history shares with many areas of recent art history a rejection of monolithic time and its presumed arrowlike progression.[18] I have also borrowed for my analysis from the French historian Fernand Braudel, for whom history is composed of layered time spans.[19] Braudel proposes a model of two simultaneous and interacting maps on which to plot the layers of time: one small and local, the other big and regional. The local map records the routines of individuals within close-knit communities, busy with issues of their day-to-day survival; the other defines a region in which structural changes are recorded that might affect the microscopic events of daily life.[20] For my purpose, the local map can constitute the ongoing acts of planning and plotting temples at a particular sacred site, town, or city, or the tracing and carving of details on stone blocks that a craftsperson may have learned to repeat from a teacher or within a guild, occasionally playing with new details or picking up ideas from a neighbor.[21] The other map connects those artistic localities and includes them in a wider sphere of interaction. This map might be invisible to the individual makers of temples, but the changes in its boundaries—perhaps because of political circumstances and exchange of ideas with other contiguous regions—affect their small, daily routine. Braudel's "spatial" model to characterize historical time is useful in describing Vesara architecture in the eleventh century as a dialectic of individual activities at various artistic centers and the regional framework of Karnataka.[22]

However, Braudel's model stands on its head in Indian art history. Braudel urges historians of Europe to study human history in terms of the slow tempos and cyclical movements of geographical and cultural factors as opposed to the attraction of short time spans and dramatic events dominating history writing of his day. But time spans in premodern India, especially as they pertain to religious art and architecture, are already so long that scholars tend to write history mostly in terms of a relatively unchanging regional matrix. Unlike the rush of revolutions in Western history to which Braudel refers, the story of Indian art has been traditionally written by scholars in terms of political dynasties that majestically come and slowly decline in various parts of India; this framework is refined recently only to emphasize the geographical base of artistic traditions.[23] Historians of Indian art are accustomed to the seemingly changeless, repetitious nature of India's religious art also because of an assumption about the conservative nature of the religions that India's temples serve. What is needed in India, then, is a sharp focus on events in which human participants become visible.[24]

I have developed a Braudelian chronology of Vesara's formation that makes their human makers visible. The chronology is based on an analysis of material facts such as ornamental motifs and profiles of architectural features, in which there is discerned a pattern of structural changes. These facts relate to aspects of craftsmanship and could be conceived as the routine of a collective group of workers. Some of these could be considered subconscious elements that did not require thought on the part of the makers; they are, however, the raw stuff of my analysis, belonging to the duration of an art historical period, which can be arranged into meaningful sequences or patterns of "time."[25]

In chapter 5, I specifically propose individuality and anomaly, usually overlooked by scholars of Indian art, as concepts that define the small map in Braudel's scheme. My characterization of "individuality," not to be confused with the modern Western myth of individualism, allows Vesara's history to be defined as a dialectic of individual acts of making. In chapter 6, Braudel interplays with models available in art history for understanding regional styles, substyles, local styles, and artistic idiom.[26] I portray Vesara as a complex, multilayered region, based on a sense of its own networks of architectural practice by ca. A.D. 1100 rather than as what had become traditionally an intellectual periphery of North and South India. My effort ultimately is to explain Vesara architecture in terms of the thinking and action of people who not only seemed to have worked under constraints but also controlled a body of regional knowledge, played intelligent games, and amazed people while negotiating formal problems in the buildings they designed to fulfill the community's religious needs.

The procedure of creating a chronology to capture the intellectual practice embodied in the material facts, leads me to reflect upon, first, the art historical production of chronology and, second, its function in an art historical inquiry. In this study of Vesara architecture, chronology is a net created out of two aspects, the absolute and the relative, the former producing a fixed time line dotted with monuments and the latter as an approximate line depending on an analysis of commonalities and differences between a close group of monuments. In the history of Indian art, fixed points, confirmed by other documentary evidence, are few. The relative chronology, on the other hand, is more precisely a field (as in magnetic field) rather than a time line, in which the net's span is largely created in relation to a few dated monuments. I have used this net strategically, intending to capture a certain ideology that may have distinguished Vesara architecture. I use the word "ideology" as a structure of values and interests that informs Vesara's representation of ideas and forms, and gives a critical edge to its procedure of absorption of ideas from outside. The pattern of absorption and use of ideas and forms of both Nāgara and Drāviḍa in Vesara, explains what become distinguishing intellectual characteristics of Vesara.[27] The relative chronology of monuments at Aihole, not the absolute dating of any monument in particular, emphasizes the initial ferment of ideas toward Vesara architecture and the ongoing experiments with North Indian ideas at that site. On the other hand, it is important to point out the contemporaneity of the two sides of a twin temple at Lakkuṇḍi (Kāśīviśveśvara and Sūrya) as well as the Yallamā temple at Badāmī—three important but remarkably different Vesara designs—in order to highlight the degree to which architects created contrasting points and counterpoints within Vesara in the same period.

In an area such as that of ancient Indian art, where so little archival record other than the monuments themselves is available, semiotics can be a useful way of analyzing the intellectual characteristics embodied by visual evidence. But semiotics is a problematic approach; it can be like clay in a sculptor's hand, taking shape and impressions only from the sculptor. In this study, semiotics serves as an interpretative tool for historical explanation, not the substance of which cultural reality is shaped.[28] It is applied to visual evidence as an aspect of formal analysis, differing from its emphasis in recent art history to formulate what one scholar has called a "radically reception-oriented approach."[29] Such an approach uses semiotics to instigate within interpretation what the scholar calls a "burst of speculative fertility," so that scholarship could arrange history as a complex of our own contemporary critical concerns. Such a creative burst, useful in exploding traditional art historical positions from the vantage point of our current intellectual climate, also overlooks that the history's subject may exist in a context other than ours. In my field of Indian art, one is cautioned against the capacity of semiotics to radicalize reception. The past of non-Western cultures such as India cannot be figured by semiotic extensions of Western subjectivities.[30] A burst of our speculative fertility in a study of Indian art could well mean appropriating it within the mythology of our interests and preoccupations.[31] This book will restrain from such a claim, using semiotics only to probe for evidence about the intellectual process embedded in these Karnataka temples.

One could argue of course that evidence is

nothing but a selection of facts that make a persuasive argument, and that the selection as well as the argument will only depend on the nature of questions the historian asks.[32] This might be true, but evidence is not arbitrary. While our intellectual horizons might be broader today and our questions sharpened by the current critical climate, not all questions are possible or can amount to an argument in a given field of research. My point therefore is that the analytical material governs the argument, not the other way around, and historical explanation is not simply a matter of the fecundity of our scholarly minds but the challenge of envisioning a possible reality to which the evidence from the past belongs.

Agency and Intentionality

A parallel case will help the book's guiding question in relation to Vesara: it is a painting whose metaphor substitutes the biological metaphor dominating so much of the writing of the history of Indian art. The 1981 painting, entitled "Revolving Routes," is by the contemporary Indian artist Gulammohammed Sheikh (pl. 2). It shows myriad, minutely detailed images juxtaposed against each other as if the canvas were not painted in oil but an appliqué fitted with small pieces of mirrors similar to folk fabric commonly made in Western India. The interconnected details, referring to the artist's personal life as well as the world of art, virtually obscure a tiny figure of the painter sitting in the center. The images surrounding the self-portrait range from references to the artist's childhood in a small Indian town in Gujarat, Western India, (in the upper left) to Rodin's *Thinker* in the bottom of a funnel-shaped enclosure on the lower right. Above Rodin, a painting by the French painter Balthus, titled *The Room,* showing a dwarf exposing a nude girl to the daylight flooding into the room, suggests at one level the artist's own creative purpose of revealing, while at another strikes an irony typical of modern life in India; the Balthus is part of a slide lecture given by an English art critic to a group of Indian students who may not have seen, or might never see, the real thing.

In the complicated additive structure of the canvas, then, the artist has captured a world of splintering diversity within which he suspends himself, like a spider in its web. A hunchbacked madman mimicking the posture in Rodin's sculpture and looking out from the middle of a world made of shifting focus and colliding perspectives, he gives the painting its many visual routes, its color and coherence. The point of this twentieth-century painting seems to be that the artist's process of defining his intrinsic being is inextricably linked with the process of knowing the outside world, here depicted in an interpenetrating, loosely connected, ironic pattern of heterogeneous visual fragments.[33]

The irony of twentieth-century India may not pertain to Vesara, although eleventh-century Karnataka may not be so different from twentieth-century India as it might at first seem. In each, heterogeneous cultural forces need to be meaningfully synthesized. Only the specific condition of the two contexts varies: Sheikh's painting draws its irony from the Third World, emerging from British colonization in the nineteenth century as well as globalization of culture, economy, and technologies in the twentieth; eleventh-century Karnataka expresses the hybridity of its geographical location. In an inscription from the Kotiśvara temple at Kuppatur, Karnataka offers a self-portrait parallel to the hunchbacked visionary of Sheikh's twentieth-century painting. The temple's architect boasts of being divine by claiming knowledge of architectural forms from different regions of India. The passage, in English, reads:

> (Within this village of Kuppatur) was built, as if by Viśvakarman himself, out of sublime devotion for the Lord of the Kailāsa mountain, the elegant, equipoise and shapely temple of Kotīśa-Bhava, freely ornamented with Drāviḍa, Bhūmija and Nāgara, and, with *bhadra* offsets manipulated in many ways.[34]

The proclamation that the maker of this temple is virtually the divine architect, Viśvakarman, is stereotypical, as is also the image of an artist as a mad visionary in the twentieth century. While Sheikh's refractive details lead to their idiosyncratic organizer in the center of the oil painting, the boast of the divine architect relates to his control of a variegated architectural tradition. It is significant that in both these cases, the identity of the makers is directly connected with knowing and responding to a world outside their individual selves, unlike the modernist stereotype of an introverted, alienated genius.

In Vesara architecture, the absorption and depiction of forms from regions other than its own is a conscious theme. The role of the architects, as they absorb and intensify the peculiarity of the region and explore new possibilities in them, has to combine in an account of Vesara's distinctive-

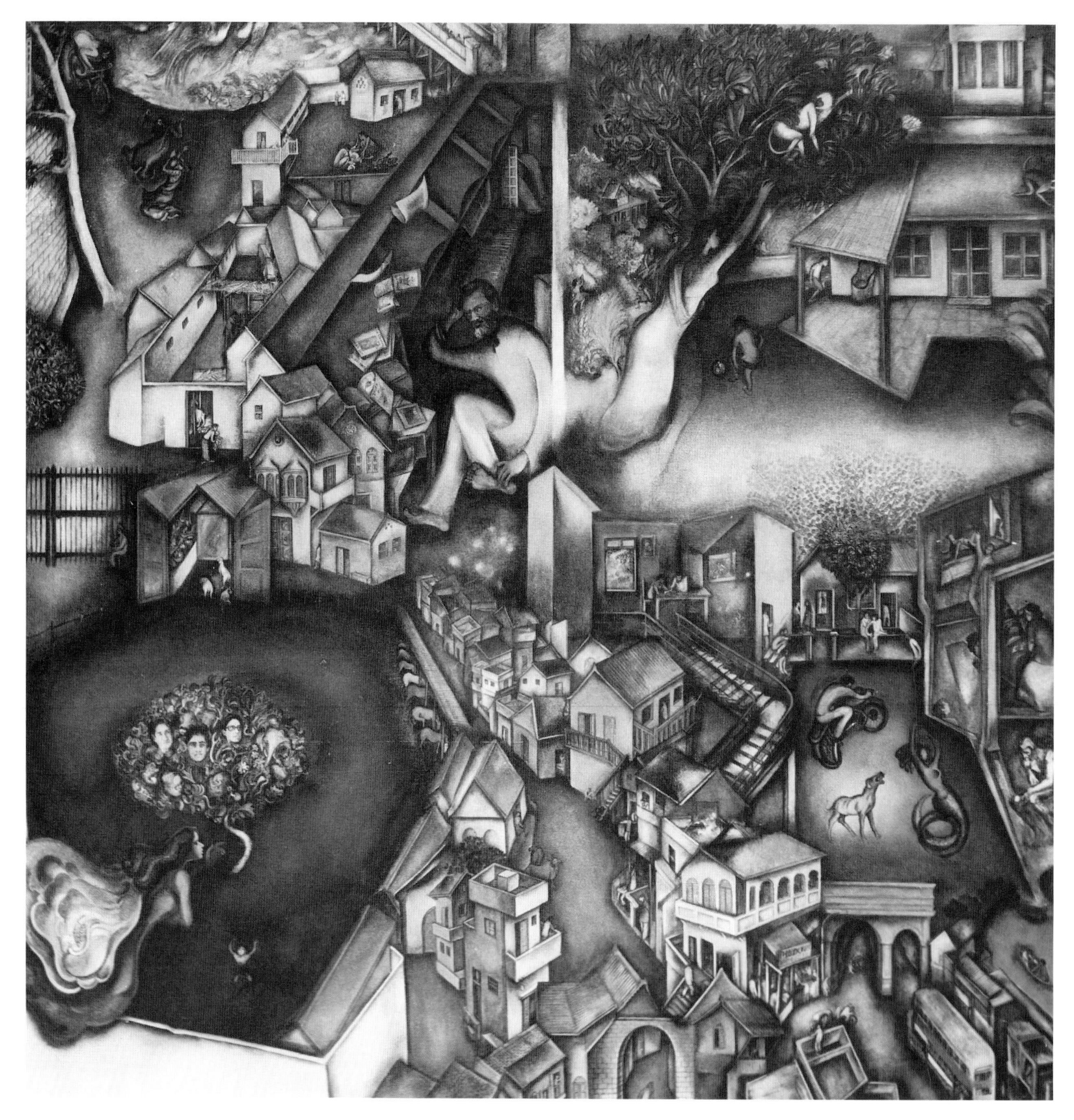

Plate 2. Gulammohammed Sheikh, *Revolving Routes,* 1981, Rupankar Museum of Fine Arts, Bhopal, India (photograph courtesy: Gulammohammed Sheikh)

ness, however limited our understanding of the region or vague our sociological knowledge about architects, craftsmen, and their guild may be when we speak of this, or any, pre-Industrial period in India. Vesara has been defined as a hybrid style, but the metaphor of Sheikh's painting presses us to ask what it might have meant for the architects to create a hybrid form. In doing so, I extend Dhaky's framework for understanding the architects' own knowledge of temple forms, discussed above, into the area of their agency and intentionality in shaping Vesara's history.

This emphasis on the artist, when applied to Indian temple architecture, may seem to suffer a modernist bias. However, introducing individuals as agents in cultural transformation does not necessarily mean an imposition of a Western, modernist concept of the individual genius. Rather, the latter notion is one culture-specific variety that need not preclude that ideas are constantly given shape and transformed by an individual agency. Nor is the individual an impediment to a study of Indian culture or society, as structuralists argue.[35] The focus of my study is the individual monuments seen as records of thoughtful acts by architects. The meaning of these acts is studied by means of an interaction between a specific body of material and structurally explainable ideas. This book's contention is that buildings are created only when those broad ideas are mediated by architects.

In emphasizing architects, I do not aim to invoke the subjective creative will or to argue for any form of Western individualism among Vesara architects, but rather to point out that a living relationship exists between the makers and their monuments. By "living," I mean that architects negotiate architectural traditions as well as religious ideas in the act of creating the formal details of their monuments. Even though the workings of the mind of the architects cannot be known, one can see their decisions reflected in Karnataka monuments. The makers of Vesara temples are anonymous, as is generally the case in ancient Indian art, so that there is almost no information about the decision-making process. Anonymity, however, cannot be taken to mean a lack of initiative, as scholars tend to think. The word "architect" in this book suggests an agency or even loosely a certain mentality that has given monuments their visual definition. The book argues for inclusion of the role of the makers in a historical explanation of these Karnataka monuments.

Eleventh-century Karnataka monuments demand to be understood as a part of the architects' process of seeing and knowing, and a sense of their self that emerges as a result, to which a few inscriptions also refer. A stone inscription dated ca. A.D.1060 in a twin temple, the Joḍa Kalaśa, at Suḍī identifies the architect who made one of its two sides. Expressing amazement at his creation, the inscription refers to the architect as an expert (Vācaspati or a master of speech) in punning (Vakrokti or deviant utterances).[36] The shrine to which the inscription refers shows a daring manipulation of southern form, a North Indian formula for its ground plan never seen in all of South India before, as well as a range of northern and southern shrine models as wall decorations (which I analyze in detail in chapter 4). Correlating archaeological and epigraphic records, rare as they might be, provides important clues to an aesthetic awareness emerging within a literate intellectual climate of cities in eleventh-century Karnataka, in which architects might have functioned as professionals.[37] The mind-set of a *nāgarika,* or a city dweller, in ancient India such as this Vesara architect seems to be, has not gained nearly as much attention in historical scholarship as urban form and the political and sociological aspects of Indian urbanism.[38] The book attempts to describe Vesara temples as a prominent record of such a mind-set in ancient India.

In characterizing Vesara's visual form as a reflection of a mentality, I also introduce issues of intention and critical purpose in the history of sacred architecture in India. The word "intention" here does not suggest a specific plan that Vesara architects consciously articulated in their mind or a project they might have set out to accomplish, rather it means a certain bend of their mind, or a course their minds took in a process of self-definition and definition of the world.[39] Sheikh's painting is useful in the way it articulates the artist's subjectivity as a two-way process of interaction between oneself and the outside world. In invoking the thinking mind, however, I do not aim to discover the subjectivity of these urban designers of Vesara and to conjure up their architectural experience, to which I have no access. My ultimate aim in posing intention is to view temple architecture as concrete, articulate things mediating the makers and their world, whose history must be told objectively, that is without tracing it unilaterally back either to the mind of those makers or to the world.[40] I may thus flip the coin of intentionality on its other side and suggest, as Michael Baxandall has explained, that "intention is the forward-leaning look of things."[41] This definition is particularly useful in Indian art because it addresses thinking as an ostensive feature of the works of art themselves, avoiding the problematic and, from the point of view of ancient Indian architects, irrelevant issue of psychological motivation. Here also the metaphor of Gulam Sheikh's painting must yield. The artist as the eye of the painting is interesting to me only in as much as it constitutes part of the painting and its circumstance. Alerting us to the agency and its cognitive practices, I will treat the intentionality of Vesara as a set of relations articulated by architecture itself.

Reflective Value in Vesara

I have emphasized architectural practice in the book against the presumed authority of sacred texts on religious structures and also the purely positivist definitions of architectural styles handed down to us in a scholarly tradition. In alluding to the architect's use of different regional forms, the Kuppatur inscription mentioned above hints at the nature of this practice in Karnataka and the role that the Karnataka architects might have played in the creation of their own regional type. While the twentieth century offers a useful analogy to address the issue of agency, it does not offer the archaeological model needed to explain the participation of this agency in the changes that led to Vesara architecture. To analyze the relationship between agency and change, I have adapted a formulation of Oleg Grabar from the Islamic context. In discussing "Islamic" as a category used for artifacts from the large and diverse Islamic world, Grabar argued that defining Islamic art in those different regions where the faith spread is not simply a matter of formally comparing their earlier, or non-Islamic, forms to those made there after the spread because the visual difference between the two is negligible given that the makers of goods in the two periods remain more or less the same. The formation of Islamic art, thus, becomes an issue of "Islamicization" of older regional traditions, which, for Grabar, has to include the new Muslim beholder that gives the artifacts already familiar in a given region now a different "sense." Islamicization is "finally a matter of defining a mind, an attitude toward the arts, a psychological motivation, and an intellectual understanding" that ultimately created within the matrix of their arts a new typology of forms.[42] Using Grabar's approach, the book explains Vesara architecture as a function of Vesarization of earlier regional architecture, which it otherwise closely resembles.

Grabar's idea of creative beholding is useful in the Indian context for understanding Vesara, for it helps us steer away from the notion of Vesara architecture as a mixture of extrinsic forms such as the Nāgara and the Drāviḍa, and gives Vesara's absorption of those forms a certain "reflective" value.[43] Dhaky's monograph also gives us some ground to think of Vesara architecture from the point of view of the reception and perception of architects. In his own explanation of Vesara, however, Dhaky seemed to ignore the responsiveness of these architects. In seeking to capture the "unmistakable flavour" of Vesara, he resorted to categories already established by earlier scholars:

> The totality of form here in Karṇāṭa has been arrested, in terms of evolution, between the late Dravidian and the proto-Nāgara; it could not move to Nāgara because it failed to wholly repeat the process which created the true Nāgara form; it lacked some of the basic elements and impulses needed for the Nāgara formulation and could not at the same time unburden those very Dravidian that were not needed for Nāgara formal organization.

From its limbo between North Indian and South Indian forms, then, Vesara achieves a strident self-confidence in the following rhetorical way:

> Did (Vesara) ever want to be Nāgara? Honestly no. The development guided by the potential and the intrinsic character of the Karṇāṭa-Drāviḍa form, as it came rushing out of the first millennium, became faster and faster till at last the building began to 'spin' (on a stellate plan) as in some Hoysala buildings. Its gene characters—exuberance and love for metallic ornateness, which neither satisfied ideal nor kind and quality—were then compelled to create its own personality, a separate reality, which is somewhat intermediate between the two, namely Nāgara and Drāviḍa, but also individualistic. It is only in this way it can be sensed and hence termed Vesara.[44]

I quote Dhaky in detail because he has synthesized many of the concerns of a long tradition of scholarship on Vesara and given it a succinct expression. Dhaky's explanation of Vesara as architecture arrested in its evolution toward a Nāgara logic is a variation of the traditional definition of Vesara as an architectural hybrid. On the other hand, his comment on Vesara's individuality relates to Cousens's characterization of the "Chālukyan" style, whereby exuberant ornamentation and the stellate plan combined to create Vesara's distinguishing qualities, although Dhaky's discussion is certainly more nuanced with textual sources than Cousens's. Dhaky also makes the ornamental emphasis and the rotating plan more than Vesara's stylistic characteristics; midway to Nāgara, these two characteristics become rhetorically charged and pull Vesara away from both Nāgara as well as Drāviḍa architecture. It is as if Dhaky perceived the dynamism of a stellate plan and the tendency toward ornamentation as Vesara's very own *prakrti* and *puruṣa*, the active and passive energies in Indian cosmogony, producing its distinctive morphology.

Instead of describing Vesara as a process of organic growth and mutation, I use Grabar's model of the creator-beholder to suggest that the presence of Nāgara in Vesara architecture is a matter of architect's choice. I do not use the presence of Nāgara as evidence of the architects' desire to replicate the North Indian form, resulting thereby into a hybrid overlaid by a decorative surface and spun by a rotating plan. Instead, I analyze the transformation of Nāgara itself within a Vesara context, that is, in terms of the receiving soil, to use Wittgenstein's idea of originality quoted in the beginning.

Chapters 4 and 5 discuss tangible evidence of Vesara architects' gesture of "beholding" North Indian temple, from the appearance of a North Indian motif early in the eleventh century to a reflection of a northern architectural logic and aesthetics by the middle of the century. With reference to the use of Drāviḍa forms in Vesara, I argue that the creator-beholder's mind-set in the eleventh century is also not the same as a century before. My point about "reception" of Drāviḍa in a Vesara context is different from attempts to look merely for formal continuities of Drāviḍa in Vesara architecture. Although Vesara architecture visibly continues the Drāviḍa mode of using stories for its pyramidal superstructure, they are manipulated in quite a different way and with a purpose that is not articulated in Drāviḍa architecture. This point will be especially made in my discussion of the Yallamā temple at Badāmī in chapter 5.

The Modality of Vesara

In Vesara architecture, although Nāgara as well as Drāviḍa are active and crucial presences, Vesara architects hardly seem to have been interested in blending and synthesizing the two. They seem to have regarded them as simultaneous morphological references in the signification of a Vesara ideology. Nāgara and Drāviḍa are present in Vesara architecture as (1) models, (2) morphologies, (3) ideologies, and (4) aesthetics. Rather than their synthesis, it is the continuing separate "function" of these two formal systems in Vesara that I find intriguing. The purpose to which Vesara architects put Nāgara and Drāviḍa references is a crucial question in recognizing Vesara architecture as a new regional type. Throughout, the book argues that Vesara architecture cannot be adequately understood either as a flourishing of Drāviḍa form or as a synthesis of northern and southern features, as our current language of visual style limits us to propose. To analyze the passage Vesara took in order to reach the new formulation by the end of the eleventh century, the concept of visual style, defined as a uniform set of visual properties shared by different monuments, is inadequate.[45] Instead, the development of Vesara architecture in Karnataka can be understood most fruitfully as a regional modality of responding to the architectural world of the eleventh century.

In Indian architecture, mode has been defined by Michael Meister as morphological consistencies that distinguish one type of structure from another.[46] I have applied this definition to characterize Vesara as a mode distinct from Drāviḍa. But modes in Meister's thinking are contemporary and interchangeable, distinct only because of other variables, for instance regions where they prevail or their social and religious function.[47] Vesara and Drāviḍa are not interchangeable in this way. Vesara distinguishes itself from Drāviḍa architecture of Karnataka as part of a historical process, for which these definitions of mode and type are only partly useful.[48] The change from an old, Drāviḍa typology to Vesara architecture in Karnataka is fundamentally a change in the "sense" (Grabar's word) given to the traditional vocabulary in the eleventh century, which has to be explained historically, not merely typologically.

To explain the history of the new meaning that Vesara architects bring to traditional forms, more useful has been Svetlana Alper's characterization of mode, which differs from Meister's. Alpers defines "mode" as a work of art's peculiar way of existing as a "mediation between the maker and his world."[49] It implies the maker's response to the surrounding world, conveyed into the visual characteristics of the works of art themselves. Using modality, I suggest that Vesara is a question of defining the difference in response of the eleventh-century makers to the typical forms of South Indian architecture they reproduce. The change in approach to southern forms is demonstrated in significant formal changes in the temple architecture of eleventh-century Karnataka.

Vesara evolved as an architectural modality by

which its makers problematized Drāviḍa's rationale of a multistoried shelter for the divine image, resulting in a range of new conceptual nuances within Drāviḍa's standard "sheltering" form. Emerging from a Drāviḍa base, this Vesara modality is also partly inspired by a North Indian, Nāgara ideology. This ideology is self-consciously and creatively used in Vesara architecture throughout the eleventh century, giving a range of elusive and unusual aspects to monuments that challenge the oversimplified conception of Vesara as an intermediate style between North Indian and South Indian architecture.

A discussion of Vesara must necessarily begin with a critique of regional theories in which so much of its historical complexity is lost. Chapter 2 offers a way in which the Vesara region can be visualized, using models from geographers and anthropologists to refute regional determinism. Chapter 3 begins the historical account of Vesara by locating tenth-century Drāviḍa temples in Karnataka that drift from Drāviḍa's conceptual logic. Chapter 4 defines the emergence of Vesara's architectural morphology by the mid-eleventh century and identifies the first Vesara temples to be built in Karnataka. This and chapter 5 emphasize the deviant nature of Vesara's chronology, analyzing the self-consciousness of the architects in creating so many anomalies and conceited, individual expressions. By the end of the century, Vesara's morphology becomes a new regional norm. Chapter 6 describes the geography of Vesara architecture from the point of view of its makers, analyzing idioms and local styles that create a network of exchange and interaction in Karnataka by ca. A.D. 1100. The intricacy of this artistic geography also contributes to the regional theory addressed in chapter 2. Chapter 7 reviews Vesara's morphology and proposes that architects, in creating the new regional type, looked radically at the meaning of sacred architecture, replacing figurative sculpture with shrine models on iconographically strategic places on the walls, and combining a Nāgara logic with Drāviḍa forms not only to re-create Drāviḍa but also to provide an expressive format for such wall shrines. The radical emphasis on architecture as an icon of measure, and the play with Nāgara and Drāviḍa figurations to emphasize its iconography, is unique to the Vesara mode. I propose that in shifting the attention from divine figures to architectural models, as well as in Vesara's various architectural experiments, architects reinvestigated the temple structure itself as Puruṣa, the universal principle at the foundation of all temples in India.

2

Regional Theory in the Definition of Hybrid

Perceptions of Region

A study of the religious art and architecture of India typically begins with fieldwork in a chosen region of India. The area of this investigation is the southwestern part of India called Karnataka. The focus is a group of stone temples built in the eleventh century in northern Karnataka, in which I trace the formation of a new temple type that dominated Karnataka and other neighboring areas for more than two hundred years. Scholars have traditionally called this regional type Vesara. My slice of time, roughly the eleventh century when Vesara was created, suggests a historical complexity challenging the way scholars have traditionally defined what constitutes a region in India.

What is the region of Vesara architecture? The modern Karnataka state is drawn up as an elongated, vertical land in the western part of peninsular India, beginning as a narrow area in the upland plateau of the Deccan in the north widening south of the major watershed of the Krishna, where its sun-scorched, rocky plains are irrigated by minor rivers, and finally having a skirt of mountains near the western coast and in the southernmost parts. The modern map defines this geographically variegated land on the basis of a linguistic grouping of people who speak Kannada with more or less consistency, distinguishing this linguistic region from other areas of peninsular India.

The linguistic concern implied in the political state is of a recent origin. Its impact on an analysis of premodern architectural history has been felt in two ways (only partly because the jurisdiction of the regional archaeological survey is defined along modern lines). First, scholars have tended to view Karnataka as a homogeneous cultural unit, connected by a common history. Second, they have overlooked the map of Karnataka through various historical periods when its boundaries have shifted to include areas outside the modern political state as well as to exclude areas that indeed are part of the modern state.[1]

Far from the homogeneity implied by the modern state, Karnataka has been a region of cultural diversity throughout its history, as it is today. In its northern limits, Karnataka's cultural and linguistic composition is closer to parts of North and Central India, while southern Karnataka shares in, and vies with, the culture of the neighboring Tamilnadu, a linguistically distinct region to the east spreading down to the tip of the peninsula (fig. 1). In the self-consciousness of its people, Karnataka is equally graded between its northern and southern parts; the northern part defining itself in relation to North India, while the southern considering itself at the center of South Indian culture, as is apparent today in a difference between areas around Dharwar and Bijapur in the north and that around Bangalore and Mysore in the south. Unified under the modern state, Karnataka indeed comprises two broadly distinct cultural areas, roughly defined as northern and southern, with the east-flowing Tuṅgabhadrā River defining a natural line of divide between their often shifting boundaries. The princely state of Mysore before India's independence from British rule in 1947 perhaps represents the cultural unit of southern Karnataka more accurately, whereas the northern part shades away more meaningfully into the culture of modern Maharashtra state, where local folks still mix Marathi and

Kannada in ways that the purists of southern Karnataka hold in low esteem.

Vesara architecture must be understood in the context of the diversity of Karnataka. In the eleventh century, its unsteady, eclectic formation north of the Tuṅgabhadrā, the core area of my investigation, seems logical. The first evidence of dynastic art and culture in Karnataka, dating to the seventh and eighth centuries, is located in northern Karnataka and relates to the Calukyas of Badāmī, who already seem to identify with the regions farther north and east from their capital city of Badāmī. Temples in both South Indian and North Indian styles are found in this period in and around the capital city as well as in the more easterly boundaries of the Calukya empire, today in the modern state of Andhra Pradesh.[2] Only in the eleventh to thirteenth centuries, do the rulers of southern Karnataka, the Hoysalas, who had been small chieftains under the northern rulers in that period, namely the Cālukyas of Kalyana, tip the balance of power on their side. History of temple architecture of the eleventh and twelfth centuries reveals that the area around the Tuṅgabhadrā River and immediately south became from then on the zone of contest, and thus the connecting link, between the north and south. The link is visible in a transmission of artistic ideas from this area to the south and a southern migration of artisans corresponding to a territorial expansion of those southern rulers into the north.

The geographer Joseph Schwartzberg has defined a region as a "perceived segment of a time-space continuum differentiated from others on the basis of one or more defining characteristics."[3] While broad enough in scope, this definition is made complex because of its emphasis on the "perceptions" of what exactly constitute the defining characteristics of the geographical segment. Using Schwartzberg and recent geographers and anthropologists, Karnataka can be seen in terms of at least three cognitive regions. One is defined by administrators and developers who since the period of British colonization of India have actively marked its boundaries for efficient rule. The changes in those boundaries relate to the political struggles between the local kings and the claimed territories of the British since the late eighteenth century. The modern state is an example of the way Karnataka's administrative boundaries finally took shape after India's independence from colonial rule in 1947. The second cognitive region might be defined as a cultural one, a region Bernard Cohn has called "subjective" in that it is studied along a pattern of social formations reflecting interaction between human culture in a given period and the constraints and possibilities of the land on which it flourished.[4] The third is what Bharat Bhatt has called a "folk region." In some ways relating to the subjective region of the social scientist, this category must include the inhabitants' own self-awareness of the region in the periods in which they lived.[5]

In discussing the architectural history of Karnataka, the first category needs to be noted only as a caution of mistaking a region of modern concerns for an ancient cultural region. The regional complexity of Vesara architecture is often missed when Karnataka is understood in today's terms. Using the model from social scientists, this book will discuss Vesara through an archaeology of networks and centers of architectural activity as they evolved in the eleventh century.[6] The book will also explore the geographical framework for Vesara architecture to specifically include the perception of regional architecture that architects themselves may have had in the eleventh century.

The "Folk" Sense of the Vesara Region

In the history of sacred art in India, evidence relating to the architects' self-awareness about their regional architecture is difficult to come by because of a lack of information. A glimpse of the folk perception of Vesara monuments can be had in Karnataka from an early thirteenth century inscription from the Koṭīśvara temple at Kuppatur discussed in chapter 1, in which the architect claims that his temple is "freely ornamented with Drāviḍa, Bhūmija, and Nāgara."[7]

The proclamation that the architect of the temple is a veritable Viśvakarman, the divine architect, may be stereotypical in a climate of competition in which Vesara architects might have functioned as professionals. But nowhere in the history of India's sacred art is a claim made about the specific knowledge of different Indian temple forms, to which the inscription refers by names, verified by different miniature temple models carved as part of the temple's wall decoration. In earlier inscriptions found in Karnataka and other parts of India, the makers of images and monuments typically claimed professional status by proving their lineage and a mastery of sacred texts within a particular genealogy of practice.[8] In emphasizing sacred texts, those makers perhaps also competed with a priestly class traditionally in charge of books. Kuppatur's claim suggests a different climate in which high value is placed on the practical knowledge and control of regional temple forms.

Beyond regional eclecticism, seen in Karnataka's monuments in general, Kuppatur's claim clearly has a contemporary ring in the eleventh to thirteenth centuries, when temples commonly employed a knowledge of diverse temple morphologies as wall decoration (pl. 51). The perception of the makers of this period about their architectural mission differs from previous periods. Showing awareness of territories beyond their immediate one, architects make monuments of their indigenous region a cognitive center within an expanded field of conscious reference. Karnataka seems to have condensed into itself all regions of India, whose typical sacred structures Karnataka's monuments embody. To assert a seemingly new nationalism of Karnataka architects is not the aim of this book, but it is my aim to explain how architecture was explored within the framework of this regional myth. By the twelfth century, Vesara was known and distinguished by name in texts and local inscriptions, as will be soon evident. Much of the narrative in the book will describe the formation of Vesara architecture from the perspective of the social scientist's "subjective" region, arguing that the new regional myth marks a moment in Karnataka when the sense of the region was cognitively changed in the folk memory of the makers. The evolution of this "folk" sense has to be combined with the history of Vesara monuments.

Linguistic Approach to Regional Architecture: Advantages and Problems

The shift from the objective to subjective region in Bernard Cohn's sense has partly been enabled by studies in temple architecture drawing upon references in religious texts. The *Kāmikāgama*, a late-twelfth-century Sanskrit religious text from South India, perhaps is the earliest critical effort to map out the territory of Vesara architecture in Karnataka.[9] According to the text, Vesara refers to temple architecture prevalent in a region between the Vindhya mountains and the Krishna River, roughly the Deccan—the plateau region between North and South India. Stella Kramrisch makes Vesara those monuments "built by later Chālukyas, in the Kanarese districts, and by the Hoysala dynasty, in Mysore," slightly south of the region designated by the Kāmikāgama.[10]

The Kāmikāgama also defines the characteristics of this regional form. Vesara, thus, is *saṅkara*, a word to which some scholars in the early twentieth century have connected an old Sanskrit usage of Vesara as "mule."[11] Kramrisch, who uses the text as a basis to understand architectural styles, explains that Vesara historically evolved in the Karnataka region later than either the Nāgara or Drāviḍa temples of North and South India, respectively, and that "certain special features of these temples result from an admixture of Nāgara detail to Drāviḍa building."[12] Kramrisch's explanation of Vesara architecture as a mixture of North Indian and South Indian architecture is widely accepted in standard scholarly literature.

It is not known whether the architects who designed temples in eleventh-century Karnataka actually called their monuments Vesara.[13] Two inscriptions that suggest an architects' awareness of architectural morphologies and terms, the one at Kuppatur discussed above and another at the Amriteśvara temple at Holal paleographically datable to the latter part of the twelfth century, belong a century or more after Vesara evolved.[14] Furthermore, while Holal mentions Vesara, Kuppatur does not. The term Bhūmija, a term not mentioned in the Holal inscription, is mentioned instead, which raises a possibility that the architects could have used the two terms interchangeably for a single architectural form.[15]

With this much ambiguity about the architects' use of "Vesara," our understanding of the term and its meaning depends on interpretations proposed by others. The Kāmikāgama is an exception in the corpus of contemporary South Indian textual sources, where Vesara is typically described as a circular or elliptical building distinguished from Nāgara, a square, and Drāviḍa, an octagonal temple. The Kāmikāgama shows an awareness of the North Indian traditions, making the text arguably from the Deccan unlike other texts that seem to be from Tamilnadu. The Kāmikāgama acknowledges a common northern usage of the architectural terms to designate the geographical distribution of temples. The term Vesara itself is not found in North Indian architectural texts, suggesting that it has relevance only in South India.

The question of terminology and its reference to architectural styles remains a point of contest among regionally based scholarships. South Indian architectural historians have tended to use the southern textual definition of Nāgara, Drāviḍa, and Vesara, according to which Vesara represents but one of the variations in the shape of a South Indian temple. These scholars have even reconciled the geographic designation of the term found in North Indian texts as well as the Kāmikāgama by proposing, for instance, that Nāgara, i.e. a square structure, may also refer to architecture in the Karnataka region, which is of course located north relative to Tamilnadu, where Drāviḍa prevailed.[16] Apsidal temples, of which evidence such as the eighth-century Durga at Aihole are found in Karnataka, are somewhat loosely designated as Vesara as are also those temples having the round form of a ribbed capping stone, āmalaka, found in northern India.[17]

An enormously valuable piece of scholarship in the context of this confused understanding of architectural terms and their application to architecture is Dhaky's monograph *The Indian Temple Forms in Karnāta Inscriptions and Architecture* (New Delhi, 1977). Dhaky's main purpose was to investigate how the architects of Karnataka may have distinguished terms such as Vesara, Nāgara and Drāviḍa, with which South Indian and North Indian texts designated various Indian temple forms. His crucial evidence was two inscriptions, namely from Holal and Kuppatur cited above, that mentioned the architects' expertise in such Indian temple forms as the Nāgara, Drāviḍa, Vesara, Kaliṅga, and Bhūmija. The inscription from Kuppatur also mentioned that the architect of that temple decorated its walls with some of those forms, which Dhaky compared with shrine models on other eleventh-to-thirteenth-century temples, pointing to a common practice.

Dhaky's investigation clarified that the confusion in the interpretations of Indian temple forms, particularly Nāgara, Drāviḍa and Vesara, prevailed in regionally based scholarship because of the different meanings assigned to the same architectural terms in the regional texts. Using the epigraphic reference on the architects' familiarity of terms as well as Kuppatur's specific pointer to the use of temple forms as wall ornaments, Dhaky compared the shrine models on that and other Karnataka monuments with descriptions of terms in both the South Indian and North Indian architectural texts. His analysis proved that Karnataka architects used Nāgara, Drāviḍa and other terms to distinguish temple forms morphologically as well as regionally, as was the case in North Indian texts and architectural practice. This conclusion strongly refuted a southern historiography in which Vesara, Nāgara, and Drāviḍa were considered merely different shapes of a South Indian temple, as described in South Indian texts. Dhaky established that Vesara was not merely a round or an elliptical temple for these Karnataka architects but a "mixed" type separate from either Drāviḍa or Nāgara. He noted that this type was indigenous to Karnataka, as Kramrisch had already pointed out on the basis of the Kāmikāgama.

Dhaky's and Kramrisch's synthesis of textual information with archaeological remains is useful but it still leaves a question unanswered: What exactly is this Karnataka type, which is a mixture of North Indian and South Indian architecture? From a very early period, artists in Karnataka, a region of South India touching many regions of North India, had naturally interacted with diverse traditions beyond its geographic limits. Vesara's mixture, according to Kramrisch:

> is natural in a region betwixt two powerful schools of which Nāgara, the first and foremost, is centered in Madhyadeśa, according to the 'Aparājitapṛcchā'—in the country bounded by the river Sarasvati in Kurukṣetra, Allahabad, the Himālayas and the Vindhya, and Drāviḍa in South India.[18]

In the seventh century, in such a temple site as Mahākūṭa, architects virtually made a point about this natural regional eclecticism. They built North Indian temples next to South Indian ones (pl. 3).

A North Indian, Nāgara temple built in Mahākūṭa in the seventh century is recognized by a curvilinear tower raised over a square sanctum and crowned by a ribbed stone, called the āmalaka (pl. 4). The central projection on the temple's wall, showing a figure in its niche, is conducted upward into the tower by a vertical band *(latā)*, as is typical of all North Indian temples. Mahākūṭa's South Indian Drāviḍa temple is distinguished from it by an arrangement of horizontal stories reminiscent of a palatial structure, capped by a dome (pl. 5). Above the walls, each story is defined by a string course *(hāra)* of miniature architectural representations. As is typical in Drāviḍa architecture of the Karnataka sort, these miniature models at Mahākuṭa are composed mainly of square-domed, hut-shaped pavilions *(kūṭas)* at the corners and an oblong, barrel-roofed hall-type *(śālā)* in the center. An arch-shaped dormer *(nāsī)* suggesting an attic window

Plate 3. Mahākūṭa temple complex, view across the tank showing Saṅgameśvara (left) and Mahākūṭeśvara (right) temples, seventh century

faces each of these miniature representations and is made especially emphatic on the śālā.

These two temple types at Mahākūṭa suggest indigenous versions of the typical North Indian and South Indian temple types, but they do not refer to any outside region from where local architects could have derived their forms. The Drāviḍa temple at Mahākūṭa is a type that is formally as well as conceptually distinguished from the neighboring Tamil region. The Nāgara in Karnataka is also a local variant and does not represent connection with regions such as Madhyadeśa (Central India), to which Kramrisch refers.[19]

While morphologically distinguishing the two regional types, Nāgara and Drāviḍa, the seventh-century Karnataka architects of Mahākūṭa combine features of one type with characteristics of the other. For example, a pavilion projecting at the center of the Drāviḍa temple's walls at Mahākūṭa is probably an idea inspired by the central projecting offset called *bhadra* in a Nāgara temple. The offset has a corresponding barrel-vaulted motif on each of its superstructural stories aligned vertically up to a pillared pavilion facing the dome, an alignment (making the śālā motif a *madhyaśālā*) in accordance with Nāgara. The bhadra of the Nāgara temple at Mahākūṭa, on the other hand, is created on a straight wall by attaching to its masonry vertical columns of stone, which stand on a projection in the base (one such detached stone column is more clearly visible on a contemporary temple at Aihole; pl. 23). These columns give the bhadra, the central projection characteristic of a Nāgara temple, an appearance of a southern wall *(pāda)* whose pilasters rest on the temple's base.

Furthermore, a sequence of moldings typically shown in North India "above" the floor level, and binding the wall, appears instead in the Nāgara temple at Mahākūṭa as a sequence of moldings "below" the floor level. This confusion of a Nāgara *vedībandha* (wall molding sequence) as a Drāviḍa *adhiṣṭhāna* (base moldings) is given a regional mark also by a swapping of individual

Plate 4. Mahākūṭa, Saṅgameśvara temple, west

Plate 5. Mahākūṭa, Mahākūṭeśvara temple, west (courtesy: American Institute of Indian Studies)

moldings, such as a faceted torus common in the local Drāviḍa architecture for the northern "pot"-shaped molding. The *adhiṣṭhāna* of the Drāviḍa temple at Mahākūṭa, on the other hand, includes the semicircular "pot" molding and the cyma *(kapotapālī)* showing dentils underneath, recalling a northern *vedībandha.*[20]

The two Mahākūṭa monuments show that Karnataka architects in the seventh century were not only aware of the typical North Indian and South Indian forms of architecture, they also created local variants by exchanging typological features of these two regional temple forms. Their eclecticism is part of the peculiarity of the region and continues to inform Vesara architecture. But to define Vesara as a hybrid ignores Vesara's eleventh-century history in favor of the natural tendency to produce hybrids in the region. The two Mahākūṭa temples are not Vesara, as all scholars agree. Vesara monuments, hence, demand more from their definition than merely a regional mixture.

About Vesara monuments of Karnataka, Dhaky has noted that they:

> are the most neglected as perhaps the more misunderstood of all the medieval architectural styles in India. Yet they are, in some ways, the more interesting, as they were relatively the least conservative of all the medieval Indian styles in the sense they allowed a far greater freedom to experiment and as a result introduced many innovations, created compelling variations, conceived newer kinds of elaborations, and also produced mutants which must seem impossible in the context of the other regional styles of that time known to us in India.[21]

Dhaky's conception of Vesara must be challenged only because Vesara is not merely a matter of the degree to which regional eclecticism was exploited; Vesara needs to be distinguished from the natural propensity to mix modes and features noted in Karnataka since the seventh and eighth centuries. The neglect of Vesara results in part because it is naturalized into a regional tendency. The implicit geographical determinism, extended linguistically to the term Vesara, absorbs Vesara's history within a unifying and stabilizing narrative for the region. The answer to Vesara lies beyond the discourse of architectural mixture that scholars have so far conducted through a reading of the Kāmikāgama and through their terminological-etymological approach to architecture. In order to examine Vesara, we will have to turn to the history of Karnataka monuments.

Archaeological Approach to Region: Advantage and Problems

Vesara monuments were known to modern scholarship at least since the 1860s, when James Fergusson drew attention to them in his monumental volumes *History of Indian and Eastern Architecture.*[22] Although Fergusson was not an archaeologist, he was a pioneer in the "archaeological" approach to Indian temple architecture that has evolved from a study of concrete examples of monuments.

Fergusson is credited for our first stylistic classification of Indian architecture. He designated the Karnataka temples not as Vesara but Chālukyan, after a dynasty that had dominated the region. As a stylistic category, Fergusson distinguished Chālukyan from "northern or Indo-Aryan" and "Dravidian" styles. The triad of architectural styles became useful for subsequent archaeological exploration and ordering of Indian monuments.

In a major monograph on Karnataka architecture, *The Chālukyan Architecture of the Kanarese Districts,* published in 1926, Henry Cousens used Fergusson's stylistic designation to define the history of architecture of the region across centuries.[23] "Chālukyan," for Cousens, was not only architecture built by the family of rulers with that name, but one that:

> embraces all that was erected within the country under their sway, either under their own auspices or that of their feudatories, or of other families who, for a time, supplanted them in the government of those districts—*for the same architects or their descendants . . . worked for all upon the same lines.*[24]

The Chālukyan style, consequently, covered a wide area, with northern extensions mixing "imperceptibly, with the remains of the so-called 'Hemāḍpanti' temples" in modern Maharashtra, and a southern version, "in its later development," found in the Hoysala territory.

Cousens's monograph is the first of its kind that discusses Vesara temples historically.[25] In emphasizing the relationship among monuments, as is appropriate for a monographic study, Cousens deliberately departed from the understanding of the Chālukyan form prevalent in Fergusson's days. In that early period of scholarship, he wrote, Chālukyan was thought to be separate from Drāviḍa and northern architecture. Instead, he painted a much broader historical picture, blurring the distinction between what Fergusson had called Chālukyan and Dravidian. Cousens believed the style in fact originated "in the older Dravidian or Pallava temples of the south."[26] For him, the Chālukyan form was the final culmination of a formal evolution in southern architecture that began, in his chronology, in the fifth century A.D.

"Dravidian" for Cousens included both monuments from the Tamil region as well as Karnataka. In fact, he often used "Dravidian" and "Pallava" interchangeably. Pallava, the name for a dynasty ruling the Tamil region in the seventh and eighth centuries, paralleled Chālukyan in thus being appropriated for stylistic definition. The map of Dravidian architecture included peninsular India as a whole, while Cousens's specific archaeological survey of "Kanarese Districts" focused on a part of Karnataka accessible to him in the late 19th century, leaving out areas within the jurisdiction of unwelcoming princely kingdoms.

Plate 6. Mahākūṭa, Bāṇantiguḍi, southwest, seventh century (courtesy: American Institute of Indian Studies)

Cousens's "Dravidian" resembles a standard, nineteenth-century, linguistic understanding of the peninsular region as a unifying matrix for a group of closely related languages distinct from those spoken in the northern part of India.

While Cousens's confusion between Pallava and Dravida no longer exists, scholars until recently have failed to make a distinction between the southern architecture of Tamilnadu and that of Karnataka. In the uniformity of this definition, scholars have also traditionally privileged the Tamil country with a normative status in the definition of the South.

For the architectural history of southern India, the category of "Drāviḍa" is too broad. Dhaky was the first to distinguish between the two regional variants of Drāviḍa architecture, which he called that of Upper Drāviḍadeśa and Lower Drāviḍadeśa, implying by the former term the architecture of Karnataka, and more broadly the upland plateau region of south India called the Deccan, and by the latter the deep south, namely Tamilnadu.[27] This distinction between the Karnataka and the Tamil variants is important in understanding Vesara architecture. A contention of this book is that Vesara could not have evolved in the Tamil region because it is closely related to the formal and conceptual peculiarities of the Karnataka variant. This variant will be called Deccano-Drāviḍa not only for brevity but also because it has relevance beyond Karnataka in the larger plateau region of the Deccan. The formal distinction made between Deccano-Drāviḍa and Tamil Drāviḍa will suggest a consistent difference in the approach to a shared architectural vocabulary.

The formal type of which temples in Karnataka and Tamilnadu are variants is called in Sanskrit texts *Kūṭina*. A Kūṭina form of temple is described by its tiered superstructure marked by kūṭa (hut, shelter) formations, evoking on the exterior face of its solid tower a vision of a multistoried mansion. While sharing this vision, the two regional

Plate 7. Badāmī, Upper Śivālaya, east, seventh century

variants of Kūṭina cannot be linked by a common chronology. Deccano-Drāviḍa architecture has both formal and ideological components that distinguish it from Drāviḍa architecture as it developed in Tamilnadu. Dwelling on these distinctions will clarify a historical and regional basis of the Vesara form.

The oldest Drāviḍa monuments in Karnataka differ in numerous ways from the Drāviḍa temples of Tamilnadu.[28] The plain stone walls of Bāṇantigudi's sanctum perhaps best express the basic conception of a Deccano-Drāviḍa temple (pl. 6). The masonry cubicle with no offset appears as if it were a cell excavated out of a live matrix of rock, as in cave architecture.[29] In temples having a circumambulatory passage (called *sāndhāra*), such as the Upper Śivālaya at Badāmī, the plain cell is surrounded by a rectangular hall, the roof of which is created by stone beams stretched between the sanctum and the outer wall, giving it a shedlike effect (pl. 7). The outer wall encloses the ambulatory and a closed hall preceding the sanctum. In this initial stage, only this peripheral wall is capped by a coping *(uṣṇīṣa)* rendered by a string course of architectural motifs *(hāra)*. The sanctum walls themselves do not have the surrounding hāra in the initial phase of their development, only the added shed wrapping around it. The inner sanctum is emphasized by a second story; at Bāṇantiguḍī, its superstructure rests on a heavy awning and reproduces the structure of wooden beams supporting a domed roof. An attic window projects from the roof at cardinal directions, framed by a dormer *(candraśālā)*. The overhanging cornice *(kapota)* supporting the roof has faint marks of the candraśālā dormers. In such temples as the Upper Śivālaya, the stories show the basic division of walls into corners and a central projecting offset, with lightly embossed dormers barely hinting the hāra's motifs on the eaves moldings. When architectural motifs finally appear on the superstructure, they seem to be defined and elaborated from the early hints of the molding itself (pl. 8).

This chronology of the earliest monuments in Karnataka suggests that a Deccano-Drāviḍa temple expressed its Kūṭina form through a gradual differentiation of what first begins as a uniform

Plate 8. Badāmī, Lower Śivālaya, northeast, seventh century

Plate 9. Paṭṭadakal, Mallikārjuna temple, ca. A.D. 745 (courtesy: American Institute of Indian Studies)

Plate 10. Mahābalipuram, Dharmarāja Ratha, south, seventh century (courtesy: American Institute of Indian Studies)

Plate 11. Tanjore, Bṛhadīśvara temple, west, ca. A.D. 1000 (courtesy: American Institute of Indian Studies)

stone cubicle. By contrast, the morphology of a developed Tamil temple is defined additively, as an arranged collection of distinct, well-formed kūṭas (pl. 10). The difference in conception is maintained in visual details. For instance, the architectural motifs along a Tamilian temple's hāra such as the square corner pavilions *(karṇakūṭas),* alternating barrel-vaulted enclosures (śālās), and dormer frontons *(pañjaras)* in between, are treated as if they were distinct miniature buildings linked by a substantially diminished, recessed corridor. Only these prominent architectural shapes, and not the linking corridor, have prominent platforms *(vedī),* often occupied by figures (pl. 11). By contrast, in a fully evolved Deccano-Drāviḍa temple, the architectural motifs as well as the linking corridor *(hārāntara)* have the same height, as if they were all receding and projecting components of a unified spatial continuum having a single roof. A uniform vedī platform above the rafter moldings *(pratikaṇṭha)* provides a single, leveled "floor" for the entire hāra cloister. On a Vesara temple (pl. 14), a continuation of this Deccano-Drāviḍa detail indicates its regional roots.[30]

The Vesara Region: Critique of the Aesthetic Criterion

Neither Fergusson nor Cousens used the term Vesara for these Karnataka monuments. Nor did they see the Chālukyan style as hybrid. Fergusson saw Chālukyan as a style belonging to the "race" that controlled the region—a style that asserted itself when that race of Chālukyan rulers grew stronger. Noting the presence of North Indian and South Indian temples in seventh- and eighth-century sites in Karnataka, Fergusson made them reflect a period of political uncertainty.

> It is as if this intrusive race adopted hesitatingly the earlier styles of the country, but that it was not till they had consolidated their power, and developed peculiar institutions of their own, that they expressed them in the style to which their name has been affixed.[31]

This chronology from hesitation to confidence is an original creation of the historian, but Fergusson developed it along the racial and linguistic lines on which all his architectural categories evolved. While Fergusson's "Indo-Aryan" and "Dravidian" reflect broad linguistic divisions of India current in his day, there is no linguistic parallel for Later Chālukyan. Fergusson imagined in it what he considered a fulfillment not only of the indigenous race of Karnataka but an innate artistic sensibility of India itself. He contrasted this sensibility with classical Greece, comparing the Hoysaleśvara temple in Halebid, which represented for him the height of the Later Chālukyan style (pl. 13), to the Parthenon in Athens. He opposed the "mathematical exactness" and mechanical precision of Greece, symbolizing the best of "pure refined intellectual power applied to the production of an architectural design," to the variety and "joyous exuberance scorning every me-

Plate 12. Belūr, Keśava temple, southwest, A.D. 1117 (courtesy: American Institute of Indian Studies)

Plate 13. Halebid, Hoysaleśvara temple, northern shrine, north wall, A.D. 1121–1160 (courtesy: American Institute of Indian Studies)

chanical restraint" in India.[32] He suggested that between these "two opposite poles, the alpha and omega of architectural design, . . . it would be possible to arrange all the buildings of the world."

The architectural "value" of the Karnataka temples within Fergusson's global perspective engendered also its local chronology, that of a continuous development toward "playful exuberant fancy" of the Halebid temple. Fergusson's chronology—not only expressing a movement from hesitation to confidence of the Chālukyan race but achieving an Indian ideal as opposed to Greek classicism—has been underplayed by Cousens, and so has Fergusson's racial determinant. But the evolutionary trend Cousens created for the style itself does not differ in any essential manner from that of Fergusson.

Although Cousens noted the presence of Nāgara architecture in Karnataka and its influence on the Drāviḍa, he traced the evolutionary trend of Chālukyan style back only to the architecture of the South. He wrote:

> [T]he style of architecture, known as Chālukyan, is an offshoot of the early Dravidian style of Southern India, so modified in its growth by western temple builders as to attain to a distinct and perfect character under their hands. The different steps in the transition from the purely Dravidian of the seventh and eighth centuries to the perfected Chālukyan temples of the eleventh and twelfth are easily traced.[33]

In the sequential development of his "Dravidian style," Cousens noted intricacy of ornamentation as a hallmark of the newly evolved Chālukyan style. In this quality, Cousens saw a destination of Karnataka's architectural history, fulfilled by a shift in the building material from a grainy sandstone—with which all temples until the eleventh century were built—to a gray, close-grained schist. This stone was soft when quarried, enabling craftsmen to carve detailed, lacelike ornaments that sandstone would not have allowed. When the stone hardened, the sharpest edges and the thinnest ridges of an ornamental motif acquired the finish of metalwork.

Cousens made the gray, closely grained stone and the resultant quality of decoration the historical determinants of Chālukyan style. The Kalleśvara temple at Kukkanūr, a sandstone temple that shows many innovations of the Chālukyan form, thus remained a Drāviḍa temple in Cousens's estimation mainly because of its material and lack of detailed carvings. Cousens dismissed the Yallamā temple at Badāmī, again a sandstone structure, as simply a ruined shrine in the end of his section on Badāmī for the same reason, although it is remarkably well preserved compared with many other temples Cousens included in his discussion (pl. 63).[34] Both the Kukkanūr and the Badāmī temples are important Vesara buildings in my estimation.[35]

The Typology of Vesara

Many scholars since Cousens have believed that Vesara (Cousens's "Chālukyan") evolved in Karnataka directly from Drāviḍa architecture.[36] Using the ambiguity in the history of the term as an argument against Vesara's form, Adam Hardy has recently dismissed the distinction between Vesara and previous monuments in Karnataka. Hardy implies that the term Vesara may at best be used for a small class of mixed structures, which he has documented from different periods of temple architecture in Karnataka, some including what Dhaky has called Miśraka, or mixed type.[37] Miśraka in his estimation might also include the eclectic, seventh-century structures of Mahākūṭa discussed above.

A lack of evidence of the term Vesara in the eleventh century, however, is not a sufficient reason to confuse it with the mixed type. The absence of the term only suggests that Vesara's architectural experiments precede their label. To be sure, the term comes into existence in the twelfth century both in architectural texts and inscriptions, acknowledging the new typology after it fully evolved.

The historical problem is hinged upon how one defines the relation between architecture in the eleventh, twelfth and previous centuries in the region of Karnataka. The book argues against the model of formal evolution as a full explanation of Vesara and analyzes those formal aspects that Vesara architecture shares in the eleventh century with previous, Drāviḍa architecture of Karnataka and ones it does not. Dhaky has pointed out that the formal basis of Vesara is Drāviḍa architecture of Karnataka.[38] His notion of "basis" introduces a way of conceptualizing the relationship between the two that differs from the prevalent evolutionary schemes. It recognizes Drāviḍa as a necessary foundation but not the determinant of the direction Vesara architecture would

Plate 14. Iṭṭagi, Mahādeva temple, south, A.D. **1112**

take. Visual analysis can show substantial differences between the two that make a contrary argument to that of smooth evolution.

For example, the walls in Vesara architecture evolve into a complex set of five offsets: a wide central offset (bhadra) that typically projects in two or three steps *(phālanās);* a pair of subsidiary offsets *(pratiratha)* set back from this bhadra and articulated usually as thick indented half-pillars having a curvaceous bell in the midregion; and finally offset corners *(karṇas)* (pl. 14). In the twelfth century, the pratirathas may be dropped. In any event, these offsets are composed to interrelate hierarchically, connected by deep, densely packed recesses between, and articulated to convey their relative emphasis. The coherence of such a wall is different from the rhythmic bay arrangement of offsets in a developed Drāviḍa temple (pl. 11).

Also, while Deccano-Drāviḍa architecture typically has a central projecting offset (pl. 9), it is never as elaborate as a Vesara bhadra. Modulated half-pillars for subsidiary offsets between the central projection and corners (pratirathas), as well as recesses with architectural motifs, are special only to Vesara. The half-pillars are introduced only since the mid-eleventh century.

The walls of a Vesara temple in the eleventh century are dominated by architectural motifs. Corners (karṇas) are faced by a pavilion motif comprising a temple tower standing above a pair of pilasters. Pratiratha half-pillars flanking the bhadra are surmounted by Vesara aediculae (kūṭas), turning these pratirathas into large *kūṭastambhas* (columns supporting temple towers). The bhadra projection shows a niche that would have housed a sculptured image. A broad awning shading this niche and a large temple tower or an elaborately carved model of a complete shrine above would have made this bhadra motif appear like a realistic subshrine. Narrow recesses separating the offsets are occupied by an architectural motif, which, by ca. A.D. 1100, is usually a Vesara temple tower on a column shown within an elaborate framework of coiled scroll spewed by fantastic, crocodile-like, aquatic monsters *(makaras)* perched on side pilasters.

While use of architectural motifs on walls is special neither to Karnataka nor to Drāviḍa, its prominent use in the basic composition of the wall is special to Vesara temples. These architectural motifs and the scrollwork in the recesses interact with the smooth masonry of the wall to produce a pulse, controlled effectively in more successful temples, such as the Siddheśvara temple at Hāverī (pl. 67), the Mahādeva temple at Iṭṭagi, and the Mallikārjuna temple at Kuruvatti (pl. 80).

A Vesara superstructure is arranged usually in four tiered stories with a square, offset dome above. The stories are marked by a string course (hāra), whose architectural motifs substantially differ from Drāviḍa. Particularly, the *madhyaśālā* (central, barrel-vaulted hall-type) is nested. This invention of Vesara, made to match the wide, staggered bhadra below, typically looks as if one barrel-vaulted motif is telescoped into another. Its vertical side panels stand taller and virtually independent of the barrel-vaulted back. Kūtas above pratiratha offsets, replacing Drāviḍa's dormer cage (pañjara), reflect the indentations of the half-pillar itself. Karṇas have square kūṭas, the only feature that asserts Vesara's Drāviḍaness in its relatively unaltered form.[39] The domed finial above shows a bold projection in the center, reflecting the serial folds of the madhyaśālās.

Such temples as the Mahādeva temple at Iṭṭagi also show a series of interlocked cavities, framed by an ornamental scroll, in the center of their superstructure (pl. 74). This opening is new both in form and conception. It is seen for the first time around A.D. 1075 on the Kāśiviśveśvara temple at Lakkuṇḍi (pl. 54). The cavities create pockets across the superstructure as much as their arched frames produce a vertical lacelike effect on the central spine of the temple.

Among moldings of the superstructure, one with beam ends (pratikaṇṭha) develops into one of the most emphatic features of Vesara's Drāviḍa-like superstructure. The emphasis on the serrated effect of this pratikaṇṭha molding seems to have evolved within Deccano-Drāviḍa architecture, where it stands prominently against the recessed necking above the molding; by contrast, the necking in the Tamil variant is made considerably taller to provide a perch and a backdrop for figures. The diminishing of that upper portion in Karnataka shifts attention to the pratikaṇṭha molding, where the beam ends are sometimes further emphasized by makara heads or *vyālas*. In a treatment unique to standardized Vesara monuments, the beam ends surround individual miniaturized motifs instead of spreading out along the length of the hāra. To summarize, Vesara features indeed evolved by progressively distinguishing themselves from the matrix of their Drāviḍa forms.

Localities of Vesara: Northern vs. Southern Karnataka

The archaeological framework to understand Vesara architecture first by Fergusson and Cousens has gone unchallenged. In fact, their emphasis on the decorative qualities of the stone surface as Vesara's "goal" continued in many subsequent survey books. I suggest that this understanding of Vesara as an ornate and florid style—and a historical account of Karnataka architecture explaining it—is based primarily on a perspective on monuments of the twelfth and thirteenth century in southern Karnataka. Those monuments, patronized by the Hoysala dynasty, had provided a ground for Fergusson's pioneering work. For Fergusson, they epitomized the Indian ideal of embellishment, which he had juxtaposed against the Greek quest for geometric clarity (pl. 13). In subsequent editions of his volumes on Indian architecture, Fergusson included monuments of northern Karnataka within the framework he had originally created for the "Chālukyan" style of the Hoysala monuments.

After Fergusson, the Hoysala monuments assumed a normative status also because of the notion of Karnataka as a homogeneous cultural unit connected by a linear history. While Cousens did not include Hoysala in his regional monograph, he operated within the framework provided by his predecessor. The status of Hoysala monuments was enhanced also by a visibility they acquired through extensive records produced by the Mysore State Archaeological Survey since the late nineteenth century. Hoysala was seen to represent the final fruition, providing a natural index for all monuments in Karnataka. Hence, all temples were judged on a scale of ornamentation derived from those monuments in south Karnataka.[40]

A look at the monuments themselves helps us test this pervasive evolutionary view. A Vesara temple such as the Mahādeva temple at Iṭṭagi, dated A.D. 1112 in northern Karnataka (pl. 14), can hardly be compared to the Keśava temple at Belūr, dated A.D. 1117 in the Hoysala territory (pl. 12). In the latter, wall surfaces seem to be stretched out and filled with figurative panels and elaborately carved vegetational motifs. At the peak of Vesara architecture in northern Karnataka, by contrast, the Mahādeva temple at Iṭṭagi shows a self-conscious restraint of ornamentation. The smooth, plain surfaces of the wide bhadra and the abstract grandeur of the corner offsets are delicately relieved by the ornamental texture of the architectural motif in the recess. The mass of the subsidiary piers between is also reduced by multiple indentations. The walls of the temple on the whole show a remarkable balance of visual effects, a controlled pulsation of ornate and plain portions.

Such effects of Iṭṭagi are not achieved at Belūr, nor are they part of its intention. Boldness of architectural features, and the dazzling intricacies of their decorative surfaces is the goal achieved there. The ponderousness of Hoysala figurative sculpture, particularly the overburdened female figures in which south Karnataka sculptors excelled, can probably serve as a measure for Hoysala structures as a whole.[41] While the rich filigree-like motifs enchant our eyes, they add a thick visual crust on the massive architectural forms underneath.

Figures dominate the walls of Hoysala temples; they are virtually absent in Vesara of northern Karnataka. On the Iṭṭagi temple, tiny figures placed at the base of the wall offsets seem like afterthoughts and suggest a scale that only enhances the loftiness of the architectural form. Although a large figure would have occupied the bhadra niche, most of the wall is plain masonry dominated by architectural motifs. The restraint that guided architecture in northern Karnataka toward architectonic effects contrasts with the energy of exuberant sculptural effects developed in southern Karnataka monuments.

The approach to Vesara form in northern and southern Karnataka should be conceptually distinguished. The difference between the Iṭṭagi and the Belūr is not merely chronological, for a five-year period that might separate the two dated temples hardly accounts for the structural elaborations and the burst of sculpture we see on the surface of the Hoysala temple. Belūr's decorative emphasis is special to a southern regional aesthetic sensibility.

Vesara architecture in northern Karnataka emphasized structural clarity. The Hoysala temples in southern Karnataka clothed their walls with layers of elaborate figural and floral carvings. The emphasis on "structure" in northern and "clothing" in southern Karnataka can perhaps be one way of distinguishing the approach of architects and sculptors to monuments in their two regions. Historically, of course, the beginnings of Vesara architecture are traced only in northern Karnataka, identified here as the Vesara heartland. In southern Karnataka, it was an architectural graft imposed on the previous Drāviḍa tradition when the local Hoysala dynasty extended its rule to the northern region.

The discussion of Vesara as regional architecture contributes to traditional scholarship on Karnataka architecture in two ways. First, it argues against evolutionary models connecting Drāviḍa and Vesara. Second, it insists on maintaining a distinction between Vesara in northern Karnataka and southern Karnataka. Both observations evolve out of a fundamentally different view on what constitutes an artistic region, extending a tiered model of the region using geography and anthropology. Karnataka must be studied not from the point of view of modern boundaries and a homogeneous culture within those boundaries but a "time-space continuum" created through the physical and intellectual effort of the architects themselves. An archaeology of the Vesara region must begin with a description of such an effort made in northern Karnataka in the eleventh century.

3

Drifts in Southern Architecture

IT MAY SEEM UNUSUAL THAT NORTHERN KARNATAKA should evolve into the heartland of Vesara architecture in the eleventh century. By most accounts, the center of architectural activity in the Deccan had steadily shifted since the eighth century to areas north and east of the areas where Vesara evolved. Our knowledge of northern Karnataka just prior to Vesara is based on small shrines in the traditional Drāviḍa mode, usually considered peripheral in importance by those standard accounts of Drāviḍa architecture. Scholars who connect major Vesara monuments of the eleventh century to the previous Drāviḍa temples labor over its relation to those centers of monumental architecture outside Karnataka, in modern-day Maharashtra, while overlooking these local Drāviḍa shrines as merely an intellectual backwater. The beginnings of Vesara architecture, however, must be traced in this local context, where tenth century temples at sites such as Aihole and Ron record a break from the mainstream of Drāviḍa architecture. Partly successful, partly failed attempts of their architects to renew Drāviḍa resulted in significant changes that created the ground for Vesara's innovations.

A study of Drāviḍa temples at Aihole and Ron shows the way architects reorganize their tradition in the day-to-day acts of making. The relationship between Drāviḍa and Vesara revealed in this documentation can be partly explained using "drift," a linguistic concept defining a gap that gradually widens between cognate languages. Applying drift to temporal movements in art history, George Kubler explains:

> This "drift," produced by cumulative changes in the articulation of sounds, can be related in turn to the interferences that distort any audible communication. The telephone engineer calls such interferences "noise." "Drift," "noise," and change are related by the presence of interferences preventing the complete repetition of an earlier set of conditions.[1]

In spite of being somewhat mechanistic, because cognate languages embody not only distortions in sound but different cultures, Kubler's idea provides a useful starting point. The presence of interferences within Drāviḍa are traced in this chapter in a group of small, rude-looking temples built in the tenth century in Aihole, a famous site in northern Karnataka. Overlooked by scholars who have tended to favor Aihole's seventh and eighth century structures,[2] these small shrines represent a period of enormous diversity when Aihole was recognized as a home of an important mercantile community far removed from the political centers of the period. The small size as well as the large number of shrines in Aihole perhaps reflect patronage of individual entrepreneurs, the international scope of whose activities is recorded in inscriptions found in many regions of South India.[3]

These Aihole temples are usually double-storied structures (pl. 15), much smaller than the grand Drāviḍa temples built in Karnataka in the eighth century, the peak of such monuments there, and are also more modest than their ninth- and tenth-century contemporaries in sites such as Sīrval and Hallūr (pl. 32).[4] These Aihole temples are *nirandhāra*, i.e. structures with no circumambulatory path around them, unlike earlier ambulatory temples. The walls of most of these temples stand directly on the basement.[5] Planned

Plate 15. Aihole, Rāciguḍi, eastern shrine, southeast, mid-tenth century

Plate 16. Aihole, Temple no. 53, Galaganātha group, south, early tenth century

on a straight plumb line *(mānasūtra),* with offsets created by cutting back the stone masonry, they are stripped of all figural ornamentation, in contrast to the Drāviḍa temples of the seventh to ninth centuries. Instead, they display an austere tendency on their reduced wall by projecting blank architectural motifs.[6] By most accounts of South Indian temples, these peculiarities of Aihole are marginal to the achievements of Drāviḍa architecture. Yet a local preoccupation with the articulation of walls and the superstructure here provides the first formal ground on which Vesara developed by the early eleventh century.

The diversity of Aihole's temples can be demonstrated by Temple nos. 52 and 53 in the Galaganātha group (pls. 16 & 17) and the eastern shrine of a triple temple called Rāciguḍi, all belonging to the beginning of the tenth century. Marking their date, as well as their Karnataka pedigree, is their base (adhiṣṭhana), which comprises a typical Karnataka set including the lowest *jagatī* (plinth, platform) curved at the upper edge; a *tripaṭṭa kumuda* (a torus with three facets); and a kapotapālī (cyma cornice typical of Karnataka), faced with wedge-shaped bosses. The torus recalls late-ninth- and early-tenth-century monuments at Kukkanūr (pl. 21) and Paṭṭadakal (pl. 19), only that in relation to those monuments, it is thinner, suggesting Aihole's slightly later date in the first half of the tenth century.

In other details, the temples vary considerably. The walls of Rācigudi's shrine rise directly above the base moldings, as is typical of Aihole's temples in this period. At Temple no. 53, a recess *(kaṇṭha)* separates the wall from the base. This recess is filled with plank moldings (called *prati*) whose

Plate 17. Aihole, Temple no. 52, south, early tenth century (courtesy: American Institute of Indian Studies)

Plate 18. Sīrval, Temple no. 4, east, early tenth century

ends are carved with elephants, composite animals (vyālas), and human figures, relating to a trend from the Tamil region of the deep south that seems to have taken root in Karnataka at Sīrval, a contemporary site (pl. 18). Temple no. 53, and the adjacent Temple no. 52, are the only two temples in Aihole reflecting Sīrval's Tamilian idiom, of which Temple no. 53 is more fully preserved. While Temple no. 4 at Sīrvaḷ, which I use to represent that site, uses a sequence of base moldings that are fully Tamilian, Aihole only adapts few details to its indigenous Karnataka type. For instance, the kapotapālī of Temple no. 52's virtually buried base shows luxurious dormer motifs (nāsī), differing from the contemporary local convention of wedge-shaped bosses. The prati moldings above the base of Temple nos. 52 and 53 have a variety of creatures, as on Temple no. 4 at Sīrval, a feature ultimately borrowed from contemporary Tamil temples.

The walls of these Aihole temples are plotted on a straight plumb line (mānasūtra), as is their base. Their offsets, marked by pilasters, are conveyed only by carving, that is, as a sculptural effect not registered on the ground plan. Thus a central segment (bhadra) shows two staggered planes, separated from corner offsets by broad recesses. In the Galaganātha temples, the niches are deeper, tending toward their Sīrval connection; at Rācigudi, they are more or less even with the ground of the offsets themselves. At Rācigudi, a pavilion motif—a pair of thin pilasters supporting an architectural dome—is squeezed between the thicker pilasters of the primary offsets. The unfinished surface of the Galaganātha temples reveals that the architectural details are created by cutting back the straight masonry walls; uncarved panels for figural sculptures exist at the same plane as the pilasters themselves.

The recesses of Galaganātha temples carry blind niches, rendered by thin pilasters split at the capital and crowned by a circular nāsī dormer, a common motif from Tamilnāḍu continuing at Sīrval. The central plane of the bhadra, called *subhadra,* also shows similar split pilasters but now supporting a decorated festoon *(toraṇa)* ris-

Plate 19. Paṭṭadakal, Jaina temple, southwest, early tenth century

Plate 20. Paṭṭadakal, Jaina temple, sanctum doorway, detail

Plate 21. Kukkanūr, Navaliṅga group, southern shrine, southeast, late ninth century

ing from two perched makaras. The makaras have drooping, foliated tails recalling the indigenous, Karnataka variant seen on the sanctum doorway to the Jaina temple at Paṭṭadakal (pl. 20) and the walls of the Navaliṅga temple at Kukkanūr (pl. 21).

The walls of both Galaganātha temples appear to be a pastiche of disconnected panels, many still to be carved, some representing Hindu deities as well as local folklore. Temple no. 52 preserves on its corners small figures of Dikpālas (the guardians of the quarters). The figurative accent of these shrines contrasts with their contemporaries on the sites such as Rācigudi, betraying a contemporary Tamilian trend of treating structural features as perches for figures.

The superstructure of these Aihole temples reflects their wall composition. The first parapet course (hāra) preserves the details most fully, following the indentations of the wall below. Corners are surmounted by a square-domed pavilion *(kūṭa)* and the wide central offset has an oblong hall-type motif *(śālā)*. On Galaganātha Temple no. 53, the proportions of individual architectural motifs of the hāra suggest a Tamil influence, particularly in the very tall neck *(grīva)* above the vedī platform on which, in the Tamil temples, figures would have been shown.[7] At Aihole, however, the Tamil ideas are absorbed within the local tradition of Deccano-Drāviḍa architecture. Thus, while the kūṭas and śālās of Temple no. 53 have the elongated proportions of a Tamil motif, the recessed space between (hārāntara) also matches their height, unlike in the Tamil region, where it would be distinctly lower. This inclusion of Tamil proportions within a Deccano-Drāviḍa formulation results in a somewhat overburdened appearance. Rācigudi relates to the mainstream of Drāviḍa temples of Karnataka and may be compared to the Navaliṅga temple at Kukkanūr or the Jaina temple at Paṭṭadakal. The proportion of the hāra of this shrine is that of the Deccano-Drāviḍa temple. The hāra's moldings are closely packed and the necking diminished so that the coping sits low on the vedī, in contrast to the tall, Tamil version of Temple no. 53. Karṇakūṭas are at the same level as the hārāntara. Madhyaśālā, however, is conspicuously magnified and has a bold *mahānāsī* fronton.

The diversity of these temples as well as the pastiche effect of the Galaganātha temples point to the degree to which interaction of architectural ideas was taking place in this period in this mercantile town. The interaction also allowed various stylistic choices. But distinct from stylistic preferences between Tamil and Karnataka details in individual monuments, we also discern common concerns and preoccupations with the morphology of Drāviḍa architecture, to which these stylistic choices apply. The interaction of stylistic choices and morphological concerns will be shown to be localized in Aihole's architectural history, characterizing what can be called Aihole's architectural idiom. It is the book's contention that Aihole's idiom provides the formal ground for Vesara architecture in the eleventh century.

Reflection on the Archetype

The tenth-century temples at Aihole are characterized by a restrained articulation of the sanctum wall. It has been pointed out that the wall offsets and recesses of the temples discussed above are not plotted on the ground plan, only created as a sculptural effect above the base moldings. The Galaganātha temples are most telling in this regard, as the recesses are much shallower than their Drāviḍa counterpart at Sīrval, and these recesses are also not carried down through the basement moldings. The eastern shrine of Rācigudi is also limited to the sanctum's cube even though the arrangement of its staggered offsets can be compared to the earlier, bolder, Drāviḍa temples such as the Navaliṅga at Kukkanūr and the Jaina temple at Paṭṭadakal. The two-storied western shrine of the twin Nādargudi is stripped entirely of any wall ornamentation or demarcations for offsets. Its late-tenth-century date can only be discerned by a large vertical slab of stone at the hāra level marking an enormous, detached dormer. The sanctum wall shows this feature only upon a bare wall made of large blocks of stone (pl. 22).[8]

The tenth-century temples at Aihole suggest an attempt to focus attention on the raw masonry cubicle. Many types of temples built since the seventh and eighth centuries—Drāviḍa, Nāgara, and Bhūmiprāsādas—also show a preoccupation with bare walls as a persistent characteristic at Aihole, giving its tenth-century shrines a local stamp. Nāgara temples in the seventh and eighth centuries for which Aihole is best known, for instance, show their typical, curvilinear Nāgara tower resting on a sanctum whose walls are essentially plain masonry cube. The central projection of the temple is conducted properly only in the base and tower. The bhadra niche, however, is created by de-

Plate 22. Aihole, Nādarguḍi, western shrine, south, tenth century

Plate 23. Aihole, Cakraguḍi, southwest, seventh century

Plate 24. Aihole, Cikkeśvara temple, south, late eleventh century

Plate 25. Aihole, a shrine south of Mallikārjuna, east view, late eleventh century

Plate 26. Aihole, a shrine north of Huccimalli, northwest view, late eleventh century

tached stone pillars standing on the base's projection and resting against the sanctum's masonry cubicle (pl. 23).

This local preoccupation with the sanctum as a stone cubicle is given a pointed expression in the eleventh century in another prominent form at Aihole we might call Bhūmiprāsāda, using Michael Meister's term for shrines that show a tower created out of layers of cornices (or condensed *bhūmis*). The top portion on all these shrines is missing, although they were probably crowned by a Drāviḍa finial (pls. 24, 25, 26).[9] These Bhūmiprāsādas are distinguished by plain stone walls, with late-eleventh-century features only revealed in the basement moldings such as a sharp *karṇikā* and low, flat kapotapālī with blank bosses. The wall's masonry blends the sanctum and the preceding vestibule, showing virtually no distinction between the two spaces it encloses except for an incised line across the uniformly surfaced stone blocks; inside, the spaces are distinguished by a doorway between them. The plain, unified stone matrix of these structures recalls cave architecture. Like those cells carved out of the mountain rock and embedded inside cavernous halls such as those in the Deccan, Aihole's cell is marked off in a delicate, sculptural fashion. Thus the minimalist form and technique utilized in these Bhūmiprāsādas reflect an archetypal cell in the Deccan, connected organically to the mountainous rock and revealed within it.[10]

Local Purpose

The stark Nādarguḍi shrine best represents this minimalist tendency at Aihole in the tenth century, fully expressing the organic archetype. More nuanced wall surfaces seem to convey only an architectural elaboration on this embedded nucleus. An interrelating, hierarchical arrangement in the massing and ornamentation of the temple's wall, distinct from the rhythm of bays in a typical Drāviḍa temple, suggests the evolution of an indigenous Aihole idiom in the tenth century.

The first hint of the architectural purpose of Aihole's idiom is seen in the eastern shrine at Rācigudi and Temple no. 53 in the Galaganātha group (pls. 15, 16). The Rācigudi shrine shows an enlarged madhyaśālā (miniature, barrel-vaulted hall-type) on its superstructure, matching the bhadra (central offset), with a visibly enlarged mahanāsī (dormer pediment) crowning the subhadra (primary face of the multiplaned bhadra offset); the Galaganātha shrine also shows a madhyaśālā corresponding to the bhadra, except now it has a crowning kūṭa (square, hut-shaped enclosure-type) instead of a mahānāsī. The two-storied western shrine of the twin Nādargudi, datable to the mid-tenth century, shows an unusual large, isolated slab of stone for the mahānāsī, dramatizing the centrality of the implied subhadra even if Nādargudi's own wall is bare of any offsetting at all (pl. 22).

The focus given to the subhadra as a feature to which the hierarchy of the wall gravitates, marked by a conspicuous, somewhat independent, crown, is part of a localized experiment in Aihole. The isolation of subhadra as a distinct feature, pulling the wall's hierarchy to itself, is signaled by Temple no. 53 in the Galaganātha group, where the wall's components are brought into a tight, hierarchical arrangement and given a central motif in the distinctive kūṭa instead of the usual mahānāsī on the large madhyaśālā. The *makara-toraṇa* (gateway pattern with fantastic aquatic creatures) created on split pilasters of its subhadra can be compared to Temple no. 4 at Sīrval, except for a significant difference between the two. At Sīrval (pl. 18), the subhadra is part of the stepped bhadra offset occupied by a blind niche motif *(koṣṭha);* at Aihole, the subhadra itself is treated as that koṣṭha (niche) framed by split pilasters. This absorption of a wall's ornament into the architectural support transforms the support itself into a potent motif, explored more fully in later temples but whose unity is already conveyed here by the unusual kūṭa above the wall.

Problem of the Wall

It seems that the question of isolating and emphasizing the subhadra as a distinct unit was first solved at Aihole in the superstructure, not a wall, by distinguishing the most central feature of the madhyaśālā. Unlike earlier temples, where the containing feature was the bhadra, the subhadra (absorbing the koṣṭha) forces the bhadra offset to widen out. The problem of expressing this expanding bhadra remains to be resolved, but the expansion itself seems to be suggested in the enlarged crowning madhyaśālā, as at the Rācigudi shrine. Also, on Temple no. 53, the miniature representations on the hāra borrowed from the Tamil region serve to magnify the parapet so that the madhyaśālā could accommodate the expanse of the renewed bhadra. This novelty is limited to Temple no. 53, making its hāra ungainly in appearance because it attempts to fit Tamil proportions—designed to distinguish miniature representations of the hāra from a low, connecting balustrade course—to a Karnataka system designed to unify architectural representations as well as the connecting balustrade at a uniform roof level of the hāra. Both temples attempt solutions to the problem of accommodating a growing, variegated bhadra, but they emphasize the subhadra on it only by juggling superstructural details, unable to expand it without jeopardizing its crowning member. The problem of the walls remains unsolved in these early tenth-century monuments.

Temples built in the second half of the tenth century at Aihole grapple with incorporating this subhadra into the overall scheme of offsets, extending the experiments of those earlier temples. Perhaps the most successful of these shrines is Ambigergudi that inscribes the primary, reconceptualized divisions on walls using only pilasters on a plain wall while also stripping it of all architectural decoration (pl. 98). The tendency to flatten the wall here is similar to that at Rācigudi, but the shrine shows features in advance of Rācigudi, arguing for its late-tenth-century date. In particular, its basement moldings have thinner and sharper features than at Rācigudi. Also as in Rācigudi, the madhyaśālā in this shrine is magnified, with its large mahānāsī blocked out to project boldly from its barrel-vaulted back.

No porch or opening could be imagined in this shrine. A seemingly monotonous array of thin pilasters along a straight plumb (mānasūtra) inflects the sanctum walls into a wide central cluster of four pilasters indicating the subhadra and *upabhadra* (subsidiary planes of the bhadra) separated from karṇas (distinguished planes of corners). The play of pilasters is reflected more boldly on the string course (hāra) of the superstructural story. The subhadra thus supports a heavy mahānāsī pediment, pilasters marking the upabhadras are aligned with the upright panels of the madhyaśālā, and the pairs of pilasters framing the karṇa support kūṭas above. The temple also

Plate 27. Aihole, triple Jaina temple opposite Virupākṣa, western shrine, south, late tenth century

removes the pavilion motifs that typically adorned contemporary Aihole temples except perhaps Nādarguḍi, which simply expresses the geometry of its stone cubicle. In its ascetic shunning of ornaments, the Ambigerguḍi is in sync with Aihole's other Drāviḍa temples, searching for a different architectural order within a Drāviḍa format. Two other temples of this period, the western shrine of the triple Jaina temple opposite Gaurīguḍi (pl. 27), and a single Jaina temple across from this triple shrine and facing it, integrate offsets and motifs in an Ambigerguḍi-like wall. These temples reflect the latter's wall formula but clearly separate the bhadra and karṇas by a recess carried through the basement. The primary faces of the offsets are decorated by a kuṭa-pavilion as in Rāciguḍi.

The Jaina shrines highlight a tension between their Drāviḍa formula and the emphasis they place on the newly evolved subhadra within it. On the walls of all these shrines, the subhadra is narrower than the karṇas. The awkwardness of a narrow centerpiece is also revealed by the Drāviḍa pavilion occupying the subhadra, shrunk and squeezed tightly into it compared with their counterparts on the corners. The tension between the desired prominence of the offset subhadra and its constricted appearance is further reflected on the superstructure, where an uneasy limbo exists between a virtually isolated central mahānāsī pediment above the subhadra that also is maintained as an integral part of the overall madhyaśālā. The block for mahānāsī is flattened on its sides as if to visually alleviate the problem of narrow subhadra. In the western of the triple Jaina shrine, a balance in the superstructure is tentatively achieved by trimming down and staggering the kūṭa crown of the corners.

The two Jaina shrines cannot be considered new solutions to a Drāviḍa wall. Rather they highlight the problem of fully developing a Drāviḍa wall within the Aihole mode. The hierarchy of their wall achieves visual coherence by means other than the control of actual wall proportions. Especially the whole śālā above the bhadra is manipulated, fragmenting the barrel-vaulted motif into its constituent parts and thus giving a new treatment to the traditional, Deccano-Drāviḍa motif. The upright side panels of the śālā show standing Jinas flanking the seated Jina in the circular cavity of the central dormer. These figurative accents on the sides shift attention from the center as well as from the volume of the connecting barrel-vaulted structure. These discrete uprights now share and complement the emphasis on the partially isolated dormer of the śālā.

In this regard, perhaps the most remarkable "aesthetic" obfuscation of the unresolved problem of coherence is seen in the single Jaina temple across from this triple shrine (pl. 30). While its second story reflects the arrangement of the wall below, its madhyaśālā is removed so that only a mahānāsī block, equal to the size of the nāsī below, occupies the center. On the otherwise slightly diminished story, this undiminished motif visually alleviates the narrowness of the feature below.

On this single Jaina temple, the differentiation and control of the hierarchy of the sanctum wall is also achieved by a play of architectural motifs. The pavilion motifs adorning its three offsets have a ranged typology of pilasters. The central pavilion pilasters on the south and north walls have plain square shafts, and on the east these are replaced by hexagonal pilasters with a large bell-shaped upper part *(laśuna)*. The pilasters used on the karṇas include four kinds: ones with indented shafts interrupted by three blocks of moldings (south); faceted pilasters having a square base faced with a candraśālā (half-moon-shaped dormer) and a *ghaṭapallava* (vase and foliage) top; a variety that seems to be designed by a vertical pile of round pots; and a fluted type with a ghaṭapallava in the top section as well as a *ghaṭa* with a *padma* (lotus) above reminiscent of a variety seen in Deccani caves (pl. 31). This array of pilasters is not arbitrary; on the three walls of the shrine, they consistently show pavilions with simpler pilasters on the bhadra and more elaborate ones on the periphery. While seemingly opposite to the relative prominence of the hāra's features, the "inverse" arrangement of simple-pillared pavilion on the bhadra and those with more elaborate types on the periphery may parallel a trend in figural sculpture in Jaina temples: for example, the Melaguḍi Jaina temple at Hallūr (pl. 32). In the Hallūr temple, the offsets of the sanctum wall are plain while a similarly organized wall enclosing the closed hall *(gūḍhamaṇḍapa)* shows standing Jina figures.[11] The Jaina shrine at Aihole shows no figures in the pavilions on the sanctum wall, but in increasing the decoration away from the center, it moves from simple architectural motifs to elaborate ones, finally showing a standing Jina in the wall adjacent to the sanctum. What began as a problem of maintaining a wall's hierar-

Plate 28. Aihole, triple Jaina temple, southern shrine, southeast

Plate 29. Aihole, triple Jaina shrine, northern shrine, northeast (courtesy: American Institute of Indian Studies)

Plate 30. Aihole, west-facing shrine opposite triple Jaina temple, south, late tenth century

Plate 31. Aihole, west-facing shrine opposite triple Jaina temple, south, wall detail

Plate 32. Hallūr, Melaguḍi Jaina temple, east, tenth century (courtesy: American Institute of Indian Studies)

chy centered on an emphasized subhadra seems in this specific Jaina context to be an iconographically serendipity.

The northern and the southern shrines of the triple Jaina temple show another major breakthrough in Aihole architects' experimentation with the wall. The northern shrine is rectangular, with only the bhadra expanded on the back wall. While the shorter wall has a bhadra composed of a subhadra and an upabhadra, the wider bhadra of the longer north wall is marked by a tertiary level. The hāra above reflects the wall division. On the shorter side, the madhyaśālā crowns the entire bhadra, with side panels boldly marking its outer pilasters. The subhadra is indicated by a prominent mahānāsī projection. Remarkably, the śālā for the longer wall is modified to match the extended wall below and has two barrel-vaulted roofs, one seemingly telescoped into the other, reflecting the two upabhadras.

The triple Jaina temple at Aihole is perhaps the first known instance of this modified superstructural feature. The "nested" madhyaśālā becomes a standard feature of Vesara temples. On the rectangular shrine, the modification of the śālā seems to have evolved almost accidentally to avoid the disproportionate length to which a single śālā would have to be pulled out to match the extended bhadra. The folds of this innovative feature allow the crowning motif to adjust to such an extension.

The southern shrine of this triple temple is strikingly different from, and more massive than, the other two shrines (pl. 28). The walls are sculpted into bold offsets, with a deep recess separating karṇas from a bhadra. The subhadra projects from two upabhadras. While a Deccano-Drāviḍa temple is often characterized by a bhadra projecting in the center of each wall, the bold central projection on this temple sports the wall rhythm of a North Indian Nāgara temple. With even the framing pilasters omitted, the plain wall is defined only by a horizontal band along its upper edge, reminding one of the decorative bands used on North Indian temples.

The nested madhyaśālā on the superstructure of this shrine seems to be used to adjust to the wall's Nāgara-like projections. In diminishing scale, these projections are reproduced on two more extant stories composing the superstructure. The nāsī continues to project boldly from the śālā back but is never detached. The nested śālā with its *nāsī* projection becomes a unit on this temple.

The most elaborate of tenth-century temples at Aihole is the so-called Temple no. 5 in the Veniyār group (pl. 33). In this temple, the experimentation of Deccano-Drāviḍa temples at Aihole comes to a fruition. On its hāra, the madhyaśālā stands much taller than that in any other Aihole temple. Its outer śālā is pulled much closer to the inner member, and the mahānāsī would have been a large separate block of stone, now fallen. The separation of the nāsī block from its *śālā* back, achieved through formal means in earlier experiments at Aihole, now also becomes an aspect of the physical construction of the temple. The stone nāsī achieves its mass in order to measure up to the width of the subhadra, not merely the motif occupying it. Its prominence on the madhya-

Plate 33. Aihole, Veniyār group, Temple no. 5, southeast, ca. A.D. 1000 (courtesy: American Institute of Indian Studies)

śālā is probably comparable to that of the shrine in Nādarguḍi. The boldly sculptured nested madhyaśālā becomes a hallmark of the Aihole idiom by the end of the tenth century.

The Veniyār temple's large, two-storied sanctum stands directly on the kapotapālī of the adhiṣṭhāna, whose sequence of moldings is comparable to the western shrine of the triple Jaina temple. The bhadra has three phālanās, as in the elaborate southern shrine of that triple temple, in this case marked by framing pilasters. In addition to the architectural motifs occupying the principal face of the offsets, this Veniyār temple also shows a kūṭa pavilion in the recesses between the bhadra and the karṇas. This is an unusual feature in Aihole,[12] and an advance over other late-tenth-century temples seen so far.

The origins of this architectural motif in the wall recess can be traced in monuments at the nearby site of Ron. There two-storied temples in the idiom of Aihole were built in the last quarter of the tenth century. These temples share with Aihole the sequence of adhiṣṭhāna moldings (the wall standing sometimes directly on the moldings without the pratikaṇṭha, as is typical of Aihole); the arrangement of wall into a broad bhadra having a subhadra with one or two upabhadras; the stocky cantoning pilasters with bulbous laśunas; and the heavy hāra with a madhyaśālā that is usually larger than other architectural motifs. The Kālaguḍi at Ron also shows a large block of stone set as nāsī in the center of a massive double madhyaśālā that recalls the temple in the Veniyār group at Aihole (pl. 34). The so-called Iśvara temple near the Anantaśāyiguḍi dramatizes the introduction of an architectural motif in the recess

Plate 34. Ron, Kālaguḍi, north, late tenth century (courtesy: American Institute of Indian Studies)

Plate 35. Ron, Iśvaraguḍi, north, ca. A.D. 1000 (courtesy: American Institute of Indian Studies)

within the arrangement of wall already developed at Aihole (pl. 101). The temple's wall shows no motifs on its offsets, only one each in its undercut recesses. Another, again so-called Iśvara temple shows shrines on the offsets as well as the recesses, as in the Temple no. 5 in the Veniyār group at Aihole (pl. 35).

Conclusion

These temples at Aihole and Ron show a new formal preoccupation within Drāviḍa architecture of Karnataka by the end of the tenth century. Architects have attempted to place a relative emphasis on offsets leading to the central projection, which has resulted in a series of adjustments in Drāviḍa's traditional architectural vocabulary. The staggering of the wall is accompanied by innovative features in the superstructure as well, particularly the nested madhyaśālā. Finally, the recesses and the offsets project architectural motifs, not images. This new preoccupation seems to be the result of a "drift" created at Aihole in Drāviḍa's conventional form.

Aihole's irregularities demonstrate a fresh critical look at a Drāviḍa sanctum. The "organic" conception of the sanctum, which in Karnataka's oldest Drāviḍa temples had resulted in Kūṭina elaborations, is given a conscious focus and articulation only in Aihole, providing a ground for modifying the traditional features of Drāviḍa.[13] Kubler's idea of "drift" and "interference" partly characterizes these piecemeal distortions of Drāviḍa, except that I would add to Kubler's linguistic model that a formal drift must also suggest a change in thinking.[14] Aihole's experimentation in the tenth century suggests a living, interactive relationship between the makers and their tradition. The chapter has assessed this active reflection on tradition by analyzing the fragmentary details of monuments. The diversity of Aihole may relate to the interregional culture of traveling merchants who must have patronized these temples. Aihole's expressive focus on the native Karnataka concept of shrine as a stark, stone cubicle reminiscent of caves may also reflect a conscious regionalism in this international context.

One model for explaining the critical, reflective thought involved in the gradation of Aihole's innovations might be derived from a notion of self in Charles Sanders Peirce. Discussing Peirce's semiotics, Milton Singer, an anthropologist of South Asia, explains that Peirce's self emerges "from the fallible inferences we all make from the observations of external facts, including the signs of the self."[15] Kublerlike "interferences" within Drāviḍa's traditional scheme, then, could be seen as Peircean "fallible inferences" through which the self gradually manifests itself. Peirce can allow Aihole's piecemeal innovations to be seen as positive acts of knowing embedded in the day-to-day acts of making.

Temples at Aihole are Drāviḍa, not Vesara. There are many features that develop in Aihole, however, that have a direct bearing on Vesara architecture. The significance given to subhadra, with a kūṭa above, in Temple no. 53 is extended into an unusual, turned offset with a turned kūṭa above in the Joḍa Kalaśa at Sūḍī (pl. 44). Aihole's use of an architectural representation as a wall ornament may not be uncommon in Drāviḍa ornamentation, but Rācaguḍi seems to be one of the first temples to show a blind Drāviḍa pavilion as its principal wall motif instead of figures.[16] Such a fundamental importance given to architectural motifs is exploited fully in the eleventh century.

The nested madhyaśālā, seen on the triple Jaina temple, as well as the development of a subhadra as the central wall projection, become standard Vesara features. At Aihole, the nested madhyaśālā offers a flexible superstructural element to an expanding bhadra. It also emphasizes the subhadra on it. The legacy of this architectural feature can be seen in the eleventh century in at least three significant ways. First, the madhyaśālā configuration on Aihole's Jaina temples, showing standing Jinas on the śālā's vertical side panels and a seated Jina in the mahānāsī dormer, provides a basis for disintegrating the barrel-vaulted shape of the śālā itself, opening a possibility of separate evolution of all its discrete components for sculptural decoration, as in the Siddheśvara temple at Hāverī (pl. 67).[17] Second, as in the triple Jaina temple as well as the single Jaina temple across, the discrete mahānāsī block, emphasized while the rest of the Drāviḍa śālā withers away, is also projected in such Vesara temples as the Mallikārjuna at Sūḍī (pl. 41) and the Sūrya at Lakkuṇḍī (pl. 59). Third, in the single Jaina temple, the independent nāsī showing a seated Jina as large as the subhadra's motif also appears above the wall connecting the sanctum to the *mandapa* in front, comparing this space to the importance of the subhadra. This likening of the antarāla vestibule to the subhadra continues in Vesara (pl. 46).

Aihole's architects developed formal features of

their temples in the context of Drāviḍa forms in Karnataka and in relation to other contemporary tenth-century temples. Yet, Aihole's inventiveness is not typical of the tenth-century monuments in Karnataka; it is localized at the site. While Aihole does not produce the first Vesara temple, I do not think architecture would have evolved from the Drāviḍa form without the mediation of Aihole's "fallible inferences."

4

The Vesara Moment

A SERIES OF ELEVENTH-CENTURY TEMPLES IN THE vicinity of Aihole shows a creative use of Aihole's irregularities to fundamentally change the formal as well as the conceptual basis of Karnataka's regional architecture. This chapter explores the moment when temples in Karnataka using a Drāviḍa formula could no longer be called Drāviḍa. Aihole's drift may suggest a slow hemorrhage in the tradition of Drāviḍa architecture. But Vesara could not have evolved simply through a weakening of the previous tradition. A wide variety of experiments in a relatively concentrated area of northern Karnataka suggests a focused search for a new organizing principle. Bolstered by a rare epigraphic record that specifically mentions an architect by name and responds to his work, the chapter will argue for the active role played by the architects in giving their regional architecture a consciously modern form.

The modernity of the eleventh-century experiments in Karnataka has been overlooked by scholars. While the term Vesara is used commonly to describe the temple type that emerged from these experiments and dominated Karnataka and neighboring regions, the relationship between Vesara and the previous, Drāviḍa architecture has never been adequately explained. Some scholars have imposed on Vesara an evolutionary model, explaining it as nothing but a late flourish in the history of Drāviḍa architecture. Others, after the twelfth-century text, the Kāmikāgama, have used the term itself (literally "mule" in Sanskrit lexicon) to describe Vesara as a regional hybrid mixing features of the typical South Indian, Drāviḍa, and North Indian, Nāgara, architecture.

Providing one argument against Vesara's derivative status within modern classification systems for temple architecture, an inscription in the Joḍa Kalaśa ("twin pot") temple at Sūḍī dated A.D. 1060 shows the excitement with which Vesara's contemporary viewers might have perceived the novelty of its experiments. Mentioning the designer of one of the two shrines of this major twin Vesara temple, the inscription reads: "Śaṅkarārya . . . constructed in the middle of the town of Śuṇḍī a dwelling for Nāgeśvara so that the finials were completed in a manner that none could possibly imagine."[1] The amazement of the scribe of this inscription is justified by many unusual features of the shrine, to be described later. First, it is important to point out in a few monuments preceding Sūḍī that Śaṅkarārya's shrine is not simply a novelty but part of a widespread change in temple architecture of Karnataka that began earlier in the century and led to standardization of the Vesara form by midcentury. The Sūḍī inscription discussed above is rare, but its tone shows an active response to architectural changes that must correspond to the level of engagement of such Vesara architects as Śaṅkarārya. Lacking the archives of documents from which historians of other periods of world architecture benefit, I propose a method of tracing the logic and purpose of Vesara's innovations in the monuments themselves.

Conceptual Shift within the Southern Form

It is true that the Kalleśvara temple at Kukkanūr, datable to ca. A.D. 1000–1025, shows all the features of a regional Drāviḍa temple (pl. 36). It

Plate 36. Kukkanūr, Kalleśvara temple, west, ca. A.D. 1025

can be related to Aihole's experiments culminating in Temple no. 5 of the Veniyār group. Kukkanūr, however, is three-storied, as none of the Aihole temples are. Its idiosyncrasies are also not found in those earlier temples.

In its solid stone tower, clearly marked by horizontal stories, the temple evokes a multistoried mansion for the divine image housed in the sanctum, as is typical of Drāviḍa architecture (pl. 5). Each story is defined by a string course (hāra) of miniature architectural representations above the walls. As is typical in Drāviḍa architecture of the Karnataka sort, these miniature models at Kukkanūr are composed mainly of square-domed, hut-shaped pavilions (kūṭas) at the corners and an oblong, barrel-roofed hall-type (śālā) in the center, the latter appearing split and staggered at Kukkanūr in a way that recalls Aihole and becomes significant in the development of Vesara architecture. An arch-shaped dormer (nāsī) suggesting an attic window faces each of these miniature representations and is made especially emphatic on the śālā.

But Kukkanūr is not simply a continuation of Drāviḍa architecture in later centuries, as a close examination shows. While fully using the architectural vocabulary of Drāviḍa, Kukkanūr introduces significant changes in Drāviḍa's basic architectural scheme. For instance, it has a wide projecting offset (bhadra) in the center of its wall, unlike the narrow feature in a Drāviḍa temple. Also unlike the latter, which is articulated as if it were a porch in which the resident deity of the mansion appears in its sculptural form, Kukkanūr simply uses a regular rhythm of thin pilasters to define evenly staggered planes of its stone masonry.

The difference between Kukkanūr and the earlier Drāviḍa temple suggests not simply a reduction of decorative details but a conceptual shift. Unlike Drāviḍa, Kukkanūr's bhadra projection is widened to span the sanctum, as is visible on plan (fig. 2). A proportional relationship is thus achieved between the inside and the outside of the temple in a way that had not concerned architects of earlier Drāviḍa temples. Instead of being merely an architectural frame for the divine figure, the expanded bhadra at Kukkanūr becomes a more positive expression of the temple's sanctum itself. The mass of the bhadra projection is especially conveyed by pinched recesses on either side, whose narrow, deeply cut lines separate it from the temple's corner piers (karṇas).

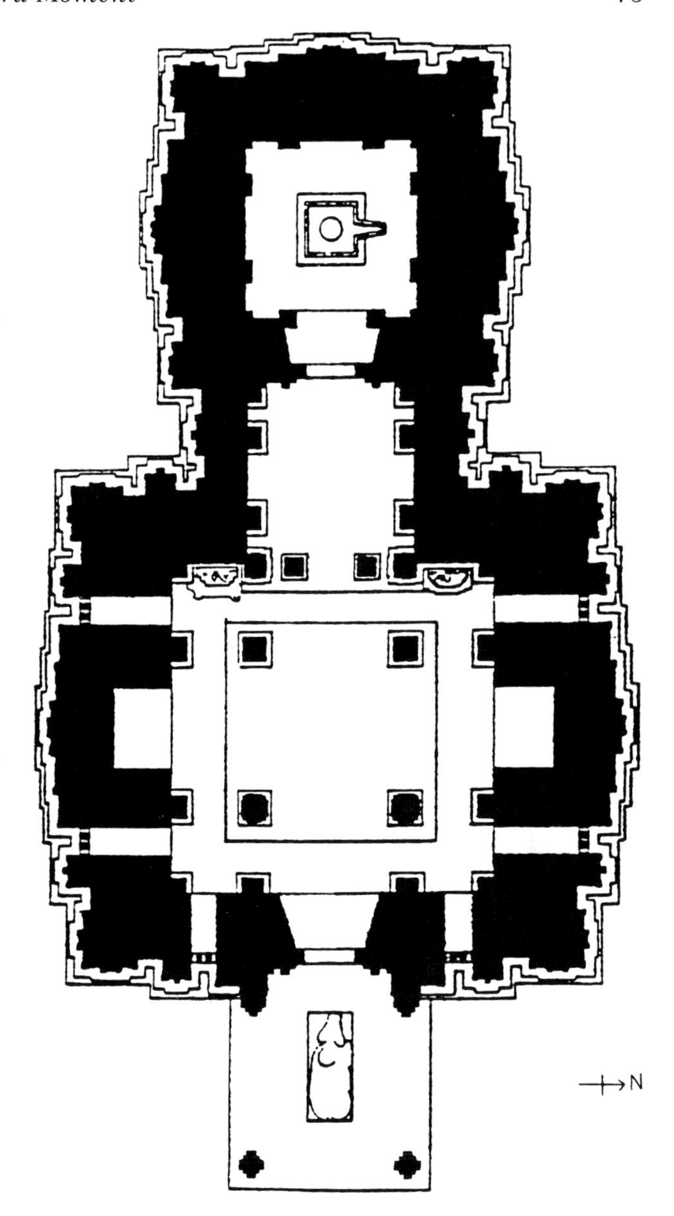

Figure 2. Kukkanūr, Kalleśvara temple, plan (Cousens, Plate LX)

Quite conspicuously, the Kukkanūr temple shows an architectural motif on the central masonry face of its bhadra instead of a figural divinity. Here it develops upon the legacy of Aihole's tenth-century temples. Carved in relief, this motif has a square Drāviḍa dome supported on a pair of tall, thin pilasters. The dome is crowned by a pot, similar to that on the temple's own finial. Such blank Drāviḍa pavilions also occupy corner piers and the depth of the recesses, providing an austere decorative scheme for Kukkanūr's exterior walls, like Aihole (pl. 38). Although Kukkanūr's decorative use of architectural motifs is not unusual in the history of Indian temple architecture, the chapter will soon show that the choice of these motifs as primary wall ornament elaborates upon Aihole and gives this specifically Aihole legacy also an unusual turn.

The superstructure of Kukkanūr is reformulated to accommodate changes on the temple's walls. The oblong, śālā motif on each of its horizontal stories (called madhyaśālā on account of its central position) is drawn out, fragmented, and manipulated to respond to the increased width and staggered offsets of the bhadra projection below. The new configuration in fact looks as if it were made up of two śālās, with the barrel vault of one of them telescoped into that of the other. The vertical side panels of this "nested" madhyaśālā are carved virtually independent of the barrel-shaped backs and shown visibly taller. The panels correspond with the thin wall pilasters below and make the renewed madhyaśālā motif compatible with the offsets of the bhadra projection. Finally, the domed finial of the temple also has divisions reflecting the serial folds of the madhyaśālās below.

The renewed Drāviḍa details on Kukkanūr's superstructure interfere with the effect of the horizontal stack of stories essential to its identity as a Drāviḍa temple. The tall panels on the side of the nested madhyaśālā, for instance, produce gentle vertical accents across the superstructure. Conspicuously, below the large, projecting dormer (mahānāsī) in the center of each madhyaśālā, Kukkanūr also has an additional dormer facing the moldings of the string course. The arbitrary pairing of dormers in the exact center of each story is unprecedented, and it violates the architectural logic that is typically maintained in a Drāviḍa temple. At Kukkanūr, however, linked dormers form a vertical spine for the entire superstructure, made emphatic also by the shortened walls for each of the stories and the resultant compression of the superstructure.

The only feature that continues to mark the horizontal stack of stories at Kukkanūr, and consistently thereafter in all Vesara temples, is the set of square kūṭas at each corner of the string course. These karṇakūṭas continue to project the temple's Drāviḍa profile in a relatively unaltered form. Within this emphatic Drāviḍa frame, however, Kukkanūr rearranges and complicates Drāviḍa details. To explain this reconfiguration as a deliberate departure from Drāviḍa, we can compare Kukkanūr with the Aḍakeśvara temple at Mahākūṭa (pl. 37), a contemporary structure that shares with it most of the formal Drāviḍa ingredients.[2]

There are, of course, minor visual differences between the Kalleśvara temple at Kukkanūr and the Aḍakeśvara temple at Mahākūṭa. For instance, the north side of the Mahākūṭa temple, which most fully preserves its features, shows a molded basement (adhiṣṭhāna) whose moldings are somewhat thicker than those at Kukkanūr, reminding one of late-tenth-century temples at Aihole. Mahākūṭa's walls also begin directly above the adhiṣṭhāna, as in those Aihole temples, without the molding of interlocked rafters (pratikaṇṭhas) present at Kukkanūr. In basic composition of wall offsets, however, the Mahākūṭa temple closely matches Kukkanūr. Both temples are distinguished by a very wide bhadra twice indented and separated from karṇas by narrow recesses. Each of their offsets is framed by pilasters that are considerably thinner than those at Aihole. The offsets and recesses at Mahākūṭa are not as deep as at Kukkanūr. The indentation of offsets is shallow and so is the depth of the recesses. Architectural motifs are also not fully encased within the recesses as at Kukkanūr. The differences between the two temples, however, can be attributed to aesthetic choice of the makers rather than chronological factors. The advancements over earlier, Aihole temples make these two monuments contemporaries in ca. A.D. 1000–1025.

The aesthetic difference between the Kalleśvara temple at Kukkanūr and the Aḍakeśvara at Mahākūṭa is conspicuous in the superstructure. Both have three stories and a dome, unlike a typical two-storied temple at Aihole in the tenth century. The manner of their upward progression, however, differs. At Mahākūṭa, the hāra right above the sanctum wall has a nested madhyaśālā; the one above it has an unmodified Drāviḍa śālā; and the topmost has only moldings supporting the hāra without the string of architectural motifs that characterize other stories. In effect, therefore, Mahākūṭa seems to show only two fully articulated stories below the dome, as in some late-tenth-century temples at Aihole and Ron. At Kukkanūr, in contrast, each of the three stories depicts a full sequence of hāra's motifs, only diminishing their size as stories ascend to the domed finial. While high walls enclosing each story give the Mahākūṭa temple a somewhat ungainly appearance, it is significant that they also maintain in the temple a Drāviḍa accent, which can only be contrasted with Kukkanūr.

The madhyaśālā of the second story especially

Plate 37. Mahākūṭa, Aḍakeśvara temple, north, ca. A.D. 1025 (courtesy: American Institute of Indian Studies)

Plate 38. Kukkanūr, Kalleśvara temple, south (courtesy: American Institute of Indian Studies)

dominates Mahākūṭa's superstructure. While at Kukkanūr the nested śālā motif on this story is only a smaller version of that of the story below, the madhyaśālā at Mahākūṭa, which is not nested, is equal to the inner of the nested śālā of the first story. This śālā also soars above the main wall of the sanctum as if it were raised on the wall of a second story directly above the inner sanctum, as in the earliest Drāviḍa temples in the region.[3] The prominence of this wall and its śālā crown asserts a Drāviḍa identity against the compressed and integrated effect of the wall so fully extended to the superstructure at Kukkanūr.

The profile of Mahākūṭa's dome shows an S curve closely comparable with Kukkanūr. The dome, however, stands over a visibly high necking, as is typical of Drāviḍa temples in the region. It also harks back to the older, Drāviḍa mode of showing a single offset on its body rather than multiple projections reflecting the arrangement of nested madhyaśālās at Kukkanūr.

The aesthetic difference between Kukkanūr and Mahākūṭa suggests a dialectical tension between two contemporary monuments that otherwise share a common architectural vocabulary. Mahākūṭa insists on a Drāviḍa form, while Kukkanūr introduces in that formal vocabulary a series of conceptual shifts that complicates its Drāviḍa identity. Dhaky suggests that Vesara architecture is poised between North Indian (Nāgara) and South Indian (Drāviḍa) architecture. While Dhaky's observation resembles a long-standing scholarly belief, namely, that Vesara is created by mixing forms from these two regional sources, he explains that "there is, in point of fact, nothing about [Vesara] superstructure that can be directly sensed as Nāgara. And yet the building can no longer be termed Drāviḍa in the sense the earlier buildings are."[4] Applying to Kukkanūr Dhaky's observation about a Vesara detail, it seems that the linked nāsīs on the central face of its superstructure coalesce almost "in the fashion of a latā [webbed central band] in a Nāgara śikhara [tower]."[5] This Nāgara cadence of Kukkanūr without an explicit use of Nāgara forms is part of a self-conscious innovation, as we shall see.

Dhaky explains that the vertical link of nāsīs in such temples as Kukkanūr is an "archaistic" reminder of "a stage, which, centuries before, the Nāgara form in its throes passed through, much before it achieved its fuller integrated and articulated form."[6] This observation should be qualified by pointing out that Kukkanūr's Nāgara-like formulation is in fact a mimicry, not an attempt, progressive or regressive, at the integrated web of a Nāgara temple's latā. The "archaistic" look of Kukkanūr continues in mature Vesara temples of the eleventh and twelfth centuries and betrays a Vesara conceit when architects also show off their knowledge of advanced, contemporary North Indian forms by rendering them accurately on walls of the same archaistic monuments.[7]

Take for instance the Kāśīviśveśvara temple at Lakkuṇḍī, a major Vesara temple of ca. A.D. 1075 discussed more fully in the next chapter (pl. 51). The temple is built in gray soapstone, the preferred material from that period onward as it gave monuments smoother surfaces and sharper details than sandstone. It has a large shrine model on its bhadra showing a type of multispired Nāgara tower known from contemporary North India. On the left karṇa of its south wall it also displays another contemporary northern variant called Bhūmija—a temple showing a vertical chain of spirelets on its tower. The temple's own superstructure, however, extends Kukkanūr's archaism. In particular, Kukkanūr's arbitrary linking of dormers in the center of each level now develops into a trefoil arch cascading across the moldings of the stories, being spewed out by a gorgon mask filling the large dormer of the śālā above. The decorative arch frames the tower of the large wall shrine underneath. While Kukkanūr's idiosyncrasy may remind modern scholars of a North Indian feature, Lakkuṇḍī's developments suggest that the idiosyncrasy is in fact perceived by Karnataka architects as a local, Drāviḍa invention from which they produce further, non-Nāgara elaborations.

Introduction of Anomaly

Kukkanūr's invention suggests the beginning of a series of unconventional ways in which Drāviḍa features are consciously manipulated. The deliberate nature of this effort is marked at Kukkanūr by an unprecedented motif inserted within the ornamental scheme of its exterior walls. This motif can be called a Nāgara kūṭastambha, consisting of a tall curvilinear tower of a typical North Indian, Nāgara temple, shown standing on a single column. The motif appears on the connecting wall between the sanctum and the closed hall in front, in the recesses of the sanctum's north wall, and a few places along the exterior of the closed hall (pl. 39).

The presence of a northern motif is unusual in

Plate 39. Kukkanūr, Kalleśvara temple, south, juncture of sanctum and *gūḍhamaṇḍapa,* detail (courtesy: American Institute of Indian Studies)

the tradition of southern architecture, to which the Kukkanūr monument belongs. The practice of building northern temples had already ceased in Karnataka more than two hundred years earlier, nor can the reappearance of this form as a wall motif be accounted for simply as an evolution within the ornamental scheme of Drāviḍa architecture. On the Kukkanūr wall, the Nāgara kūṭastambha is an anomaly.

I define anomaly as an intrusive term applied to the prevalent architectural framework so as to alter the logic on which the framework was originally based. Anomaly is an irregularity, but not all irregularities are anomalies. Irregularities are created as a matter of human routine, based on which scholars have traditionally described slow, stylistic changes over time. In Fernand Braudel's model (of two maps for plotting history discussed in chapter 1), all irregularities can be recorded on the small, local map of daily work, accounting for little changes that occur even when identical monuments are intended; in that model, anomaly is a function of the regional map, suggesting systematic changes in regional architecture. An anomaly can be like any irregularity an idiosyncrasy, a playful gesture, a motif introduced from a neighboring region, but in order to qualify as an anomaly such unexpected occurrences will need to be explained in terms of their function within the ongoing tradition of practice.

Kukkanūr's kūṭastambha is borrowed from a North Indian source, especially Bhūmija temples, where such a motif was commonly used to create a vertical chain of spirelets on the superstructure (pl. 55).[8] The use of this borrowed motif on temple walls, however, is original to Kukkanūr, where

Plate 40. Guḍur, Rāmaliṅgeśvara temple, north, ca. A.D. 1025

it is distinguished from the general array of Drāviḍa motifs. While a Drāviḍa motif recalls an open pavilion, with a pair of pilasters supporting a square dome similar to the temple's own finial or the kūṭa roof in the corner of each story, the anomalous Nāgara kūṭastambha is distinguished from such a Drāviḍa kūṭa pavilion by its slender tower as well as its single columnar support.

The use of Nāgara kūṭastambha on walls signals a change in the conceptual framework of Drāviḍa at Kukkanūr. On temples earlier than Kukkanūr, the ubiquitous Drāviḍa kūṭa pavilion motif could have been read as an abstract representation of the sheltering form of the temple itself, making the monument and the ideograph on its wall directly reflect each other. At Kukkanūr, this earlier, modular relationship between the structure and its ornament is qualified by the presence of a Nāgara kūṭastambha. Adjacent to the Drāviḍa kūṭa pavilion, the Nāgara kūṭastambha motif evokes a different reference. In its single column supporting a northern tower, the motif represents an irreducible form of a Nāgara temple, imagined in its North Indian context as an ornamental stone casing for a column of smoke and fire rising above the temple's symbolic altar platform.[9] As an embodiment of this basic northern imagery, the Nāgara kūṭastambha differs fundamentally from the shelter form of a Drāviḍa ideograph. The play of wall motifs at Kukkanūr creates a tension within the temple's Drāviḍa matrix, whose resolve results in the emergence of the new regional form of architecture we know as Vesara.

Kukkanūr is the first known temple in Karnataka showing experiments that depart radically from the tradition of Drāviḍa architecture. In the Rāmaliṅgeśvara temple at Guḍūr, the anomalous, northern motif introduced at Kukkanūr is fully integrated into a decorative scheme of the sanctum wall (pl. 40). On a Kukkanūr-like wall composition, simplified to a bhadra having only two rather than three stepped offsets, this small temple, datable to ca. A.D. 1025–1050, shows the Nāgara kūṭastambha uniformly occupying all wall recesses and distinguished from the Drāviḍa kūṭa pavilions on projecting offsets.

For about fifty years following Kukkanūr and Guḍūr, temples built in their vicinity in northern Karnataka showed a pattern of deliberate play between Nāgara and Drāviḍa references, evolving into a conceptual logic different from that of earlier Drāviḍa architecture. The term Vesara should properly refer to this change within Drāviḍa, not simply a regional hybrid, as it is presented in current scholarly literature. The features of Vesara's new conceptual logic will be revealed first in an elaboration and systematization of the visual formula introduced at Kukkanūr, and then in two different, anomalous treatments of the Drāviḍa forms.

Elaboration of Kukkanūr into a Vesara System

The Mallikārjuna temple at Sūḍī, northwest of Kukkanūr, elaborates on the visual formula of the Kukkanūr temple, and is datable to ca. A.D. 1025–1050 (pl. 41).[10] Within a Kukkanūr-like scheme of the wall, the Mallikārjuna temple introduces an additional offset between the bhadra and the karṇas called the pratiratha, providing additional projecting as well as receding surfaces for more shrine motifs. The pratiratha is surmounted by a large nāsī pediment, repeated on each story of the superstructure. The additional pair of offsets is indicated in the temple's finial, whose profile otherwise is remarkably close to that of the Kukkanūr temple.

The Mallikārjuna temple is boldly sculptural in its massing. Its walls are made lofty in effect by pavilion motifs that reach only half the walls' height—a characteristic it shares with the Aḍakeśvara temple at Mahākūṭa. The addition of *pratiratha*s also increases the lateral stretch of Mallikārjuna's walls. As a result, the superstructure sits on a very broad base, from which it rises in a distinct stride of stories to a small dome. The walls of each of its stories are pulled inward to enable the quick, upward progression toward the dome. The stepped, wavy outline of the superstructure created by the silhouette of curved kūṭa roofs on corners is different from the harmonious pyramidal profile of Kukkanūr.

As in Kukkanūr, the Mallikārjuna temple has three full stories on its superstructure, except that above the third it also has the wall segment and a set of lower moldings of a typical string course of an additional story, on which then the temple's domed finial rests. The nāsī pediment facing the finial is also small enough to continue the sense of graded rhythm of the stories, unlike the large mahānāsī facing Kukkanūr's dome, which distinguishes the finial from the lower stories. The Mallikārjuna's dome appears to be an incipient fourth story. Its indented face also corresponds to the width of the staggered bhadra of the temple.

Plate 41. Sūḍī, Mallikārjuna temple, west, mid-eleventh century

The central spine of Mallikārjuna's superstructure is conceived in a way different from Kukkanūr. While at Kukkanūr the entire nested madhyaśālā continues on each of its stories in a progressively diminished scale, in the Mallikārjuna, only the block of stone with a mahānāsī pediment (some left uncarved) persists in the center of each story. On the second story, this nāsī is backed by a simple, barrel-vaulted śālā rather than its nested variant. On the third story, only the mahānāsī block remains. This formula of removing peripheral elements of the madhyaśālā motif in order to accommodate the narrowing of stories seems to correspond to the Aḍakeśvara temple at Mahākūṭa. Here, however, it achieves the opposite result. Whereas Mahākūṭa emphasized distinct stories in a Drāviḍa manner, Sūḍī helps condense the stories and even integrate the finial within its wavy profile.

The decorative scheme of the wall that began at Kukkanūr and Guḍūr is given a systematic form in the Mallikārjuna temple at Sūḍī. Wall offsets and recesses are filled with two types of blank architectural motifs. Drāviḍa pavilions occupy projections as well as the inner pair of recesses, flanking the staggered bhadra. Nāgara kūṭastambhas only fill the outer pair of recesses, those between the pratirathas and karṇas.

In using a Nāgara motif only in the outer pair of recesses, the Mallikārjuna temple at Sūḍī provides early evidence for an emerging Vesara morphology. Reflected also in other temples of the mid-eleventh century, the scheme was expressed perhaps most fully in ca. A.D. 1075 in the Kāśīviśveśvara temple at Lakkuṇḍī. In the complexity of its wall surface one continues to see dwarfed Nāgara kūṭastambhas clearly marking recesses between the karṇas and pratirathas (pl. 51).

The Kāśīviśveśvara temple at Lakkuṇḍī has a five-part wall as in the Mallikārjuna temple at Sūḍī, comprising a pair of karṇas, pratirathas, and a staggered bhadra projection showing a niche. Against the advanced composition of the wall, however, Lakkuṇḍī's ground plan reveals a simpler, tripartite division recalling Kukkanūr and Guḍūr in its single, expanded central projection distinguished from a pair of corner piers (fig. 3). The components of this basic layout are further emphasized on the basement moldings, where three gateway patterns (toraṇas) face each of the three primary offsets. The primary division of the plan is maintained by distinguishing wall recesses. The outer pair, separating the central mass from the corner piers, are carved deeper than the inner pair, immediately following the bhadra. More significantly, only those outer recesses are filled by (dwarfed) Nāgara kūṭastambhas embellished now also by a variety of highly decorative surrounds.

At Sūḍī, the primacy of these outer recesses was shown only by the northern ornament. Distinguished sufficiently from a general array of southern motifs, the Nāgara kūṭastambha systematically defined the five-part wall of that Vesara temple into a central cluster of offsets, which included the pratirathas, and corner piers. Lakkuṇḍī quite literally includes the wall's pratiratha offsets within the projecting mass of its central cluster. I call the combined bhadra-cum-pratiratha projection that evolves on these and other mid-eleventh-century temples a "bhadra cluster," because it corresponds to the effect of an expanded bhadra projection developed first at Kukkanūr.

The bhadra cluster is an original Vesara conception, created by inducing a shift of focus within Drāviḍa's formal vocabulary. The significance of Sūḍī's Mallikārjuna temple is that it indicates the new conceptual frame using Nāgara motifs to stake out the central cluster of offsets. Lakkuṇḍī extends Sūḍī's Vesara logic by massing out the bhadra cluster on a tripartite plan, visually binding its components by a remarkable tracery of interwoven architectural motifs. The bhadra cluster provides Vesara architects a basis to organize a complex and varied formation of the temple's elevation on a relatively simple underlying plan. Lakkuṇḍī's projection of overlapping structural motifs around a Nāgara wall shrine is one of the many expressions of the bhadra cluster expressing the inventiveness of Vesara architects in ways that are quite unlike any known Drāviḍa temple.

The Vesara Formula

In the second half of the eleventh century, Vesara developed into a new regional formula for temple architecture. Absorbing the conceptual logic demonstrated in the Mallikārjuna temple at Sūḍī, Vesara clearly distinguished itself from Drāviḍa architecture. The achievement of a new type is best expressed in one of the two shrines of a twin temple at Sūḍī popularly called the Joḍa Kalaśa (twin-pot).

Sūḍī is called "rājadhānī" in contemporary inscriptions, which may at least suggest a major city if not one of the capitals built under the Chālukya

Plate 42. Sūḍī, Joḍa Kalaśa, south, ca. A.D. 1060 (courtesy: American Institute of Indian Studies)

rulers of northern Karnataka. In any event, it certainly was a principal site for building projects in the middle of the eleventh century, having at least two large temples—the Mallikārjuna and the Joḍa Kalaśa—as well as an extensively carved step well. The two shrines of the Joḍa Kalaśa, known as the Western and the Eastern, share an open pillared hall having conspicuously drooping eaves (pl. 42). The Western shrine completes the formative period of Vesara architecture; the Eastern shrine is an anomaly discussed in the next section.

A foundation inscription in the temple makes the Joḍa Kalaśa a concrete chronological touchstone for this period. The inscription, from the reign of the Chālukya king Someśvara I and dated Śaka A.D. 981/1060, mentions that the army general *(daṇḍanāyaka)* Nāgadeva, who seems to have been a native of Sūḍī, constructed a temple there named Nāgeśvara after his own name, "attached to the Nagareśvara."[11] The two shrines of the twin temple may thus properly be designated as the Nagareśvara ("Lord of the City") and the Nāgeśvara shrines. It is the Eastern shrine of the Joḍa Kalaśa (right) that might have been referred to as the Nāgeśvara in the Sūḍī inscription. Although the Western shrine (left) to which it is attached shares some features that suggest that the two parts of the twin temple belong to the same period, the Eastern shrine might be marginally later, a fact to which the inscription seems to refer.

The Western shrine of Joḍa Kalaśa gives the architectural elaborations of mid-century temples such as Sūḍī's Mallikārjuna temple a formal coherence similar to Kukkanūr. The shrine shows five projecting offsets on its walls, separated by recesses (pl. 43). For pratirathas it uses thick, molded half-pillars, which provide a more robust frame for its bhadra cluster than the thin framing pilasters for offsets in the Mallikārjuna temple. These intermediary half-pillars hereafter become a typical feature of Vesara temples in Karnataka.

For the first time, the superstructure of the Western shrine has four fully articulated stories of a typical Vesara temple. These four stories are well integrated by the diminishing of individual units of each story so that our eyes are smoothly led up to the dome. In particular, the nested madhyaśālā is maintained as a whole unit reduced gradually in subsequent stories, as at Kukkanūr but differing from the treatment at Mallikārjuna where the śālā around the mahānāsī block was gradually whittled off. In the Western shrine, the dome also stands apart from the four stories and is made to harmonize with the sloping profile of the superstructure by an increase in its size. Its

Plate 43. Sūḍī, Joḍa Kalaśa, western shrine, south, ca. A.D. 1060

forehead is marked by a large dormer as at Kukkanūr, distinguishing it from the gradual progression of each level of the superstructure.

The Western shrine of Joḍa Kalaśa employs the Nāgara kūṭastambha motif uniformly in each of its wall recesses, obscuring the motif's systematic use to indicate the bhadra cluster at Mallikārjuna. This "overuse" at Joḍa Kalaśa might suggest a fascination with what might have been considered a modern motif in a period of tentative explorations. The excess may also indicate an aesthetic choice. The slender Nāgara ornament fits more comfortably in recesses that have become narrow with the introduction of massive pratirathas, and that consequently could have become cluttered by the pair of pilasters and the square finial of a Drāviḍa pavilion motif.

Of course, a motif need not always be limited to its original function; while marking the evolution of an architectural principle when first introduced, the motif is more likely to vanish or transform when the principle is internalized.[12] The overused northern motif may in fact be a sign of an internalized Vesara standard. While giving sufficient hint of the bhadra cluster embedded in the systematic Vesara composition at Sūḍī's Mallikārjuna temple—a composition strengthened by thick half-pillars on the Western shrine—the Nāgara kūṭastambha motif is now also treated as a decorative device. Occupying the shrine's recesses, the slender motif regularly alternates with the more rectangular Drāviḍa pavilion facing wall offsets. If such a use of the Nāgara ornament obscures its systematic function, it also sets a pattern for standard Vesara temples of ca. A.D. 1100, when Nāgara towers are replaced altogether in recesses by a steady refrain of Vesara towers standing on their single columns.[13]

Irregularities of the Formative Period

In contrast to the Western shrine, which represents a development of earlier experiments into a new architectural norm, the Eastern shrine of Joḍa Kalaśa at Sūḍī preserves one of the most daring experiments of Vesara, its audacity recognized and remarked upon by contemporary viewers. The shrine shares its basic composition with the Western shrine except that it is smaller and has three instead of four stories on its superstructure (pl. 44). Nevertheless, it exploits the extended wall surface available with the addition of pratiratha offsets far more than the Western shrine (pl. 46). The shrine is especially distinguished by its array of architectural motifs, which are far more varied in type. On karṇas and in recesses, large shrine motifs stand on paired pilasters, those on the half-pillars of pratirathas stand on single thick columns. Some are simply towers, some are full-blown shrines with walls. They all seem to fold into each other, multiply, and shift on the wall as if seen through a prism. Small kūṭastambhas are embedded into each of the large motifs on offsets, except on the bhadra, which itself is radically transformed.

Among the temple types depicted on the walls of the Eastern shrine, large Nāgara towers occupy the easterly recesses on the south wall and Bhūmija form—recognizable because of small spirelets strung together on the tower—appears as a small kūṭastambha embedded in a Drāviḍa motif on the western pratiratha (proper right of bhadra). The Drāviḍa motifs also vary in forms. The east karṇa of the south wall has a double-storied Drāviḍa structure with a śālā roof; the western karṇa has a broad-based, single-storied temple with a square cupola. The recesses flanking it have a pillared wall section reminiscent of the Dharmarāja Ratha at Mahābalipuram in Tamilnadu—showing awareness of Drāviḍa variant of a neighboring region. The pratiratha adjacent to this karṇa has a shrine, the dome of which is reminiscent of the Lower Śivālaya in Badāmī—showing a local regional memory.[14]

The bhadra of the Eastern shrine is rendered in an unusual way. Its most conspicuous feature is its most central face (subhadra) having a projection that is turned at a forty-five-degree angle to the shrine's orthogonal plan. A thin pilaster clinging to it marks the exact center of the bhadra. To either side of the central mark are Vesara kūṭastambhas, also at a sloping angle.[15] The wide subsidiary level behind the subhadra shows a partly hidden oblong pavilion, carved in detail with a shaded, second-story veranda with setback cells and a barrel roof with lions at each end.[16] The framing pilasters of the whole bhadra support a barrel-vaulted śālā at the level of the string course of the superstructure.

The superstructure, preserved most fully on the east side, responds to the overlap in the features of the wall. Above the subhadra the thin cornice (kapota) of the horizontal story—usually having a quarter-round profile—is turned into tapered eaves. Thicker than the kapota cornice, the eaves projects into a pointed ridge providing shade to the angled fold of the subhadra. Above

Plate 44. Sūḍī, Joḍa Kalaśa, eastern shrine (Nāgeśvara), east

it, and instead of the components of the usual nested madhyaśālā, is a square kūṭa inscribed against a single śālā back. The kūṭa shows a projection in the center, turned at an angle. Two tiny corner pavilions on either side of a turned third in the center enhance the nested, folded arrangement of kūṭas. The ruffled dome of the temple fully reflects the composition of the wall as it is conducted through the superstructure. The dome is unusual in that it also shows a dormer on either side of its ridged bhadra, corresponding to the temple's dormer-topped pratirathas.

The angled subhadra and its kūṭa crown appear as if they were part of a projecting corner from another shrine imaginatively embedded in the main temple. Such an imagery of embedded shrines, conducted as a theme also through the miniature models on the walls, becomes the basis for Vesara's many bold and innovative experiments with the bhadra cluster. At Sūḍī the architect dared to manipulate the structural parts of the temple to make this kind of statement for the first time.

The foundation inscription from the Joḍa Kalaśa discussed above mentions the architect of the Eastern (Nāgeśvara) shrine, stating that "this Śaṅkarārya, a *vakroti-vācaspati,* a teacher to the loyal, undertook the charge and constructed in the middle of the town of Śuṇḍī a dwelling for Nāgeśvara so that the finials were completed in a manner that none could possibly imagine."[17] The unusual experiments of the Eastern shrine must represent the only novelty to which the scribe could refer.

The Sanskrit phrase "vakrokti-vācaspati" used in the inscription to describe the architect has been translated as "the master of punning phrases."[18] "Vācaspati," the second term in the phrase, means a "master of speech" in the same way that *sthapati,* a term commonly used for architect in India, might literally mean a "master (creator) of place." "Vakrokti," the first term, refers to a concept from Indian literary criticism that implies a twist of phrase in speech that reveals unexpected meanings. Some Indian aestheticians regard vakrokti, or this quality of deviance, to be the heart of poetic language.[19] The use of the phrase "vakrokti-vācaspati" in the inscription may thus reflect the reaction of a sophisticated, literate member of the urban public who wrote it. It is significant, however, that the literary phrase is used here to refer to an architect, conveying the scribe's sense of wonder about his architectural creation.

The finials that the writer of the Sūḍī inscription noted with amazement must first refer to the temple's exceptional superstructure. However, the reference may also be to the impressive display of various architectural models used as ornaments for this monument, including some elaborate, contemporary North Indian towers, appearing for the first time in the region. But there is more to evoke the writer's amazement.

The temple's central wall offset and the superstructure were unlike anything seen in Karnataka or in the entire Drāviḍa tradition of South India. Experimentation with such a turned offset had only been seen in the North Indian architectural tradition. Sūḍī's central projection might compare, for instance, to the bhadra of the Śiva temple at Dhobini built in Eastern India (pl. 45).[20] At Sūḍī, however, the North Indian formula is made fully consistent with the southern architectural vocabulary. In calling Śaṅkarārya a "master of poetic deviance," the literate writer of the Sūḍī inscription may even have been referring to the northern interpretation the architect of the Eastern shrine has given to his southern monument.

The Eastern shrine of Joḍa Kalaśa is anomalous within the Drāviḍa tradition. Its idiosyncrasy sets a precedent for Vesara architecture in the latter half of the eleventh century. The rotated central offset makes Joḍa Kalaśa perhaps the first temple in Karnataka to attempt a deviation on the wall to give it a prismatic effect (pl. 46), one that is further articulated by turning pratiratha piers in the Sūrya temple at Lakkuṇḍī (pl. 60). The shrine motifs used as ornament on the Eastern shrine reveal a knowledge of a variety of temple forms, including—for the first time—Bhūmija, which we also see later on the Kāśīviśveśvara temple at Lakkuṇḍī. Finally, this temple's somewhat overburdened layering of architectural motifs on offsets is reproduced in a formulaic way in a Jaina temple at Lakkuṇḍī (pl. 47), while its effect of embedded shrines is given greater conceptual refinement in Lakkuṇḍī's twin Kāśīviśveśvara and Sūrya shrines.

The Brahmadeva temple at Savaḍī, another of Vesara's anomalies built farther west from Sūḍī, provides yet another link in Karnataka with North Indian architectural experiments, breaking ties with its Drāviḍa precedents (pl. 48). Built in ca. A.D. 1050–1075, the Brahmadeva temple provides one of the earliest examples for a fully stellate temple in northern Karnataka.[21] Its date is supported by a comparison with Sūḍī. For instance,

Plate 45. Dhobini, Śiva temple, east, ca. A.D. 700 (courtesy: American Institute of Indian Studies)

Plate 46. Sūḍī, Joḍa Kalaśa, eastern shrine, south wall

Plate 47. Lakkuṇḍī, (Nīlakaṇṭheśvara) Jaina temple east of the Jaina Basti, late eleventh century

Plate 48. Savaḍī, Brahmadeva temple, south, late eleventh century

the adhisthāna of the Brahmadeva temple compares with those on the Joḍa Kalaśa at Sūḍī. Also, the walls are exaggerated in height to fit figurative panels in the upper section, but the shrine pavilions on them stand low, unlike temples after ca. A.D. 1075.

The temple's sanctum uses four rotated squares to create sixteen corners on which the karṇas piers of the temple are located. The wall shows a column wedged between the karṇa piers. The column is created within the boundaries of the rotated square by simply carving back the recesses around it, while the monotony of its excessive height is broken by plain ribbons along the shaft.

Like Sūḍī, the Savaḍī temple abounds in its reference to North India (pl. 49). All recesses are filled with a Nāgara kūṭastambha, an excess Savaḍī shares with the Western shrine at Joḍa Kalaśa. Karṇakūtas above at the superstructural level are also faced by a Nāgara kūṭastambha. Although ruined, the moldings of the hāra above the sham column between the karṇa piers suggest that it would also have been crowned by a Nāgara tower, so that the entire string course above the wall would then have had a row of such northern ornament.

The emphasis on North Indian architectural models is unusual in this temple only because it is overdone. All karṇas piers are faced by Bhūmija shrine models—a form that was introduced on the Eastern shrine at Sūḍī in a much diminished detail. In his study of architectural models on Vesara temples in relation to two architects' inscriptions that discuss these, Dhaky has noted an ambiguity between Vesara and Bhūmija.[22] The Bhūmija shrine, occupying a place on the karṇa typically reserved for Vesara pavilions in later temples (except Bhūmija on the south side of the Kāśīviśveśvara temple at Lakkuṇḍī) suggests that this ambiguity between a Vesara and Bhūmija temple that Dhaky noted might have a basis in real confusion.

Savaḍī reinvents the components of a Vesara

Plate 49. Savaḍī, Brahmadeva temple, northwest, wall detail

temple to fit the needs of its rotating plan. Staked out by Nāgara kūṭastambhas in adjacent recesses, its sham columns suggest a series of bhadra clusters collapsed into emblematic, pratiratha-like half-pillars. Karṇa piers are also activated as never before; alternating and multiplying, they open up the core of the temple to reveal the condensed bhadra cluster through their facets.

The Eastern shrine of the Joḍa Kalaśa at Sūḍī and the Savaḍī temple, built not far from each other and datable to ca. A.D. 1050–1075, represent two different kinds monuments created from shared ideas. Sūḍī's shrine could have been planned by a single rotation of the square diagram of the temple to create central wall offsets turned at a 45-degree angle, as at Dhobini in eastern India. Savaḍī is a fully developed, stellate temple having sixteen corners created by rotating the diagram four times. Sūḍī's angled subhadra is articulated as if it were the karṇa of a hidden shrine, with its implied karṇakūṭa revealed at the hāra level against the temple's śālā. The rotated plan at Savaḍī creates serial folds of alternating karṇas and bhadras. The contemporaneity of these two diverse temples suggests that they are not part of an internal development of regional architecture. In both cases, their architects seem to be looking outside the region, perhaps in the neighboring regions of eastern and central India, for formulas to modify their Drāviḍa tradition. In using those borrowed formulas for quite distinct results, these two irregular temples demonstrate the originality of the Vesara experiment in Karnataka.

Conclusion

Scholars after Henry Cousens's first monograph on Karnataka temples have usually identified Vesara, or in Cousens's view the "Chālukyan style," with a distinct interest in detailed tracery of surface ornamentation, for which temples mainly in the twelfth and later centuries in southern Karnataka are well known. Cousens related Vesara's achievement to a shift in its building material from sandstone to a gray soapstone, soft when quarried but hardening gradually because of exposure to weather. In explaining Vesara in terms of a new stone surface, the archaeologist hardly understood the originality of these early Vesara temples discussed here, which are all made in sandstone.

The profusion of ornament is hardly an issue in defining Vesara. If we compare any of the monuments discussed above to Karnataka's Drāviḍa temples during their high point in the eighth century (pl. 9), we may find it far more accurate to make a reverse statement. A more significant point emerging from this chapter is that early Vesara temples show a reduction, not an increase, of surface details, and adorn a visual austerity contrasting with both the earlier Drāviḍa monuments in the region as well as later schist monuments. This remarkable "dip" in the arrowlike history of ornamentation in Karnataka has gone unnoticed, and the architectural and intellectual breakthroughs that have taken place precisely at this moment have been overlooked.

The traditional reliance on building material can easily be challenged. Both early Karnataka monuments (that is, primarily Drāviḍa) and the eleventh-century temples (that we have defined as Vesara) use the same material, sandstone. The material used in all periods of Indian art relates to regional geography and local availability. While sandstone remains common in northern Karnataka, schist becomes a prominent material for temple building as one moves southward; the boundary between the two can roughly be located around Lakkuṇḍi. In the next chapter, I identify in Bādāmi, north of Lakkuṇḍī, one of the most significant Vesara temples of the late eleventh century, built in the local sandstone of that area in contrast to its prominent contemporaries at Lakkuṇḍī.

This chapter introduces a series of snags in the argument that Vesara architecture is merely a late, flamboyant version of Drāviḍa. It is true that a Vesara temple in the early eleventh century shares all its architectural elements with contemporaneous Drāviḍa temples. To become Vesara, it does not replace features of Drāviḍa architecture with typology of new forms;[23] instead, it insists on a Drāviḍa profile by especially maintaining the kūṭas at the corner of each of its distinct stories.[24] But it is a mistake to consider Vesara only as a late, eclectic stage of Drāviḍa architecture. Vesara emerges only as a result of conceptual and formal changes applied to Drāviḍa architecture. This crucial experiment is recorded in this group of sandstone temples.

The complexity of Vesara's architectural play is not sufficiently explained by our current classification system for Indian temple architecture, in which Vesara is given an intermediary status between North Indian and South Indian forms. While temples in Karnataka have commonly combined borrowed features since an early period, the deliberate nature of Vesara's innovations in the eleventh century as well as their architectural purpose must be underscored against such tendency toward eclecticism naturally shown by temples in Karnataka.

The formation of Vesara architecture is marked by a daringly unprecedented play with regional architectural conventions. In distinguishing their designs both from previous monuments in the region and from temples elsewhere in India, these Karnataka architects convey in Vesara a sense fundamentally different from its current explanations. Their monuments and inscription analyzed in this chapter argue for Vesara as an expression of self-conscious modernity. The opening up of a South Indian, Drāviḍa temple in a way that incorporates North Indian, Nāgara references suggests Vesara's mode of departure from its native tradition. By introducing Nāgara within its formal matrix, Vesara architects changed Drāviḍa architecture from an inheritance to be preserved and reproduced into a problem to be explored. Nāgara architecture, used as a motif in the decorative scheme of a Vesara temple, as an aesthetic reference in the overall organization of its elevation, and as a formula to transform its ground plan, shows various means by which eleventh-century Karnataka architects achieved a tension within their Drāviḍa tradition. Their experiments, including anomalies as well as highly irregular structures, permanently changed the character of Drāviḍa architecture in the region.[25]

5
Individuality and Agency in Vesara Architecture

VESARA IS A SYNTHESIS OF ARCHITECTURAL ANOMAlies within Karnataka's Drāviḍa tradition. The deliberate shift in the framework of Drāviḍa and a public awareness of the innovations recorded in contemporary epigraphic evidence draw attention to the active human efforts involved in such a change. Vesara architecture offers a unique opportunity to analyze the participation of human agency in the history of sacred art in India, for which "Individuality" is a useful concept. Individuality is proposed here not only to emphasize the importance of day-to-day acts of knowing through which broader patterns of regional changes are produced but also to capture the sense that every building activity is a highly localized renewal and synthesis of the totality of previous knowledge, as temples discussed in this chapter will show.

Individuality here should not be construed as a plea for the individual identity and subjective will of these anonymous Vesara architects but as an argument that traditional norms are shaped by thoughtful action of the makers of monuments. Far from the romanticized value of individualism in Western art, individuality is invoked in the context of the sacred art of India as a feature that pushes the tradition toward its possibilities. Vesara architecture is an expression of an active participation of the human makers who produce the fluid, heterogeneous tradition of the region. The "effect" of this participation is recorded sometimes in small, incremental changes and sometimes in exceptional monuments, giving two views on individuality: that it is an expression of day-to-day thought embedded in the making of all temples and that it is an expression of a moment when architects far exceed the imaginative possibilities of previous traditions. Two idiosyncratic temples, both datable to ca. A.D. 1075, are my examples of this latter "excess": one is a twin temple at Lakkuṇḍī known generally as the Kāśīviśveśvara but that in fact includes a large shrine of that name as well as a small Sūrya shrine attached to it; the other is called the Yallamā temple at Badāmī. Their remarkably divergent designs challenge us to move beyond the account of irregularities and anomalies of Drāviḍa to consider the individual choices and inventions within Vesara, and their contribution to the understanding of India's sacred art in terms of the intellectual challenges their makers confront within inherited traditions.

THE SOUTHERN FORM "AS IF" A NORTH INDIAN TEMPLE

Lakkuṇḍī is one of the most important sites for our understanding of Vesara architecture. Its prolific output of temples in the eleventh and twelfth centuries suggests a strong economic growth for this city.[1] Among about 15 temples and two step wells that survive in the village today, the Kāśīviśveśvara complex, comprising the Kāśīviśveśvara and the Sūrya shrines, is part of the earliest group of temples built on the site, datable to late eleventh century.

The two shrines face each other across a raised platform that once was an open hall (pl. 50). They are built on a plinth *(pīṭha)* whose profile is unusual in Karnataka temples. According to M. A. Dhaky, the feature was possibly borrowed from Western India.[2] The uniform stretch of this plinth

Plate 50. Lakkuṇḍī, (twin) Kāśīviśveśvara and Sūrya temples, southwest, ca. A.D. 1075–1100

suggests that the shrines it supports at the two ends were planned as part of a single complex. Differences seem to have been introduced in it only at the time of carving, as in the case of toraṇa motifs framing a Nāgara kūṭastambha applied to corners and the central offset of the plinth moldings on the Sūrya side (pl. 56) but not on the Kāśīviśveśvara side (pl. 51).

In format, the twin temple at Lakkuṇḍī depends directly on an earlier model in Karnataka. Efforts to create linked shrines can be traced back at least to the tenth century in such temples as Aihole's Rāciguḍi, where accretions of new shrines and a connecting hall can easily be discerned from an older fabric. By the Joḍa Kalaśa at Sūḍī, a convention of building two conjoined shrines seems to have stabilized (pl. 42); triple shrines were standardized only in the twelfth century. Like Sūḍī, the Lakkuṇḍī shrines were planned to be conjoined.

Because the two sides of the twin temple at Lakkuṇḍī seem to be part of a single architectural plan, their radically different form is puzzling. The similarity with the Joḍa Kalaśa at Sūḍī is again striking. The Kāśīviśveśvara compares with the Western shrine at Sūḍī in that it is also the western of the two shrines, is the larger of the twins, and is directly related to previous Vesara experiments, of which it mostly represents an excess. The Sūrya shrine is comparable to the Eastern shrine at Sūḍī in that it is also the eastern extreme of the complex, smaller of the set, and shows an unusual experiment with turned offsets. The major difference between the two twin temples seems to be that the Lakkuṇḍī shrines are built in a gray soapstone, which becomes a standard material for Vesara temples from now on, while the Sūḍī shrines are in sandstone.[3]

The architectural features of the twin temple at Lakkuṇḍī support its date of ca. A.D. 1075. The adhiṣṭhāna (basement) moldings are an advance of the temples at Sūḍī (pl. 52). Especially the flat-edged karṇikā is now thinner, and close to the Jaina Basti nearby, which is only marginally earlier than the twin temple. New motifs, however, are intermingled with traditional features of the basement. On the Kāśīviśveśvara's side, the jagatī (the lowest "earth" molding) has carved lotus petals above. The kapotapālī is generously faced with foliated candraśālās. The basement is faced by cusped toraṇas, with beaded coils spewed by makaras who stand on short circular pillars. These toraṇas carry stationary human figures within their frame on the Sūrya shrine's side and more animated human and bird figures on the Kāśīviśveśvara. Such a toraṇa against the moldings takes the place of the niches against the vedībandhas (binding wall moldings) of Nāgara temples. The South Indian basement with its curved padma shoulder, karṇikā, and the luxuriant kapotapālī also resonate with the suggestion of the *khura-kumbha, kalaśa* and kapotapālī of a North Indian temple's vedībandha, although all of these moldings at Lakkuṇḍi retain a southern, Drāviḍa form.[4]

The walls of the Kāśīviśveśvara stand directly on its adhiṣṭhāna, without the usual pratikaṇṭha recess, suggesting an archaism relating to tenth-century temples at Aihole and the Aḍakeśvara temple at Mahākūṭa (the Sūrya shrine replaces the prati molding with a frieze of muscled figures, underscoring the conceit). The pratiratha half-pillars are of the thick variety introduced only at Sūḍī (pl. 53). On the Kāśīviśveśvara, the mass of the pratiratha half-pillars is reduced by their serrated section, an effect that contrasts with the turned, pierlike quality of pratirathas of the Sūrya.[5] Weight-bearing dwarfs *(bhāraputras)* float almost weightlessly in the middle region of these pilasters. Their posture compares to some of the *haṃsa*s (geese) depicted above the central niche and also under the kapotapālī at the base of each hāra of the superstructure.

The two Lakkuṇḍī shrines are the first to show miniature kūṭa crowning the pratiratha instead of the pañjara seen at Sūḍī (pl. 54). On the Kāśīviśveśvara, the kūṭas have a central porch with tiny figures and a tower showing three *śṛṅgas* (spirelets) facing its main *phāṃsanā* (tiered, pyramidal roof-shape) superstructure and a large ghaṇṭā (bell-shaped crown).[6] On the Sūrya shrine the kūṭas respond to the angle of the half-pillars and have a tower of stacked cornices faced by large dormers (pl. 59). Exploring the new detail in their various ways, the shrines began a pattern of treating the engaged pratiratha column as a large kūṭastambha common in monuments after A.D. 1075.[7]

The wall ornaments of these Lakkuṇḍī shrines reveal conscious eclecticism. Remarkably, the Kāśīviśveśvara uses miniature architectural motifs that represent temple types from different regions of India. Prominent among these is a contemporary North Indian, Bhūmija pavilion on karṇas of the north and south walls, first introduced in Karnataka in the Eastern shrine at Sūḍī but shown here with greater precision of details (pls. 53, 55). The bhadra has a large multispired Nāgara tower. On the opposite end of the complex, the Sūrya shrine projects large makara toraṇas on corner piers (pl. 58). Far from representing a conservative tradition, the motif deliberately recollects an old region-specific motif. The toraṇa resembles a type seen in the ninth century (pls. 20, 21). The layered foliage of the makara tail, characteristic of Karnataka, is seen in many Lakkuṇḍī temples including the Kāśīviśveśvara. But nowhere is it reproduced so boldly as on Sūrya's corner piers. Against the shrine motifs from different regions on the Kāśīviśveśvara, the toraṇa only gives the Sūrya shrine a consciously regional, Karnataka mark.

Both Lakkuṇḍī shrines continue the basic morphology of a Vesara temple as it was developed at Sūḍī. They each have a five-part wall, comprising a pair of karṇas, pratirathas, and a staggered bhadra projection, only that the bhadra now has a conspicuous niche. Underneath the advanced composition of the wall, however, the Lakkuṇḍī's shrines reveal a simpler plan of tripartite division recalling Kukkanūr and Guḍūr, comprising an expanded central projection separated from corner piers by recesses (fig. 3). The basic layout is emphasized on the basement moldings, where three toraṇa gateways face each of the three primary offsets: one applied to the central projection and two facing the corner offsets. On the Sūrya side, toraṇa motifs are also applied to the plinth, each framing a Nāgara kūṭastambha. Above, the primary tripartite division is maintained by distinguishing wall recesses. On the Kāśīviśveśvara, the outer pair, separating the central mass from the corner piers, is carved deeper than the inner pair, immediately following the bhadra. More significantly, only those outer recesses are filled by Nāgara kūṭastambha motifs, as in the Mallikārjuna temple at Sūḍī, but now embellished also by a variety of highly decorative surrounds (pls. 53, 54). On the Sūrya, both inner and outer recesses are deep, except that the inner pair is linked by an oblong pavilion whose sloping roof spanning out to the recesses is visible behind the bhadra niche (pl. 56). As at Kāśīviśveśvara, only the outer

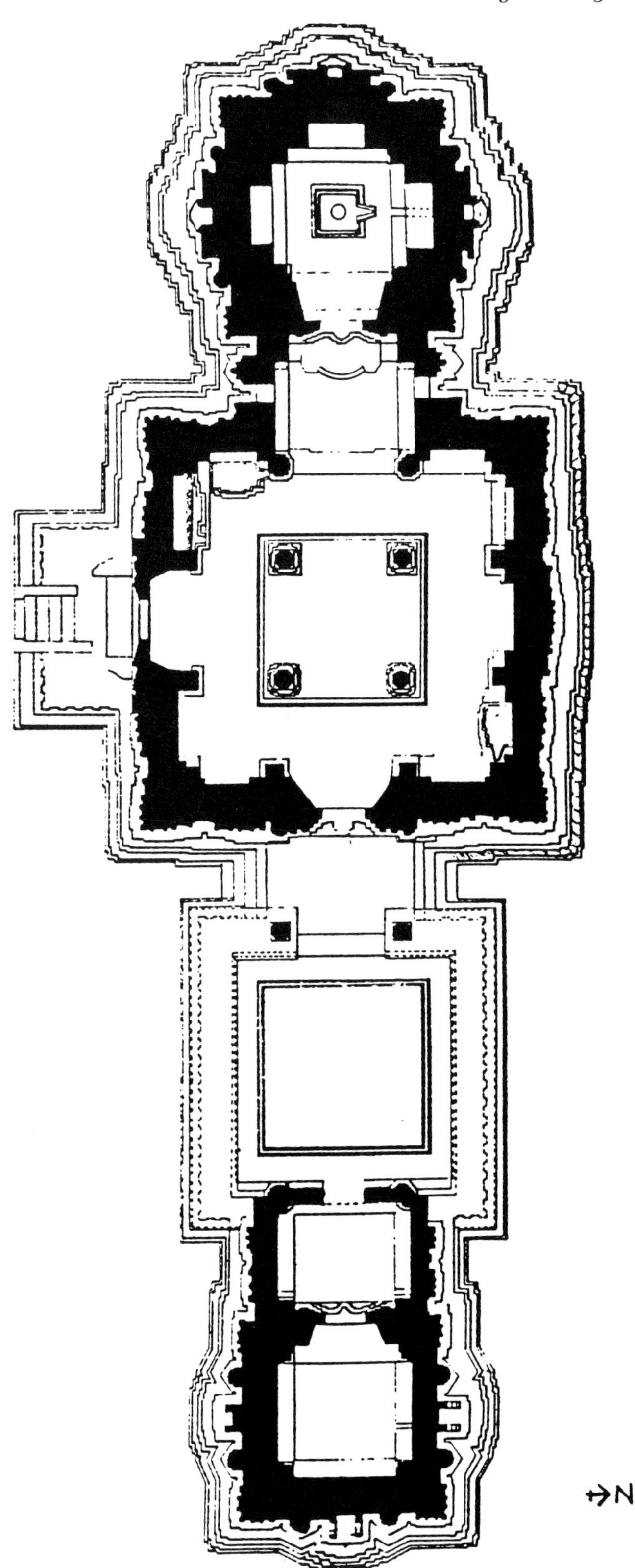

Figure 3. Lakkuṇḍī, the twin Kāśīviśveśvara and Sūrya shrines, plan (Cousens, Plate LXII)

niches have a Nāgara motif, now a kiosk with standing figures having a short conical roof that mimics a Nāgara tower (pl. 58).

In other words, the Lakkuṇḍī shrines reflect what I have defined as the bhadra cluster, the primary indicator of Vesara morphology first achieved at the Mallikārjuna temple at Sūḍī discussed in chapter 4. Instead of only using the Nāgara motif to mark off the central cluster as at Sūḍī, Lakkuṇḍī quite literally masses out the projection of the central, composite cluster on a tripartite plan and emphasizes its perception with additional ornamental motifs. The Sūrya shrine also integrates the cluster by using an oblong pavilion motif behind the bhadra niche, extending between the niche and the pratiratha half-pillars.

The Kāśīviśveśvara integrates the bhadra cluster by creating an elaborate architectural vision across it (pl. 53). First, the central projecting mass is unified by the treatment of the half-pillars of the pratirathas. Projecting in a high relief from the outer recesses and casting deep shadows, their serrated section is graded more gently toward the level of the shallow, inner recesses. Flying dwarfs in their midregion, suggesting supports for brackets even where there is no evidence of the brackets themselves, further diminish their architectural weight, tying them more closely to the interwoven relief work of the cluster. Second, just like the oblong pavilion behind Sūrya's bhadra niche, a makara toraṇa seemingly stretches behind Kāśīviśveśvara's, its pillared supports, makaras, and wavy springers filling the shallow recesses between the pratirathas and the bhadra.

The bhadra projection and its niche is integrated with the cluster, contributing to its remarkable, picturesque imagery (pl. 54). The niche is framed by a balcony, recalling North Indian temples, showing a balustrade with a sloping seat back. The outer face of the balustrade shows figural panels, some identified as mythological narratives. The south wall shows dwarfs surrounding an elephant surmounted by three figures, each with an umbrella, on the right. The left panel shows a large elephant attacked by a warrior while an archer aims from his chariot on the left corner and a row of smaller elephants turn away in confusion. The west wall shows on the left Rāvaṇa at battle with the army of Indra, and on the right Rāvaṇa shaking Mount Kailāsa.[8] On the north wall, the left panel perhaps shows dancing Cāmuṇḍā with a host of emaciated attendants; that on the right shows Śiva Gajāntaka, dancing with the elephant skin and trampling a

Plate 51. Lakkuṇḍī, Kāśīviśveśvara, south

Plate 52. Lakkuṇḍī, Kāśīviśveśvara, wall connecting sanctum and *gūḍhamaṇḍapa*, turned pier

Plate 53. Lakkuṇḍī, Kāśīviśveśvara, south wall, left detail, *karṇa* showing a Bhūmija tower, recess showing a dwarfed Nāgara *kūṭastambha*

Plate 54. Lakkuṇḍī, Kāśīviśveśvara, south, detail of wall and superstructure

Plate 55. Balsāne, Triple temple 1, southwest, ca. A.D. 1100 (courtesy: American Institute of Indian Studies)

human figure, flanked by dancing Gaṇeśa and Kārttikeya. Visually, these narratives of spiritual, moral and military conquests dramatize the overlapping architectural motifs of the bhadra cluster. The North Indian balcony on the bhadra, as well as narrative panels to surround it, is unique in Vesara architecture.

While Lakkuṇḍī's elevation maintains a five-part wall articulation, the bhadra cluster massed out on plan is visually integrated by the shimmering, illusionistic relief work of overlapping structural motifs and narratives. Only the recesses between the pratirathas and the karṇas are cut deep enough to visually separate the offsets, and they show dwarfed Nāgara kūṭastambhas with elaborate variations on the toraṇa motif. The tension Lakkuṇḍī maintains between the plan and the elevation, and its mode of conveying the bhadra cluster through relief work, is unique to Lakkuṇḍī. In later Vesara temples, Lakkuṇḍī's tripartite plan is simply assumed, and sometimes represented in a formulaic fashion.

The culminating central feature of Kāśīviśveśvara's bhadra cluster is a deep niche, shown for the first time on a Vesara temple only at Lakkuṇḍī. The niche allows an image of a divinity to be housed within, as if in a real, free-standing shrine. The realism of this representation is enhanced by thick projecting sidewalls faced by a doorway pattern and a threshold distinguished from the temple's adhiṣṭhāna. Above the bhadra niche is a straight, ribbed awning on which stands a large anekāṇḍaka (multispired) Nāgara tower comparable to a type found in Western India in the 10th century. The niche relates to a prior century-long practice of showing blank architectural pavilions on the exterior wall, except it seems to flesh out those blank motifs into a lifelike shrine whose tower pierces beyond the cornice level of the temple's superstructure and projects through a dark cavity at the level of the hāra.

The Kāśīviśveśvara is the first Vesara temple to create a cavernous opening in the center for its principal shrine motif. The opening continues to be reflected in different ways in temples hereafter. Kāśīviśveśvara's bhadra niche is gouged out from the physical mass of the projecting wall, and its hollow interior imaginatively deepened also by the thick layer of the surrounding architectural imagery on the bhadra cluster, from which it is treated differently.

Contrasting with architectural motifs on other parts of the wall—such as toraṇas, pavilions, half-pillars, all presumably having reference in timber construction of urban architecture—Kāśīviśveśvara's niche is enclosed by thick masonry stone walls. On the Sūrya shrine, a similar stone encasement for the divine image includes more direct suggestions of cave architecture. The representation of "stone" niche is remarkable at Lakkuṇḍī, for when Lakkuṇḍī's practice of bhadra niches continues the niche reverts to representing a pavilion on a pair of pilasters, with awning and shrine model carved above pillar supports recalling timber construction. Those later examples, thus, absorb the niche within a more straightforward, Drāviḍa tradition of pavilion motifs, only giving realistic expressions to the abstract, timber-based Drāviḍa pavilions used as wall ornaments at least since the tenth century. Lakkuṇḍī's deliberate choice conveys into a wall ornament the mystery of a mountain cavelike aura for divine manifestation as it has been captured in Karnataka and elsewhere in India in the design of the raw, masonry cell of a free-standing temple.[9]

Kāśīviśveśvara's bhadra shrine is embedded in a dark, cavernous enclosure, enhanced by an unusual framework at the superstructural levels (pl. 54). On the madhyaśālā, a bold mahānāsī dormer crowned by a fleshy *kīrttimukha* ("face of glory") mask, shows another larger, chubbier kīrttimukha emerging from its arched cavity. The latter mask spews out a cusped, trefoil vault cutting the moldings of the hāra and framing the tower of the wall's shrine model. The mask also vomits a chain of various motifs: pearl chains as well as makaras leaping on either side, who in turn spew vyāla (fantastic, composite beasts) or human figures. Drooping lotus buds enhance the cusps of the vault below. Fanciful though it might seem, Lakkuṇḍī's frame is related to the Kukkanūr temple (pl. 38). The elaborate, linked motif surrounding the tower of the wall's architectural model only extends the idea of pairing dormers so idiosyncratically presented within the Drāviḍa format at Kukkanūr.

Lakkuṇḍī's bhadra thus presents a realistic shrine through a cavelike opening on the exterior. The vaulted opening as well as the embedded shrine is repeated on the remaining two levels of the superstructure. While formally relating to Kukkanūr, Lakkuṇḍī's mode of unfolding these cavelike apertures could not have been anticipated by the latter. The depth and mystery wrapping around miniature towers of the shrines is increased as the cavity gets narrower in upper stories.

The most remarkable feature of Kāśīviśveśvara's superstructure is a simple, unfragmented madhyaśālā on the first level instead of Vesara's standard nested motif. The choice is striking because it harks back to a pre-Vesara, Drāviḍa detail, but its archaism is deliberate, given unusually numerous references to North India in the architectural models used on its walls. The conceit of the architect is fully revealed when the enormous size of Kāśīviśveśvara's Drāviḍa śālā is contrasted with a complete omission of the motif on the Sūrya shrine across from it.

On subsequent stories, the Kāśīviśveśvara shows no śālā, only the dark, hollow sheath containing a Nāgara tower. The trefoil "cavern motif" remains a constant and prominent feature of the superstructure, following a scheme of whittling off other details of the madhyaśālā seen earlier on the Mallikārjuna temple at Sūḍī. As with other motifs, these frames shrink in size adjusting to the narrowing of each subsequent story. On the third level, the karṇakūṭas also probably disappeared; the paired pilasters that would have supported kūṭas are replaced by single pilasters that bind the wall portion of the story.[10] The pratirathas probably retained their kūṭas but are pulled in close to the central cavity. The cascade of central cavity motifs matches the chain of dormers at Kukkanūr. The temple's finial is missing, but it would have been close to the Sūḍī temple.

The conceit of the Kāśīviśveśvara temple at Lakkuṇḍī is revealed in the way it absorbs a North Indian conceptual logic fully within a South Indian architectural vocabulary. All Indian temples are conceptually "monuments of manifestation"[11] in that through worship a living divinity comes into existence within the sanctum (thus called *garbhagṛha*, or womb chamber). In North

Plate 56. Lakkuṇḍī, Sūrya temple, south (courtesy: American Institute of Indian Studies)

Plate 57. Lakkuṇḍī, Sūrya, north wall

India, however, this ritual logic was fully realized through the architectural features of a Nāgara temple. Thus, a projection of the sanctum's exterior wall into the central bhadra offset suggests the swelling of the inner sanctum, while the divinity manifesting inside appears fully formed in a deep niche cut into the projection.[12] Following this northern logic, the central opening at Lakkuṇḍī conveys on the exterior wall the depth of its sanctum, while the bhadra shrine, complete with its own realistic cell originally containing an image, appears as a fully formed divinity. In manipulating archaizing Drāviḍa features so fully as if it were a Nāgara, this conceited temple at Lakkuṇḍī stands out as a primary example of Vesara's originality.

The Sūrya temple stands in stark contrast to the Kāśīviśveśvara across the courtyard. Kāśīviśveśvara's interwoven tracery of motifs are replaced here by few bold elements against whose solidity the temple shows many types of architectural enclosures. The overall effect of the Sūrya temple at Lakkuṇḍi is that of a mountain made of interlocking, rocky boulders (pl. 56). The projections and recesses on the elevation, the short and heavy wall elements such as the cantoning pilasters, and the elaborate high pīṭha and adhiṣṭhāna, contribute to this solid mass of the temple.

The Sūrya temple's walls comprise a simple bhadra, flanked by pratirathas, and rectilinear karṇas. The pratirathas, in contrast to the delicately rendered half-pillars on the Kāśīviśveśvara, are thick pillars turned at a 45-degree angle. Recesses show kiosklike enclosures occupied by standing figures that alternate with solid offsets. Karṇas are massive and appear even wider because of the outstretched and drooping tails of makaras perched on paired pilasters. The toraṇas frame tiny figures.

The five distinct offsets of the Sūrya temple's walls contrast with the illusionistic overlapping of forms created on the Kāśīviśveśvara temple (pl. 57). The moldings underneath the wall offsets replace the usual recess with rafter ends

Plate 58. Lakkuṇḍī, Sūrya, south wall, *pratiratha* and *karṇa* detail (courtesy: American Institute of Indian Studies)

Plate 59. Lakkuṇḍī, Sūrya, south, superstructure, detail

(pratikaṇṭha) having a variety of discrete animated figures. The bhadra has galloping horses, appropriate for a niche that may have contained Sūrya, the sun god whose vehicle is a chariot driven by horses. Pratirathas show load-bearing dwarfs and the karṇas have leaping vyālas. This variegated molding does not appear on the Kāśīviśveśvara. On the Sūrya, it adds muscle to the temple's architectonic features (pl. 58).

The kapotapālī of the hāra also distinguishes the offsets (pl. 59). It has a straight edge above the pratirathas and bhadra but a sloping edge over the karṇas. This differs from the Kāśīviśveśvara, where the highly characterized array of architectural motifs of the hāra is still connected by a uniform kapotapālī molding. Furthermore, the pratikaṇṭha of the Sūrya temple has rafters with makara heads for the bhadra and karṇas but vyālas above the pratirathas. These are arranged to leap radially from a kīrttimukha mask and to support kūṭas instead of nāsīs. These kūṭas are turned at an angle like the pratiratha pier itself and stand out from the surrounding architectural motifs. The kūṭas appear to be Nāgara, and they are made of seven stacked-up kapotas faced with *rathikās* containing small figures.

The absence of madhyaśālās in the Sūrya shrine's superstructure is remarkable. For an architect working within the framework of Drāviḍa architecture in Karnataka, an emphasis on this feature had helped distinguish that architecture from Drāviḍa elsewhere in South India. In the Drāviḍa temples of Karnataka, offsets usually build up to a central bhadra projection with its wide madhyaśālā, a convention the Kāśīviśveśvara addresses. A nāsī instead, visually connecting also with a trefoil dormer above the niche, now emphasizes an isolated subhadra (the central projecting offset of the bhadra) in a way that reminds one of the central, projecting niche in a Nāgara temple. Also extending the effect of a turned pratiratha down to the pīṭha animates the ground plan of the Sūrya temple in a way unlike any previous Drāviḍa temple (pl. 60).

Angled pratiratha offsets originated in an experiment in many pre-Nāgara and Nāgara tem-

Plate 60. Lakkuṇḍī, Sūrya, east

ples in North India, where the square basis of a temple's ground plan was geometrically rotated, as Michael W. Meister has analyzed. The resultant faceted temples are seen in many regions of North India, given a special attention in a group of seventh-and eighth-century temples in Dakṣiṇa Kośala.[13] These northern experiments seem reflected directly in the monuments in Karnataka. We already saw one in the previous chapter, namely the angled subhadra in the eastern shrine at Sūḍī, which surprised its contemporary, southern viewers (pl. 44). The angled pratiratha of the Sūrya temple at Lakkuṇḍi reflects another from Dakṣiṇa Kośala, that of the Indal Deul at Kharod (pl. 61).

However, the turned half-pillars of the Sūrya are not a result of an experiment with the plan but only a visual effect. Sūrya's plan includes the pratiratha within the mass of the bhadra cluster (fig. 3). The half-pillars are square in shape, not reflecting the geometrical maneuvers as in the Dakṣiṇa Kośala temple's plan. They seem to be individually turned, pulled out beyond what the plan would allow, and finally enhanced also by the deep recess cut straight back to the base wall. On the pīṭha, the turned segments of the pratiratha become the sloping sides of the wide, integrated bhadra cluster. The emergent three major divisions of the moldings are faced by a makara toraṇa with a Nāgara kūṭastambha. Another set of toraṇas continues to indicate this tripartite framework at the adhiṣṭhāna level. The complexity of reading this temple involves recognizing, on the one hand, the absorption of the five *rathas* (karṇas, bhadra, and the pratirathas) into three essential parts at the base and, on the other hand, their distinctness as maintained and emphasized above that level.

The framing wall of the bhadra niche projects dramatically from the base wall. The niche is articulated as a subshrine with freestanding porch whose disengaged pillars are still to be seen on the north wall (pl. 57). This wall shrine has thick walls and is double-storied, the upper story treated like a narrow, deep balcony. Its roof shows an elaborate trefoil dormer supported on columns. The tall central pair supports a large dormer, while two short columns support side flanges. Elephants and leaping vyālas are seen on either ends and standing figures appear within this architectural frame.

The trefoil dormer creates a solid stone facade above the cavernous balcony of the temple's bhadra. At one level, it may recall a śukanāsa (barrel-vaulted pediment) characterizing Drāviḍa temples in Karnataka.[14] The feature is much reduced now, however, and its details are also quite unusual. The shaft of the pillars used are piled pots, with laśuna (bulbous upper part) above and a large, distinct, cushion capital reminiscent of a type commonly used in Deccani caves in the fifth to seventh centuries. The motif also recalls the original architectural context for these dormers, namely the facades of early Buddhist *caitya* halls excavated in the mountains of the Deccan, represented somewhat realistically here by spatial depth and small standing figures between pillars. Sūrya, thus, vividly recalls a Deccani archetype, contrasted with a more advanced, foreign, Nāgara tower on the Kāśīviśveśvara.

While the Kāśīviśveśvara's niche shrine sets a trend, Sūrya's reference to cave architecture is an exception. This specific architectural reference is not repeated elsewhere on its superstructure. The two remaining stories show just the central mahānāsī as if they were cubical blocks of stone, comparable in effect to the Mallikārjuna temple at Sūḍī, showing a seated figure in their cavity. The mahānāsī blocks are rendered in diminished scale and flanked by angled kūṭastambhas. (The third story of the temple is now haphazardly pieced together with carved stones, including pieces that do not belong to the temple or its period.)

The twin Kāśīviśveśvara and Sūrya temples at Lakkuṇḍī far exceed Drāviḍa while playing with its possibilities. The absence of a madhyaśālā on the Sūrya temple is made conspicuous by the enhancement of this feature in the Kāśīviśveśvara. Both create contrasting effects using the format of the bhadra cluster. Kāśīviśveśvara opens a cavity on its integrated bhadra cluster; Sūrya projects discrete features including the central niche. The jagged roughness and facets of the latter contrasts with the delicacy of interwoven parts on the former. In unfolding a niche, both embody a North Indian logic, exploring new relationships with Drāviḍa's architectural details. The Kāśīviśveśvara also abounds in northern references, while the Sūrya asserts its Deccani roots, creating points and counterpoints within a shared Vesara format.

Sūrya's experiment with turned pratiratha half-pillars can be considered anomalous in that it is an early experiment, along with Sūḍī, that is not simply limited to these two individual creations. The turning of offsets caught the imagination of other architects once it was introduced in the re-

Plate 61. Kharod, Indal Deul, south, seventh century (courtesy: American Institute of Indian Studies)

Plate 62. Lakkuṇḍī, Pārśvanātha temple next to Jaina Basti, west, late eleventh century

gion. Their use of half-pillars and offsets is reflected in at least two different circumstances. One, the formula of giving angles to offsets framing the bhadra, for instance, is repeated in the designing of sanctums in the plain, unfinished Pārśvanātha temple at Lakkuṇḍī built perhaps in the last quarter of the eleventh century (pl. 62). While its walls follow an orthogonal plan, showing staggered bhadra, pratiratha offsets, and karṇas, the adhiṣṭhāna shows a pointed edge projecting in the center of the bhadra's innermost face, namely the subhadra. The pratirathas are also angled.

Second, the half-turn of the half-pillar catches attention in many Vesara temples especially on the wall of the vestibule (antarāla) connecting the sanctum to the hall in front, serving perhaps as an architectural knuckle between the worshiper's space and that of the worshiped divinity (pl. 52). The Kāśīviśveśvara temple, which we have contrasted with the Sūrya, shows such an antarāla pilaster with its central section turned into a pointed edge, an experiment also reflected later (pls. 76, 92). Lakkuṇḍī's Pārśvanātha temple limits the turned detail of the antarāla only to the unusual adhiṣṭhāna on which its thick, indented pilaster stands. In a way, this molding reflects the dynamic scheme of the sanctum itself. A cylindrical shape carved on its central face is flanked by raised and pointed edges that blend into the straight sides of the regular molding, showing an original Karnataka condensation of the North Indian experiment. Fully stellate temples such as the Brahmadeva at Savaḍī discussed in the previous chapter (pl. 48) or the Doḍḍa Bassapā temple at Ḍambhal discussed in chapter 7 (pl. 106) appear to be grafts of a contemporary Bhūmija formula rather than a local evolution relating to Sūḍī and Lakkuṇḍī, but the two temples could suggest an early regional need for varying the Drāviḍa features in this way.

The faceted richness of the Sūrya temple and its use of kūṭastambhas at each level of the superstructure suggest a comparison with a contemporary parallel in North India, namely, Bhūmija (pl. 55). In Bhūmija, however, the projecting, even accentuated, bhadras, enormous *śūrasenas* (circular pediments), and intricately webbed *madhyalatās* (central bands), stand out against other storied offsets. Karṇas are pulled back and reduced to match other subsidiary offsets; their superstructural features—chains of kūṭastambhas—are not distinguished from those of other offsets. This is not the case in the Sūrya temple. Karṇas remain firm, pierlike features, and karṇakūṭas continue the typical southern profile of the temple's superstructure. The earlier Dakṣiṇa Kośala temples seem more relevant for the northern connection at the Sūrya temple than a comparison with contemporary Bhūmija forms. Some might argue also that Bhūmija developed in Central India and Western India as a mode in part influenced by Drāviḍa arrangements of stories.[15]

Although the kūṭastambhas on the Sūrya temple's superstructure compare with a Bhūmija temple, and their particular tower forms are clearly not Drāviḍa, they fit logically within a conception of a Vesara hāra. The coiled-up vyālas at the base of the pratiratha's kūṭas relate to the typical pratikaṇṭha moldings of Vesara architecture, missing in Bhūmija temples, even in their Maharashtra variant, where southern elements are used.[16]

This comparison between Bhūmija and the Sūrya temple at Lakkuṇḍī demonstrates that both Vesara and Bhūmija temples are contemporary experiments with some tempting similarities. Although Bhūmija was certainly known in the Karnataka region by the late eleventh century,[17] and some late Vesara temples might be influenced by that form, similarities between the Sūrya temple at Lakkuṇḍī and Bhūmija cannot be understood as influence of one over the other. A comparison of the Bhūmija shrine model so accurately represented on the Kāśīviśveśvara temple at Lakkuṇḍī (pl. 53) and the Sūrya shrine just across from it can point only at the difference between the two.

Direct and self-conscious interaction with North Indian ideas and forms is pronounced in the Lakkuṇḍī temples. The use of North Indian forms seems a result of direct contact and knowledge, as can be evidenced by the accuracy of the Bhūmija and Nāgara models on the Kāśīviśveśvara. These late-eleventh-century monuments of Lakkuṇḍī are strongly marked by characteristics that reflect an ecumenical cultural environment brought about during the reign of Someśvara I (A.D. 1042–68) and Vikramāditya VI (A.D. 1068–1124). The two Cālukya rulers of Karnataka campaigned in various regions of North India, including Dakṣiṇa Kośala, from their new capital at Kalyāṇa. Innovations at Sūḍī, Savaḍī, and Lakkuṇḍī may be attributed to the beginning of this northern contact.[18]

The Vesara monuments that these Lakkuṇḍī architects created do not imitate northern models, however. North Indian ideas and elements were incorporated into the Vesara form with a Vesara purpose. The morphological base of Vesara architecture is Drāviḍa. If Vesara is seen simply as evolving from it, however, the twin Kāśīviśveśvara and Sūrya temples at Lakkuṇḍī would truly be exceptional. The Lakkuṇḍī shrines emphasize their distinctiveness by deliberately challenging their "Drāviḍaness." The variety of Nāgara-like ways in which architects maneuver Drāviḍa features, and in fact display this variety, shows the extent to which the possibilities of the new Vesara format was explored in the eleventh century.[19]

Vesara "As If" a South Indian Temple

It is striking in the context of the strong, northerly trend established by the time of Lakkuṇḍī that the Yallamā temple at Badāmī, built ca. A.D. 1075–1100, maintains a strong Drāviḍa appearance (pl. 63). Still made in sandstone, not the gray soapstone, the Badāmī temple can be related stylistically to the earlier sandstone temples such as at Kukkanūr and Sūḍī. But unlike those temples, the Yallamā temple at Badāmī avoids all overt affiliation with Nāgara. The monument's seemingly stark Drāviḍa appearance especially contrasts with the bold display of Nāgara ideas and forms found at Lakkuṇḍī, with which it is contemporaneous. A detailed analysis of the Yallamā temple can also show how this Vesara monument problematizes its Drāviḍa identity.

This temple has hardly received the attention it intellectually deserves. In 1877, J. F. Fleet published an inscription found in front of the temple and casually remarked that the temple itself was "of no size or architectural pretensions." Henry Cousens only commented that this temple was ruined.[20] Dhaky, on the other hand, designated the Yallamā temple as of the "formative phase" of Vesara architecture, dating it to ca. A.D. 1025 and used it to test the accuracy with which miniature shrine models had represented the Vesara form on temple walls.[21] Actual discussion of the temple itself, however, he postponed to a forthcoming volume of the *Encyclopaedia of Indian Temple Architecture*.[22]

Although Dhaky did not elaborate upon the reasons for his early date for the temple in his monograph, one hint available from his text is the attention to the presence of only Drāviḍa shrine motifs on the temple's walls.[23] He may also have considered this temple as part of "the formative phase of Chālukya architecture"[24] because it is made of sandstone, not schist. Its seeming simplicity made him place it before the mid-eleventh-century temples at Sūḍī, which also lack the "exuberance and love for metallic ornateness"[25] for which Vesara monuments have commonly been known.

I argue that the Yallamā temple is a mature and sophisticated example of Vesara architecture and must have been built in the last quarter of the 11th century at a time when major schist monuments, such as the Kāśīviśveśvara temple at Lakkuṇḍī, were under construction.[26] I propose that the Yallamā temple's Drāviḍa form and the austerity of its ornamentation are part of a "conceit" rather than a chronological marker, which must be studied in the context of the Lakkuṇḍī temples.

The east-facing Yallamā temple stands on the west bank of a large tank in Badāmī. It commands a significant location in terms of the modern layout of the town. The current name of the temple, "the mother of all," also indicates its significance in the consciousness of the present townsfolk. A small, well-crafted temple, it gains grandeur as one approaches it. This is not only because the temple is located above a stepped embankment on one side of the tank and high from the main road but also because of the formal means used to create it.

There are a number of features on this temple that make a strong case for the temple belonging to A.D. 1075–1100. The temple's adhiṣṭhāna includes a narrow jagatī with a sensuous padma above. A narrow, recessed necking and a fillet separates it from a *kumuda* with a curved, cushionlike profile. The final kapotapālī molding rests on a short *ūrdhvacippikā*. Above is a *pratikaṇṭha* and *vedikā*. In general, this sequence compares to that of the Joḍa Kalaśa at Sūḍī (pl. 43; particularly in moldings such as the kumuda torus) except that the individual moldings are narrower.

The wall of the Yallamā temple comprises a bhadra that projects in three bold stages on the ground plan, a pair of narrow pratiratha offsets stepped back a little from the bhadra, and karṇas (pl. 64). Deep and narrow recesses separating these offsets remind one of the sheath-like quality achieved by the recesses of the Kalleśvara temple at Kukkanūr. The pratiratha offset has cantoning pilasters, as in the Mallikārjuna temple at Sūḍī (ca. A.D. 1050), rather than a half-pillar common in temples after A.D. 1075. The choice of the older form for the pratiratha contributes to the restraint of the wall and the harmony of its offsets.

The principal face of the wall offsets as well as the recesses is occupied by pavilions, whose paired supports create a close clustering of vertical uprights on the wall (pl. 65). Their towers dominate the upper section and reach differing heights against the masonry wall. Their eaves, however, make an even line slightly above the middle point of the wall.[27]

All the models that decorate the walls of the Yallamā temple are Drāviḍa, except for the central offset, where the Vesara variant is recognized in the faceted dome (pl. 66). This arrangement is in contrast to the pronounced use of Nāgara models in earlier Vesara temples. By limiting the wall ornament to pavilions of a single, indigenous type, leading the hierarchy toward a large Vesara tower, the Badāmī temple distinguishes itself from earlier monuments, setting a trend for later, when Vesara models themselves are fully used as wall ornaments.

The superstructure of the Yallamā temple consists of four stories, an upper vedikā platform, and a narrow domed roof. The four stories are each marked by a hāra consisting of a string of architectural forms corresponding to the offsets of the wall. The base molding of this hāra consists of a kapota heavily marked by undecorated wedge-shaped bosses, as on the Sūḍī temples.

The moldings of the hāra are tightly compressed. In particular, the rafter ends (pratikaṇṭha) are packed close to each other so as to produce a dense, toothlike effect. These rafter ends form separate bases for each miniature unit of the hāra rather than forming a straight, continuous chain across. This compact clustering of the pratikaṇṭha under each of the hāra's architectural motifs is in advance of Sūḍī and can better be compared to later temples (pls. 67, 74).

The Yallamā's most notable advance from Sūḍī is in its treatment of the architectural models of its hāra. The barrel-vaulted back of the nested madhyaśālā is diminished (the mahānāsī slab and the upright frames for the madhyaśālā on either side are more than twice its height). In earlier temples, including Sūḍī and the Kāśīviśveśvara temple at Lakkuṇḍī, the side panels are lower and do not obscure the wall of the story behind. On the superstructure of the western shrine of the Joḍa Kalaśa at Sūḍī, a block of stone projects from the barrel-vaulted back of the madhyaśālā with

Plate 63. Badāmī, Yallamā temple, west, ca. A.D. 1075–1100

Plate 64. Badāmī, Yallamā temple, southeast

Plate 65. Badāmī, Yallamā temple, west wall

the mahānāsī dormer inscribed on it in such a way that the latter appears to be a projecting attic window of the śālā (pl. 43). On the Yallamā temple, the cavity of the mahānāsī is even larger than its śālā backing. This diminishing of the barrel vault and the lengthening of the framing panels into independent uprights necessitates a date for the Yallamā temple late in the eleventh century.

The slab on which the dormer's cavity is carved has become an independent upright panel. The vertical panels have the same effect as the arched nāsī panels of the Siddheśvara temple at Hāverī (pl. 72). The vertical frames of the madhyaśālā and the rectangular pañjara slabs above the pratiratha match the height of the mahānāsī, and the karṇakūṭas are diminished to match the back of the madhyaśālā. That these roofs are aligned with the coping of the hāra is typical of Deccano-Drāviḍa architecture. This coping, however, has been transformed by the vertical features seen on the Yallamā temple.

Significant differences between the temples at Sūḍī and the Yallamā temple are size and proportions. In terms of sheer size, the Yallamā temple is small. The stories of the superstructure are compressed and obscured behind the hāra and this vertical compression matches the compactness of the wall. The coping of each hāra is diminished, as are the roofs of its architectural motifs. The side panels of the madhyaśālā are pulled close to each other and to the mahānāsī slab, adjusting to the narrow, staggered bhadra and the other tightly graded offsets of the wall.

This gemlike precision in the facets of the Yallamā temple clearly represents a sense of form far different from the bold massing of the Kalleśvara at Kukkanūr or the temples at Sūḍī. If the architectural vocabulary used in the Yallamā remains essentially that of other sandstone temples of the midcentury, this shift of a sensibility marks a change in the monuments in this region, comparable to such temples as the Siddheśvara temple at Hāverī.

While the Yallamā temple may be small in size,

Plate 66. Badāmī, Yallamā temple, west *bhadra,* detail

the proportional balance between its wall and the superstructure creates a monumental effect (pl. 63). The thick forest of closely packed pilasters and shrine pavilions open up the masonry wall. Although the offsets and their motifs are held closely together, graded projection of the walls' offsets creates an illusion of expanding form. The superstructure soars up, tapering to the dome, which is conspicuously shallow compared with Sūḍī and more closely integrated into the tower's profile. The vertical band of nested madhyaśālās adds strength to the tower and continues as a central projection on the dome. The wall's width equals the superstructure's height. The interacting proportions of the wall and the superstructural elements, not size, give the Yallamā temple its grandeur.

In contrast with Sūḍī, the Yallamā temple avoids the use of North Indian shrine models, choosing to use only the southern variety. The overall features of the temple, however, deliberately obscure its Drāviḍa morphology. For example, the madhyaśālā of the superstructure largely loses its barrel vault. Its discrete vertical elements instead become a part of a nuanced decorative grid across the temple's superstructure and walls. It seems that the architect of the Yallamā temple intended to make the Drāviḍa identity of the decorative features he uses problematic. Unlike the earlier Drāviḍa temples in Karnataka, and to a large extent also Sūḍī, the Yallamā temple represents no palatial structure that could possibly have been built. The compression of stories, the abstraction of the hāra's elements, the articulation of vegetal growth on the imaginatively recreated central spine of the superstructure, the boldly projecting, staggered central wall offset, and the sense of vertical growth show a systemic shift. The temple's features are potent with imaginative inflections that tend toward abstraction, or, perhaps a different order of representation. Even the toothlike plank moldings in the superstructure might suggest compressed and abstracted superstructural stories as on a Nāgara tower (pl. 4).

It would be inaccurate to compare these closely ribbed plank moldings placed at the base of each level of the Yallamā's superstructure to the āmalakas (ribbed stones) that crown *bhūmikhaṇḍa*s (segments marked by ribbed stones along the curved tower) of a Nāgara temple, yet they have a similar marking effect. (No such direct equation can be made between any feature of the Yallamā temple and a Nāgara structure.) While remaining an emphatically Drāviḍa feature, the plank molding perhaps still was intended to refer obliquely to the North Indian āmalaka.

Dhaky points out that the central chain of mahānāsīs on the superstructure of the Yallamā temple coalesces almost "in the fashion of a *latā* in a Nāgara *śikhara* archaistic though it seems."[28] He implies that the architect's attempt might be to produce a Nāgara temple with Drāviḍa elements, very much as had "proto-Nāgara" temples in North India.[29] The use of Drāviḍa forms in a Nāgara fashion, however, is a "problematization" of Drāviḍa, broadening the scope of its expressions. Southern architects in the early Calukya period already had shown their capacity to produce a Nāgara temple. The rigor of a Vesara temple, by contrast, is in its continued use of the Drāviḍa vocabulary, a fact on which the Yallamā temple seems stubbornly to insist.[30] This insistence is self-conscious and particularly poignant at a time when experimental temples such as those at Lakkuṇḍī insist on an overt use of Nāgara models. On the Yallamā, the chain of mahānāsīs only interprets the Nāgara form in a southern way, as does the plank molding.

That Vesara architects may have used architectural elements for such conscious interpretations of the north is hinted in an inscription dated A.D. 1060 on the Joḍa Kalaśa at Sūḍī. The inscription mentions that the architect "Śaṅkarāya, a vakrokti-vācaspati, a teacher to the loyal, undertook the charge and constructed in the middle of the town of Śuṇḍī a dwelling for Nāgeśvara, so that the finials were completed in a manner that none could possibly imagine."[31] The unusual treatment of the temple bears out the amazement shown in the inscription (cf. chapter 4). The inscription describes the architect as an "expert of punning phrases (vācaspati)."[32] This can be taken to mean that the architect is capable of creating a certain deviance in architectural form. Both Sūḍī's inscription and its "punning" monument provide precedence for the suggestion of Nāgara created in the Yallamā temple's Drāviḍa form.[33]

The elusive quality of Vesara is captured by Dhaky in eloquent negative statements. He says that there is no feature of the temple "that can be directly sensed as Nāgara. And yet the buildings can no longer be termed Drāviḍa in the sense earlier buildings are." However, he goes on to write, "A close examination reveals that there is a vague similarity, a faint but unmistakable flavour that distantly reminds one of the Nāgara, despite the absence of genuine and typical Nāgara features."[34] Dhaky's perceptions are liberally borne out by the Yallamā temple. Its play with Nāgara is not at a formal but at a rhetorical level. Its rejection of Nāgara motifs, which were employed systematically on earlier Vesara temples, seems an intentional conceit.

We do not know whether the architects of the Yallamā temple or other monuments of the eleventh century called their architecture "Vesara." It is possible that they simply understood what we call Vesara *as* Drāviḍa. Inscriptional evidence for the term Vesara as used by architects comes only from the late twelfth century, and, as Dhaky's discussion shows, that also is left to inference.[35] One might therefore argue that the eleventh-century architects may well have designated their buildings Drāviḍa.[36]

Whatever their designation, the Yallamā temple permanently changed the terms by which Deccano-Drāviḍa architecture could be understood. By so fully integrating the formal experiments with a Nāgara aesthetic of earlier Vesara temples within a format so self-consciously Drāviḍa, it demanded an awareness that the meaning of a Drāviḍa temple in Vesara architecture had never simply been that of a palatial structure as might seem true in early Kūṭina structures. This "nuanced" and significant rendering of Drāviḍa in the Yallamā temple created a firm basis for the standardization of Vesara toward the end of the eleventh century.

Individuality and Change

The irregularities of Lakkuṇḍī and Badāmī reveal deliberate conceits of their architects. These monuments are, however, more dramatic instances of only normal practice of intellectually engaging with architectural traditions. Individuality, as is defined here, characterizes architectural practice in terms of an involved human agency.

Making individuality a key concept in an understanding of change raises an issue of method in art history dealing with religious art in India. Artistic innovation is hardly assumed a natural part of change in this field, given the conservative tendencies associated normally with religion and with the art serving it. Incremental changes in monuments are treated not as willful experiment but as reflection of the natural inconsistencies of the human hand, or an effect of political change in the region of temple making. These changes are traditionally inventoried under the "style" of broadly construed geographical regions.

Recently, Michael Meister has provided a framework to explain change in regional temples using "idiom" in relation to regional styles of Rajasthan in Western India.[37] Meister's interaction between idiom and style is modeled after a two-tiered system developed in the history of science whereby paradigms of an age are defined in relation to local experiments that refine and alter it. The value of Meister's two-tiered system in art history is that it emphasizes the process of making, providing a microscope to analyze local artistic practice and a method to characterize regional style in a context-bound way. In chapter 7, Meister's "Idiom" will be used to lay out Vesara's artistic region from the point of view of the makers of these public monuments, but Karnataka also provides a vivid example of conscious thought and willful action in a way Meister's area does not.[38]

"Individuality" contributes to our understanding of making because it takes us a step further into the microscopic view, allowing an explanation of Vesara *before* its regional idioms could develop. As will be shown in the next chapter, it is possible to speak of the idioms of Vesara only after ca. A.D. 1100. Previous to that, in the eleventh century, individuality is key in the explanation of the irregularities and anomalies that change the makeup of regional, Drāviḍa architecture. Finally, individuality always remains erratic and idiosyncratic in relation to traditional knowledge; anomaly is regularized into a historical pattern. Lakkuṇḍī and Badāmī stretch individuality toward expressions of deliberate conceits. The Yallamā temple at Badāmī is anomalous only in that it provides the necessary breakthrough leading to the standardization of the Vesara type by ca. A.D. 1100.

6

The Geography of Vesara Architecture: Karnataka in ca. A.D. 1100

OUT OF THE UNCERTAINTY OF THE ELEVENTH CENtury, when some monuments might have simply appeared to be extensions of Drāviḍa (as with Kukkanūr) or exceptional temples (Lakkuṇḍī), progressive monuments (Mallikārjuna temple at Sūḍī) or regressive ones (Aḍakeśvara at Mahākūṭa and the Yallamā temple at Badāmī), Vesara emerged as a new regional type of temple. By ca. A.D. 1100, it was unmistakably different from Drāviḍa of previous centuries, and it dominated Karnataka and the neighboring regions. One evidence of a public recognition that the new type was a distinct regional reality is the appearance of the word Vesara in texts and inscriptions from the twelfth and thirteenth centuries.[1] The Kāmikāgama's reference to Vesara as architecture of the Deccan region and its definition there as a hybrid of North Indian and South Indian temple form can be seen as a critical attempt to place the new type in a national context.

ARTISTIC GEOGRAPHY

Through a network of exchanges and interactions among various local traditions, Vesara became a noticeable, regionwide phenomenon by ca. A.D. 1100. Vesara's geographical spread, however, cannot be construed as regional style, if by "style" is meant, to use Michael Meister, "an accumulation of general characteristics that reflect a broad cultural grouping."[2] The use of "style" to group and order artifacts has been part of a necessary procedure in India, where artifacts often stand without any other supporting documentation.[3] But style in Indian art history is typically characterized as an art historical parallel to political and geographical divisions. Meister refines this framework, using style to describe awareness and receptivity of local makers within an interactive field, a model I partly use here.

To probe style as a result of interaction of craft guilds and individuals, Meister uses "idiom," partly developing on a model of "Interacting Sphere" by Irene Winter. Winter borrowed the idea originally from Joseph Caldwell and defined it as a "network of relationships within which diverse cultures engage in the material exchange of finished goods, stylistic concepts, and raw materials."[4] The model of interaction treats artifacts as products of human exchanges, making the human participants in those exchanges visible even where precise information about them may not be available, as is usually the case both in India and Winter's field of the ancient Near East. Winter uses "interaction" to analyze "the effect of one artistic tradition on another" in a context of "growing interconnectedness of things." Her concept of "local style" explains the changing artistic makeup of a locality absorbing elements from an "international style" that rides on the expanding sphere of regional interconnectedness. For Meister, "idiom" too identifies the makeup of local artistic traditions responding to styles that dominate their region. For Meister, however, "interconnectedness" does not suggest an exchange between artistic/imperial centers and peripheral localities, as in Winter's Near Eastern example, but rather a "continuity of habitation and craftsmanship, with local traditions shading from one geographically rooted community to another."[5] The chapter uses this framework of style, local style, and idiom to analyze the artistic geography of Vesara architecture around ca. A.D. 1100, but Karnataka also challenges the conclusions reached by the two scholars.

STANDARDIZATION: A CRITIQUE OF STYLE

For both Winter and Meister, style is a way of defining a coherent archaeological set based on a measurable average of visual properties deduced from a region's works of art that might otherwise vary in specific details. At no point in the history of Vesara architecture in Karnataka can such an average be demonstrated. An argument can perhaps be made from the Karnataka example that "style" has very little archaeological relevance, and it might as well be primarily, if not only, a category in the eye of the art historian.[6] In the eleventh century, Vesara's anomalies evolved in an active response to the regional, Drāviḍa mode. In architecture of the late eleventh and early twelfth centuries, it becomes possible to describe variants of the Vesara mode in different localities of Karnataka. But no single variant gained precedence with Vesara's spread, reinforcing perhaps Meister's sense of India as a connected chain of local traditions.

Archaeologically, what is demonstrable in Karnataka is a chain of idioms and local styles, responding to a new standardized type the Kāmikāgama has called Vesara. By "standardization" is meant that a tacit agreement or consensus seems to have been reached among architects in this period, signaled in a few late-eleventh- and early-twelfth-century temples, which nevertheless continued to be as diverse visually in this period of standardization as in the earlier period of experimentation. In the eastern shrine of the Joḍa Kalaśa at Sūḍī, discussed in chapter 4, the earliest sign of an implicit Vesara standard was first analyzed.

In ca. A.D. 1100, the implied agreement is indicated by at least two visual signals. One is that monuments in this period do not overtly display an interaction of Drāviḍa and Nāgara, the two frames of references evoked so consciously in monuments since Kukkanūr. After an early broad interest in a wide variety of contemporary regional sources as well as Nāgara, the standardized Vesara form affirmed its regional Drāviḍa base (pl. 67).

The Yallamā temple at Badāmī provides a crucial breakthrough for this "return" to the Drāviḍa base (pl. 63). In contrast to its contemporary at Lakkuṇḍī, the Badāmī temple absorbs a Nāgara reference fully within a self-consciously Drāviḍa form, defining in the archaism of its choice a proper southern analogy for Nāgara.[7] The renewed emphasis on Drāviḍa becomes a useful part of the chronology of Vesara only when the breakthrough at the Yallamā temple is fully understood.

The other forcible marker of Vesara's standardization in ca. A.D. 1100 is a kūṭastambha in recesses that shows a Vesara kūṭa instead of Nāgara śr̥ṅga (pl. 68). This Vesara kūṭastambha motif, seen for the first time on the Siddheśvara temple at Hāverī, indicates a major turning point given the well-developed and systematic use of Nāgara kūṭastambhas in the group of early-eleventh-century temples in sandstone and at Lakkuṇḍī.[8]

Numerous temples in this period of standardization only have a simple tripartite wall comprising a wide central bhadra and karṇas.[9] Ones that do show pratirathas distinguish it as an offset half-pillar with a Vesara kūṭa at the hāra level. This kūṭa differs significantly from the Drāviḍa kūṭas on corners of the string course. Its narrow dome dramatically steps up to a central projection and sometimes shows a vertical chain of dormers along the entire motif. The plank molding (pratikaṇṭha) wraps around the motif, as in Badāmī, and its rafters are often carved with vyālas leaping in centrifugal ways, unlike the makara heads for bhadra and karṇas.

HĀVERĪ AS A TYPE SITE

Early examples of standardized Vesara monuments are located in a region along the Tuṅgabhadrā River, which was the southern boundary for Vesara in the eleventh century. The Hāverī temple seems to be the most expressive of these monuments. It relegates a Nāgara tower to its *maṇḍapa* wall, in stark contrast to the Kāśīviśveśvara at Lakkuṇḍī, a major monument of the period of experimentation whose centerpiece is a Nāgara model. Hāverī uses only Vesara shrine models on its sanctum walls, so conceptually distinguished as to suggest a mode of self-reflection; the only exception to this usage is a Bhūmija shrine on the temple's south bhadra, which seems to be a deliberate counterpoint to those Vesara meditations.

The Siddheśvara temple at Hāverī is the earli-

Plate 67. Hāverī, Siddheśvara temple, east, ca. A.D. 1100

est known example of a standardized typology for Vesara—a temple with bhadra projections dominating the hierarchy of wall offsets and conducting the central emphasis through a series of nested madhyaśālās up to the dome.[10] The bhadra niches are surmounted either by a miniature Vesara shrine or a Vesara temple tower. Karṇas are always solid piers faced by architectural pavilions having Vesara towers. In Hāverī, the wall is separated from the superstructure by a curved stone awning; other Vesara temples may enlarge the kapotapālī of the first hāra itself, as if to suggest its dual role as a molding as well as an awning for the temple wall (pl. 73). The madhyaśālā on each of the four stories commonly has a paired nāsīs, one above the other, evoking a vertical chain of interlocking motifs reminiscent of Kukkanūr. The upper dome (śikhara) reflects all the offsets of the walls and stories below.

The Hāverī temple and the shrine models on its sanctum's bhadra—all Vesara except for a Bhūmija on the south wall—explore possibilities of extending this typology in the last quarter of the eleventh century. The shrine models are carved as if they were realistic versions of free-standing temples. That on the temple's north bhadra differs significantly in articulation and proportion from that on the east wall (pls. 69, 70). It stands on a wider base, has a shorter wall and has a heavier superstructure than that on the east. The adhiṣṭhāna is left plain, suggesting ramparts of a fort. Karṇas and pratiratha half-pillars are at angles from the bhadra, a fact reflected in a ridge on the karṇakūṭas.

The bhadra of this miniature model shows a Nāgara motif. This is, however, far less conspicuous than that on the Kāśīviśveśvara temple at Lakkuṇḍī, yet it cannot be missed. What was explicitly the theme of the Kāśīviśveśvara seems thoroughly absorbed and subordinated to Vesara form at Hāverī.

The superstructure of the model on Hāverī's north bhadra is also exaggerated in its width. An illusion of great height is created by mahānāsīs facing the madhyaśālās of its four stories. These are square and detailed on the lowest story, but smaller, taller, and reduced in detail on the upper stories. Additional wide planks on the *gṛhapinḍī* walls enhance the projections as well as the overall mass of this superstructure. The domed śikhara literally looks as if it were a kūṭa hut, with a tall necking, cornice, and curved roof.

The architectural model on the east bhadra is delicate in comparison with the massive faceted model on the north. Its low, compact adhiṣṭhāna matches that of the temple itself. The pratiratha is a thick half-pillar beyond which, strangely, is another thin cantoning pilaster. The four stories of the superstructure reflect this idiosyncrasy in uprights beyond the pratiratha-kūṭa.[11]

Both of these models are idiosyncratic figurations, different from each other and from the main temple itself. The temple, for instance, has bhadra niches with a low, curved awning above, unlike the models. On each level of the superstructure, this niche is hinted at by a similar awning, in itself an unusual feature. Also, unlike the circular nāsīs paired to create a central emphasis on the superstructure of both the models, the madhyaśālā of the temple has an arch form facing the pratikaṇṭha and a shallow vertical niche above embroidered with a floral scroll. The cavities of these niches are framed by a pair of standing figures set on stepped-back vertical panels.

The presence of Bhūmija on the south wall at Hāverī has the effect of a deliberate architectural point and counterpoint (pl. 71). The shrine models on earlier monuments, such as the Kāśīviśveśvara temple at Lakkuṇḍī, also had displayed their architects' knowledge and control of Bhūmija among other various regional types. At Hāverī, however, the Bhūmija on the south matched with prominent Vesara variants on other walls highlights a tension between these two contemporaneous but regionally different architectural forms, which also differ in mode. Bhūmija's multiplicity of towers on the superstructure might have seemed to the architect to be parallel to the proliferation of shrines on a Vesara temple, but the morphological components of a Vesara temple are distinguished from its North Indian parallel. Bhūmija's multiplication and fragmentation of wall into ever minute offsets is not shared by the Vesara variants, whose karṇas maintain their pierlike position. Idiosyncratically angled karṇas of the Vesara model on the northern wall only emphasize the corners even further.

Although the inscriptions M. A. Dhaky has discussed leave some ambiguity in our understanding of the textual terms Vesara and Bhūmija,[12] the Hāverī architect has made a clear distinction between the two in his shrine models, associating the morphology of Bhūmija with North India. He shows the shrine having a North Indian pīṭha and vedībandha, treats the central projection like a proper northern bhadra, that is, without cantoning pilasters, and depicts a creeperlike madhyalatā (central band) on the superstructure rather than paired nāsīs as on Vesara models or the temple itself.[13] A southern architect's hand is betrayed only by such details as the model's *śūrasenaka,* a vine creeper rather than a proper *jāla* (net) for the madhyalatā, and a large kīrttimukha that idiosyncratically faces the basement of this Bhūmija model.

Hāverī's models seem to articulate imaginary possibilities of Vesara, as if they were in an architect's sketch book in which Bhūmija also intellectually participates. The difference between these experiments and earlier Vesara temples is that while earlier experiments related to a wide variety of heterogeneous details through which Vesara is formulated, these modify a fully developed type, suggesting a chronological mark of accomplishment relating to a standardized typology. As the new typology gains root, variants of Vesara resolve themselves into time-tested formulas.

Idiom and Local Style

By about A.D. 1100, at least three contemporary variants of Vesara temples can be distinguished in northern Karnataka, associated here with three type sites: the Siddheśvara temple at Hāverī, of approximately A.D. 1075–1100; the Mahādeva temple at Iṭṭagi, dated A.D. 1112; and the Mallikārjuna temple at Kuruvatti, datable to ca. A.D. 1100. The three variants and their combinations built under different local rulers define the geographical spread of Vesara in Karnataka.[14]

Emerging through the Vesara experiments of the eleventh century as time-tested options rooted in different localities of northern Karnataka, these variants can be considered the three idioms of Vesara. "Idiom" suggests syntactical and morphological peculiarities that distinguish closely related monuments in a region.[15] The important point in this definition is that idiom draws upon the structures of language and is an integral whole, like language, active at a microscopic level. Like language, idiom must demonstrate a pattern of use, hence it is an aspect of standardization. While Vesara's standardization is achieved by a combination of Drāviḍa vocabulary and a new kind of thinking, Vesara's idioms reproduce such a combination at a local level. Strictly speaking, the Vesara shrine models at Hāverī do not constitute an idiom even if they suggest varying possibilities. On the other hand, the temple itself does because its peculiar visual formula generates a pattern of repeated use.

The artistic geography of a region in India is envisioned by Meister as an interconnected tissue of local, contiguous practices. That tissue in Karnataka seems to be variegated between idioms and what Winter has called local style. "Local style" is produced by "emulation," which Winter explains as a process of active absorption on the part of a receiving locality.

In some ways, northern Karnataka compares with Winter's Near Eastern context. Around A.D. 1100, this region came increasingly under the political control of Hoysala rulers of southern Karnataka, making a circumstance of political expansion an occasion for the flow of stylistic concepts. The only difference might be that the Hoysala ruler at that time, Viṣṇuvardhana, was a Chālukya feudatory before he overpowered his overlords and extended his empire northward. In any case, this political instability in the region created an increase in the "Interaction Sphere" in the north, incorporating the southern, Hoysala style. This style of architecture may be generally characterized by its emphasis on surface decoration, composed into clearly defined levels: base moldings covered by layers of lace-work and registers of figurative motifs, and walls showing architectural enclosures whose awnings divide it into two sections—above is a row of towers, below which the wall bristles with figurative panels (pl. 13). Karnataka, however, demonstrates that as political domination of the Hoysalas allows an expansion of the sphere of artistic interaction, it is not the Hoysala style but the regional idioms of northern Karnataka that provide a basis for local styles to emerge. Idioms thus are of primary significance in the development of a Vesara region.

Vesara's Idioms: Hāverī, Iṭṭagī, Kuruvatti

The Siddheśvara temple at Hāverī is different from the Vesara variants of its shrine models in that it is actually built (pl. 67). It is also one of the most exquisite of Vesara temples to be constructed in the last quarter of the eleventh century. Its elegantly proportioned gemlike sanctum is connected to a *raṅgamaṇḍapa* (open type of pillared hall) in such a way that the shrine's antechamber and the hall's eastern porch overlap (fig. 5). A lofty śukanāsa (barrel-vaulted antefix) over this space, stepping up the four stories of the sanctum, provides an appropriate transition from the sanctum to the controlled expansiveness of the open hall. The antechamber is enclosed by a

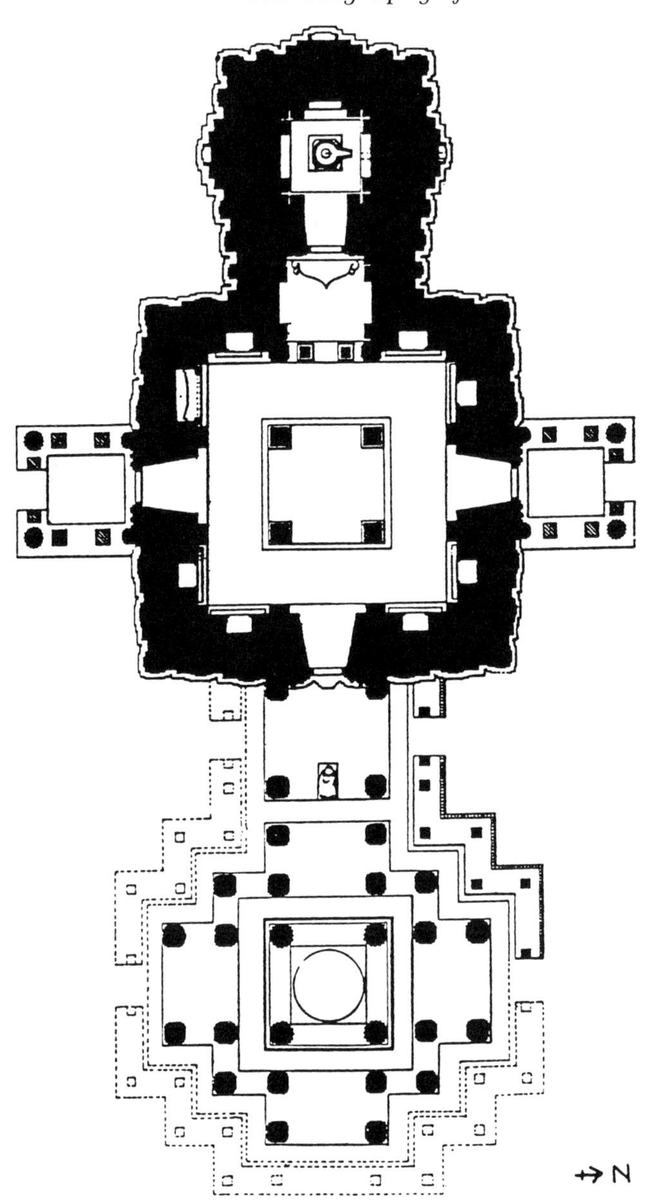

Figure 4. Iṭṭagi, Māhādeva temple, plan (Cousens, Plate CV)

wall, plain on the inside but showing offsets with architectural motifs on the outside rhythmically related to the sanctum. The antechamber wall extension reaches the raṅgamaṇḍapa's side porches and has deep niches—virtually subshrines—facing the antechamber.[16] This partially walled raṅgamaṇḍapa produces a rather abrupt transition on plan, yet this arrangement sets a pattern for the raṅgamaṇḍapas of large Vesara temples after ca. A.D. 1100 (compare fig. 4).[17]

The raṅgamaṇḍapa has a central bay and three entrance porches, and it is surrounded by broad seats with ornate seat backs. A large, curved awning extends far beyond the seat backs of the maṇḍapa, supported by thin pillars located on the seat slabs. These thin pillars set well back on the seat slabs have proved insufficient support for the outstretched awning,[18] yet this engineering risk directly relates to the effect desired. Small in actual size, the raṅgamaṇḍapa seems spacious but with a low, cavelike depth. This sensation of containment is emphasized also by clarity in the design: the mass of the pillars is carefully underplayed in relation to the intercolumnar spaces. Pillars economically provide accents, unlike later, much heavier Vesara elaborations.[9]

The peculiar combination of a comforting intimacy with a sense of restrained expansiveness is achieved also in the sanctum. The walls of the sanctum stand on a low adhiṣṭhāna with a knife-thin karṇikā. A bulging padma above the shallow jagatī and bosses that project from a virtually flat kapotapālī shift attention from the moldings (pl. 68). The large pratikaṇṭha is packed with rafter ends carved with leaping lions, elephants, and other motifs. The motifs at the ends of each proj-

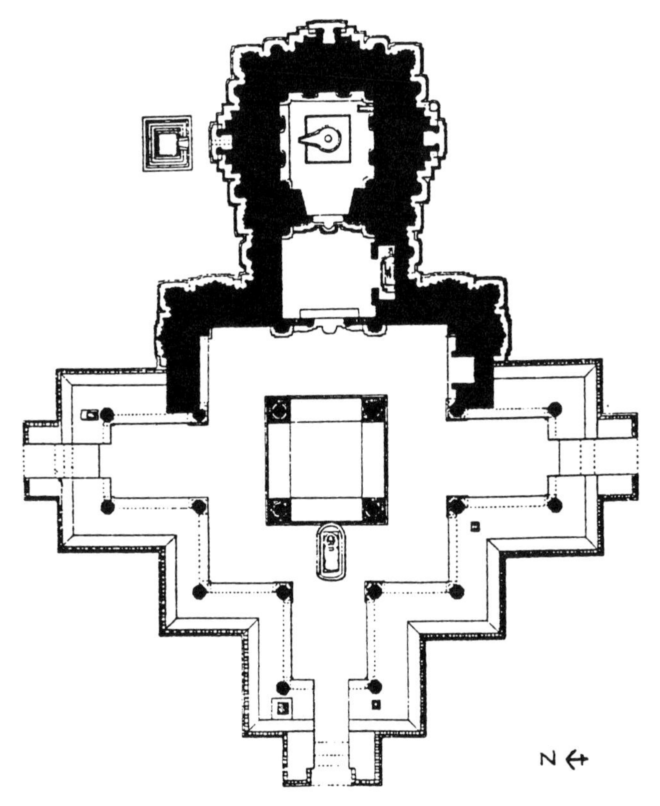

Figure 5. Hāverī, Siddheśvara temple, plan (Cousens, Plate LXXIV)

Plate 68. Hāverī, Siddheśvara temple, north wall (courtesy: American Institute of Indian Studies)

ecting offset are out-turned, as if radiating from a center.

The walls stand on a wide vedikā platform. The cantoning pilasters are precisely reflected in the pratikaṇṭha and in the bosses of the kapotapālī underneath, as if the architectural components were part of real wooden structure and the uprights were actually drawn through the vedikā base and locked into corresponding rafters below. Such precise alignment of the wall and adhiṣṭhāna will more frequently be found in Hoysala territories than in the northern Karnataka region; Hāverī in northern Karnataka, however, seems an early precursor of that feature.

The wide wall is clearly marked off from the superstructure by a curved awning. Neatly squared-off blocks of stone masonry enhance the wall's design and provide a visual grid for its adorning features. The precision of knife-sharp masonry joints contributes to a seemingly intellectual quality of the grid. The cantoning pilasters carved on them seem even to describe units of measure or at least the concept of measure. The varying sizes of the shrine models and kūṭastambhas on the wall and the thick pratiratha pilasters all seem proportionally linked and visually synchronized by the carefully controlled dimensions of the masonry blocks by which they are made.

Considering the height of each block of stone as one unit, the height and width of the bhadra is six units. The width of the bhadra's niche at its opening is one unit; its inner measurements (also the inner edges of the central cantoning bhadra pilasters that it overlaps) is two; and that including the outer walls of the niche is three. The awning of the niche spans four units as far as the cantoning pilasters of the first upabhadra. The height of the adhiṣṭhāna is three units, making the ratio between these and the wall above 2:3. The overall wall's height in relation to its width is 10:16 units.

It is remarkable how much these proportions become palpable, made so as much by the expressive interweaving of motifs as by the grid work of masonry. The awnings of the shrine models mark the wall's midpoint with a straight line precisely on a masonry joint.[20] As the uprights extend down to the rafters, they also continue the grid into the adhiṣṭhāna.

While conveying the mathematical rigor of the wall's design, these motifs gracefully balance and relieve it. The muscular kūṭastambhas in recesses mingle with the organic lushness of the scrolls above them. The shrine models on the bhadra have exaggerated, curvaceous profiles complementing the curved laśunas of the cantoning wall pilasters and pratiratha half-pillars.

The bhadras have niches cut deep into the wall, faced by a door frame whose prominent feature is a decorative pilaster (pl. 69). The folds of heavy curved awnings above the niches seem like upturned petals of lotus flowers, showing shrine models in the center.[21] Decorated with beaded tassels, these awnings make the bhadra niches appear as if they were low and deep entrances to a mountain cavern.[22]

The superstructure of the Hāverī temple comprises four stories (pl. 72). The mahānāsīs are carved on a rectangular slab and may have contained standing images. Each mahānāsī is framed by a scroll and crowned by a large kīrttimukha mask. This slab is flanked by additional uprights stepped back from it and showing standing figures.[23] This configuration reflects a shift in aesthetic preference from the square, blocklike nāsīs, seen at Sūḍī and Lakkuṇḍī, to more vertical elements recalling the Yallamā temple at Badāmī.

The "Hāverī" type seems to have developed in the Tuṅgabhadrā River-belt region that marks the southern boundary of northern Karnataka. The Siddheśvara temple at Hāverī is, as far as we know, the first available example of this type. In ca. A.D. 1100, the extensions of this type can be seen in the Mukteśvara temple at Caudadāmpur and the Kalleśvara temple at Huvināhaḍagali (pl. 73). In the twelfth century, this also became widespread in a transformed version in the Hoysala territories farther south. The Lakṣmī Nārāyaṇa temple at Lakkuṇḍī shows a northern limit of the Hoysala version of this type, perhaps built when the Hoysala rulers actually occupied the city in the late twelfth century.

* * *

The Mahādeva temple at Iṭṭagi—type site for the second idiom—contrasts with Hāverī. These two types of temples are best distinguished by the differing effects used to form their decorative surface. While Hāverī tends toward a cozy intimacy, Iṭṭagi tends toward loftiness (pl. 14).

The contrasting effects of the two temples are led through many details. In Iṭṭagi, the rhythmic undulation of the wall culminates in the bhadra, where sloping sides of the awning above the niche raise the eye up to framed openings cut vertically across the superstructure. The height of the temple wall and the slow progression of separated stories of its superstructure toward the finial convey its grandeur.

In Hāverī, the upward movement of the eye is halted by an awning that clearly separated the wall from the superstructure. The accent seems to be on the wall's lateral stretch, given especially by the elongated awning above the bhadra niche. A low basement brings the wall motifs down to eye level. The condensed and unified stories of the superstructure also convey a sense of containment.

The two types also vary in their sculptural conception. Hāverī is characterized by a more interlocked, muscular effect of densely textured walls. Architectural motifs are tightly fit into offsets and recesses, with awnings that stretch beyond and overlap cantoning pilasters. Iṭṭagi's masonry work, on the other hand, offers broad spaces, marked lightly by slender cantoning pilasters, between decorative details. While Hāverī's half-pillars are robust, having a particularly meaty bell-shaped upper section, those flanking Iṭṭagi's bhadra are reduced in mass by serrated edges.

Figurative sculpture is more likely to become an integral part of the ornamental play on the Hāverī than the Iṭṭagi type of temple. Although the central niche of both would have been occupied by figures, panels fitted into the central niche of Hāverī's madhyaśālā would also have carried figures. The uprights flanking this panel show standing female figures in them, and the dormer cavities of the architectural motifs of the hāra are filled with dancing dwarfs. The dense

Plate 69. Hāverī, Siddheśvara temple, north *bhadra,* Vesara shrine

Plate 70. Hāverī, Siddheśvara temple, east *bhadra,* Vesara shrine

Plate 71. Hāverī, Siddheśvara temple, south *bhadra,* Bhūmija shrine (courtesy: American Institute of Indian Studies)

Plate 72. Hāverī, Siddheśvara temple, superstructure, east (courtesy: American Institute of Indian Studies)

pratikaṇṭha of the basement, the dormers facing wall and superstructural motifs, the clearly separated components of the madhyaśālā, all become frames for figures in this type of temple.

One of the most conspicuous marks of difference between Iṭṭagi and Hāverī types is the configuration of their madhyaśālā. In the Iṭṭagi type, the madhyaśālā is faced by a slab showing a vinelike version of a mahānāsī dormer. A kīrttimukha in the central cavity of this mahānāsī spews a vertical pendant and a long scroll looping across the moldings of the hāra, terminating at the lower edge of the hāra. The cusps of the loops show floral buds. This scroll frames a deep cavity created in the hāra moldings. In the Iṭṭagi temple, this scroll would have been aligned with leaping animals on the wall below, presumably supported by the sockets on either side of the bhadra's shrine model. The whole configuration would have appeared as an elaborate frame for the bhadra's shrine model. On the stories above, smaller shrines are encased by scrolled cavities of each madhyaśālā.

At Hāverī, the mahānāsī and the toraṇa scroll of Iṭṭagi are replaced by a pair of slabs, one above the other. The lower, facing the pratikaṇṭha molding, has a curved arch embroidered by a floral band. The larger slab above is upright and also bordered with a floral band. The two vertically aligned slabs would have contained figures in them. The architectural solidity of this configuration, producing a vertical spine across the superstructure, differs from the open, lacy appearance of the motifs on the Iṭṭagi type.

The central nāsī panel of the madhyaśālā replaces the circular nāsī of Iṭṭagi and is flanked by additional, vertical panels stepped back from it and carved with standing figures or floral scrolls.

Plate 73. Huvināhaḍagali, Kalleśvara temple, north ca. A.D. 1075

Plate 74. Iṭṭagi, sanctum, superstructure, south, detail

Plate 75. Aṇṇigeri, Amriteśvara temple, south, ca. A.D. 1100

Plate 76. Gadag, Sūrya shrine in Trikūṭeśvara group, south wall, ca. A.D. 1100

These subsidiary uprights match the side panels of a nested madhyaśālā. The accent on these vertical decorative panels creates a staggered, outward progression that matches the expansiveness of the wall below. The expressive quality of the Hāverī type inheres in this sideways offsetting as the bhadra itself pushes forward; that of the Iṭṭagi type inheres in the way in which a rhythmic progression of the wall collects at the bhadra and is projected up towards the finial.

Iṭṭagi is more or less contemporary with the Hāverī temple and its twelfth-century variants, but it shows a different kind of preoccupation with the composition of the wall, the centrality of the bhadra, use of architecture as wall ornament, and effect. Iṭṭagi tends toward monumentality, Hāverī toward snugness. Iṭṭagi shows a chain of cavities that open the bhadra, giving a strong sense of an upward movement in the superstructure; Hāverī has a horizontal awning above the wall that prevents that movement, suggesting an outward and sideways expansion of the wall, complemented by a tapering profile of a well-condensed superstructure. The toraṇa frames for the superstructure's cavities at Iṭṭagi are replaced at Hāverī by slabs of *nāsīs* flanked by the uprights as central motifs on the superstructure.

The "Iṭṭagi" type seems to have developed in the northernmost areas of northern Karnataka out of a lineage of monuments ultimately relating to the Kāśīviśveśvara temple at Lakkuṇḍī (pl. 51). Monuments such as the Amriteśvara temple at Aṇṇigeri (pl. 75), the Sūrya shrine in the Trikūṭeśvara temple at Gadag (pl. 76), and the Banaśaṅkarī temple at Amargol (pl. 77) represent its spread in the eleventh and twelfth centuries,

Plate 77. Amargol, Banaśaṅkarī temple, northern shrine, east, dated A.D. 1119

while the Tārakeśvara temple at Hanagal marks its southern extension in the late twelfth century (pl. 78).

* * *

The Mallikārjuna temple at Kuruvatti represents a third idiom in the region (pl. 79). Here, it seems to have developed out of the Lakkuṇḍī-Iṭṭagi lineage but as a variant distinct from Iṭṭagi. The boldness and monumentality of this temple impresses one here as in Iṭṭagi. Kuruvatti's sanctum walls are of course higher, with offsets narrower, and distinguished by delicately carved motifs that are balanced by smooth wall masonry (pl. 80). This elegant restraint in the temple itself, and the slenderness of cantoning pilasters, conveys the wall's loftiness in a way unparalleled in the history of Vesara architecture.

The Mallikārjuna temple at Kuruvatti belongs to ca. A.D. 1100, and an elaborate inscription mentioning a grant of land, taxes, and money made for the service of the god Abhinava-Someśvara is dated A.D. 1099.[24] This may refer to the Mallikārjuna temple, whose other names include Āhavamalleśvara.[25] Both names recall the Chālukya emperor Someśvara I (r. 1042–68), who is known to have given up his life by drowning in the Tuṅgabhadrā at Kuruvatti in A.D. 1068 and in whose memory this large temple could possibly have been built on the eastern bank of the river. The memory of Someśvara I's voluntary drowning, "amidst din of waves and of all manner of musical instruments,"[26] seems to have been kept particularly alive during the reign of his son, Vikramāditya VI, who considered himself the heir to his father's empire. The inscription of A.D. 1099 also records elaborate institutional arrangements for the upkeep of the temple Abhinava-Someśvara, gives detailed genealogies of the political participants in the town, and establishes Kuruvatti as an important Kālāmukha center.[27] The temple could have been built between ca. A.D. 1070 and 1100.[28]

The temple is comparable to Iṭṭagi, but in the

Plate 78. Hānagal, Tārakeśvara temple, north, twelfth century

Plate 79. Kuruvatti, Mallikārjuna temple, south, ca. A.D. 1100

Plate 80. Kuruvatti, Mallikārjuna temple, south wall

Tuṅgabhadrā River-belt area, it represents a southern variant distinct from Iṭṭagi in the north. Both show the bhadra's shrine model framed by a looped toraṇa whose lineage can be traced back to the Kāśīviśveśvara temple at Lakkuṇḍī. However, they conceptualize the motif differently. At Iṭṭagi, the toraṇa is integral to the elements of the superstructure, locked into the dormer of the madhyaśālā as it cascades down, cutting across the moldings of the hāra. In Kuruvatti, the looped toraṇa is isolated as a distinct motif, a makara toraṇa with makaras spewing the loops upward. The toraṇa is also treated as part of the wall, so that the spewing makaras are shown perched on wall pilasters and the loops, taking a much more triangular profile around the wall shrine's tower, only reach the lower edges of the superstructure. The superstructure of Kuruvatti is covered with modern plaster, but the structural elements do not seem to suggest the possibility of repetition of the wall toraṇa, which differs from the vertical series created on the superstructure of Iṭṭagi.

That the idiomatic distinction between Iṭṭagi and Kuruvatti was made by craftspeople can be understood in the treatment of the same idea in two different twelfth-century temples: the Sūrya shrine in the Trikūṭeśvara complex at Gadag, near Iṭṭagi (pl. 76), and the Kalleśvara temple at Āmbli, east of Kuruvatti in the Bellary district of modern Karnataka (pl. 85). The Gadag temple reflects the Iṭṭagi-like toraṇa frame, treating it like a vegetal vine hanging from a kīrttimukha facing the dormer of the madhyaśālā. Āmbli shows the Kuruvatti-like makara toraṇa.

In the Tuṅgabhadrā belt, the Mallikārjuna temple at Kuruvatti represents an idiom adjacent to Hāverī. Kuruvatti's elevation contrasts with Hāverī's snugness. Its loftiness compares with Iṭṭagi and may be seen as its southerly version. Both are enhanced by minutely carved, spatially complex shrine models over the bhadra (pl. 80). Kuruvatti further emphasizes height and spatial openness. Iṭṭagi's bhadra shrine, for instance, has a heavy awning weighing down the niche; Kuruvatti's awning is less ponderous, and shrine models above are tall and airy, framed by openwork toraṇa low-

Plate 81. Kuruvatti, Mallikārjuna temple, north *bhadra,* detail

Plate 82. Kuruvatti, Mallikārjuna temple, east doorway half-pillar, detail with bracket figure

Plate 83. Kuruvatti, Mallikārjuna temple, *gūḍhamaṇḍapa*, pillar

Plate 84. Belūr, Keśava temple, *raṅgamaṇḍapa*, pillar (courtesy: American Institute of Indian Studies)

Plate 85. Āmbli, Kalleśvara temple, south, twelfth century

ered to the wall level. And finally, scaled by tiny Dikpālas (guardians of quarters) at the bottom of the karṇa pavilions, Kuruvatti's walls achieve cosmic dimensions.

The expressive focus of the Mallikārjuna temple's wall is the bhadra. The deep niche in the center is framed by projecting walls with facing pilasters. These niches provide an enclosure for images set on pedestals (pl. 81). The northern bhadra shows Narasiṃha, the western only the upper fragment of a divinity, while the southern niche is now empty.[29]

These niches are shaded by curved awnings supporting intricately detailed miniature shrine models (only a tower on the north). These are tightly framed by triangular makara toraṇas. The makaras carved here are embodiments of sheer lushness: their frothy tails reach beyond the bases on which they stand; a branch laden with fruits (or buds) forms a canopy for tiny figures seated on their backs. The creatures swirl buds in their trunks; a clump of vegetation escapes their gaping mouths as they throw up beaded scrolls grasped by a kīrttimukha. These triangular makara toraṇas are a southerly variant of the looped toraṇa that frames the bhadra models at Iṭṭagi.

The temple's large sanctum is preceded by a vestibule (antarāla) faced inside by makara toraṇa set on a thin, molded circular pillars, as in Iṭṭagi.[30] Its spacious gūḍhamaṇḍapa has a central bay supported by four large pillars (pl. 83). The voluminous bells of these pillars have a restrained S curve; the upper bulge of three out of the four pillars has a beaded girdle instead of medallions as seen in earlier temples (Lakkuṇḍī). This pillar seems a bolder version of the type at Iṭṭagi; its mass contrasts with those used in Hāverī. Pillars of such massive proportions become common in Hoysala temples except that the later ones usually have an ornamental chain around the circular cushion above the shaft (pl. 84).

It is not Iṭṭagi but Kuruvatti that became the basis of further variants when the new political power, the Hoysala rulers of southern Karnataka, began to extend their empire in these upper regions of Karnataka. The ponderous gūḍhamaṇ-

Plate 86. Nilagunda, Bhimeśvara temple, west, twelfth century (courtesy: American Institute of Indian Studies)

ḍapa interiors in Hoysala temples reflect Kuruvatti's configuration. The "metallic" quality in the carving of the makara toraṇa within (as well as the bhadra's models) is also a characteristic for which Hoysala monuments became generally famous.[31] The female bracket figures typical of such major Hoysala monuments as the Belūr were seen for the first time on the eastern doorway to the gūḍhamaṇḍapa at Kuruvatti (pl. 82).[32]

The tapered makara toraṇa framing shrine models on Kuruvatti's bhadra was closely reproduced in the twelfth century on the Kalleśvara temple at Āmbli (pl. 85). Conceptualized as an independent motif, Kuruvatti's triangular makara toraṇa is also adapted to other architectural features. For instance, it faces the basement of the Someśvara temple at Gadag (pl. 92). The Kaṭṭeśvara temple at Hirehaḍagali shows such a toraṇa on wall offsets and miniature, semi-detached makara toraṇa standing on its own pillar supports to face the madhyaśālā of its superstructure. The Bhimeśvara temple at Nilagunda in the Bellary district also uses the motif to face the pratikaṇṭha of its superstructure, adapting it to a Hāverī-like circular panel (pl. 86). The Rāmeśvara temple at Gadag uses a circular variant on its superstructure, fitting the Kuruvatti toraṇa even more closely to a proper Hāverī mold (pl. 90).

Local Style

The idiomatic base of Hāverī and Kuruvatti is reflected around ca. A.D. 1100 in varying combinations in many monuments in the Tuṅgabhadrā region. The twelfth century in northern Karnataka also shows absorption of artistic ideas spreading in the region due to an increasing domination of the southern, Hoysala dynasty to produce what Winter calls "local styles." Three monuments—the Mukteśvara temple at Caudadāmpur, the Someśvara temple at Gadag, and the Kaṭṭeśvara temple at Hirehaḍagali—provide grades of such interaction in northern Karnataka between these idioms and Hoysala style.

Huvināhaḍagali

First, however, the Kalleśvara temple at Huvināhaḍagali (pl. 73) also provides a caveat to the above formulation of idiom and local style, as well as demonstrates what Winter called a "feedback model."[33] Unlike Caudadāmpur, Hirehaḍagali, and Gadag, this temple does not represent local style, a term I reserve for examples that demonstrate "emulation," or "absorption" of the idiom into a new kind of structure. Huvināhaḍagali is a variant of the Hāverī idiom, a different possibility within the scope of Hāverī. Such an extension cannot be defined either as a different idiom or a local style. The temple may suggest the function of individuality (viz. Chapter 5) even in the period of standardization.

The Kalleśvara temple at Huvināhaḍagali,[34] located on the east of the Tuṅgabhadrā River in the modern Bellary district, provides many points of comparison with the Hāverī temple. The temple is datable slightly before A.D. 1071 on the basis of an inscription near the south wall of the temple. This records that Vikramāditya VI granted in that year the village of Kotiganūru (in Halpola twelve, a subdivision of Kogali 500) to the temple of Kālideva at Puvinapaḍagili (Huvināhaḍagali) at the request of the mahājanas of that village who had gone on deputation to the king to bless him.[35]

The temple has only bhadra and karṇa offsets, and only three stories of its superstructure survive. The hāra immediately above the sanctum wall is distinguished by a prominent kapotapālī, combining, as it were, the function of a molding as well as of a proper awning. This temple reflects the idiom of Hāverī, giving it a different expression.

Its superstructure offers the closest comparison with Hāverī. The arrangement of centrally paired nāsī slabs relates to Hāverī. The karṇakūṭa roof of Huvināhaḍagali is similar in articulation to the main dome of the Hāverī temple, showing a thin molding separating its roof from its sloping sides. As in Hāverī, Huvināhaḍagali also has a low hāra coping, prominently marked with dormers filled with seated or dancing dwarfs. The pratikaṇṭha on Huvināhaḍagali's superstructure is also rigorously toothed with closely gathered vertical blocks carved with leaping vyālas.

As on the Hāverī temple, each superstructural story of Huvināhaḍagali shows a central projection with a curved awning below the hāra's nāsīs. The awning continues from temples such as the Kāśīviśveśvara at Lakkuṇḍī on which the bhadra shrines are reproduced in cavities created on each level of the superstructure (pl. 51). While paired nāsī slabs on the hāra of both Hāverī and Huvināhaḍagali do not allow for openings for shrine models, the vestigial awnings imply the presence of these bhadra shrines.

This awning, however, is less elaborate at Huvināhaḍagali than the serrated one at Hāverī. It is also conceived somewhat differently than Hāverī. It is connected to the hāra's kapotapālī and directly supports the arched nāsī above. The awning on Hāverī is distinctly lower than the hāra and conceived as part of the wall's ornament similar to the one that shades the bhadra niche below.

There are other differences in Huvināhaḍagali. Leaping lions and elephants on its pratikaṇṭha are limited to upper stories of the superstructure; the pratikaṇṭha of the adhiṣṭhāna and the hāra above the wall have gaping makara heads instead. The latter variation may recall pratikaṇṭhas of such monuments as the Sūrya at Lakkuṇḍī.

The Huvināhaḍagali temple can either be interpreted as being a geographical boundary where such features combine, or at a chronological point in the 1070's, when the older northerly motif of gaping makara heads, for example, is being replaced by a newer (and southerly) motif of lions and vyālas. The chronological moment is reinforced by one other superstructural feature of the temple, the articulation of the madhyaśālā's end motifs. If in earlier temples the nested madhyaśālā shows upright panels on the outer sides, in Hoysala buildings of the twelfth and thirteenth centuries these uprights are replaced by square dormer blocks showing kīrttimukhas on their corner tips. The dormer, articulated on both sides of the block, is commonly filled by a floral motif or a figure (pls. 89, 97). Huvināhaḍagali is one of the earliest temples where this feature appears. Here these corner dormer blocks have lotus, resembling the flowers on flat lotus ceilings of Hāverī's raṅgamaṇḍapa.

Huvināhaḍagali is an extension of the Hāverī idiom with innovations that are further absorbed and developed in Hoysala monuments. A single motif may demonstrate this movement of artistic ideas. Huvināhaḍagali shows a limited use of tasseled border on upper parts of the superstructure (the kapotapālī of the second and third stories, but not the hāra above the temple wall). At Hāverī, this embroidery exists on the awning of the bhadra niche (pl. 69). The Kaṭṭeśvara temple at Hirehaḍagali, discussed later as a monument of ca. A.D. 1100 nine miles away from Huvināhaḍagali, uses it widely on the awning above the wall, in the superstructure, and in the shrine models (pl. 93). Such laced borders are commonplace in Hoysala monuments.[36] Thus, this feature seems to have originated in the Tuṅgabhadrā belt in the last quarter of the eleventh century as a peculiarity in the idioms of Hāverī and Huvināhaḍagali, to have only later gripped the imagination of Hoysala craftsmen. When Hoysala conquests moved northward, artistic ideas seem to have moved south toward the Hoysala homeland.[37]

CAUDADĀMPUR AND GADAG

The Mukteśvara temple at Caudadāmpur and two shrines at Gadag, namely the Someśvara and the Rāmeśvara, provide proper examples of "local style." Built probably in the mid-twelfth century, both temples use idioms of the Tuṅgabhadrā region to reflect a Hoysala aesthetic. In their combination, however, the monuments differ significantly, suggesting an ambiguity inherent in Winter's term.

The Mukteśvara temple at Caudadāmpur closely emulates the Hāverī idiom (pl. 87). The temple has low walls separated by an awning from a tapered superstructure. The bhadra niche sits low on the wall, as at Hāverī, and is surmounted by an outstretched awning. The hāra's configuration and its integrated profile are also comparable to Hāverī.

Caudadāmpur, however, differs from Huvināhaḍagali in its relationship to Hāverī in that it is not an extension only of the possibilities of that idiom. Made for the local Gutta dynasty of Guttal, this temple uses the Hāverī idiom to reflect a Hoysala aesthetic. For example, the thin adhiṣṭhāna moldings compare with Hāverī but are laced with floral bands that recall the more elaborate ornamental bands in major Hoysala temples of mid-twelfth century.

Caudadāmpur modifies features of Hāverī in a manner characteristic of many Hoysala temples of the twelfth century. With only a wide bhadra and karṇa offsets, its wall below the awning seems to prolong it sideways, which vertical floral scrolls filling upabhadras seem too delicate to balance (pl. 88). The superstructure's nested madhyaśālās are also exaggerated in their span. The horizontal emphasis is echoed in dense layers of hāra's moldings as well as a ridge on the coping of each hāra that mimics the articulation of Hāverī's dome. The superstructure has only three stories, as opposed to Hāverī's four. The elongated uprights of the madhyaśālās, however, help it maintain its narrow, tapered look that recalls Hāverī.

The temple closely maintains the Hāverī typology, in which the Hoysala style is only shown in glimpses. The vertical scrolls filling the bhadra's

Plate 87. Caudadāmpur, Mukteśvara temple, south, twelfth century

Plate 88. Caudadāmpur, Mukteśvara temple, south wall, *bhadra*

Plate 89. Amritāpura, Amriteśvara temple, south, A.D. 1196 (courtesy: American Institute of Indian Studies)

Plate 90. Gadag, Rāmeśvara temple, west, twelfth century

Plate 91. Gadag, Someśvara temple, south, twelfth century

Plate 92. Gadag, Someśvara temple, south, detail

offsets are original interpretations of the Hoysala-like emphasis on surface decoration, so that the "international style" is not only "emulated" in a "local style" but thoroughly transformed. Caudadāmpur's unusual rendering of the bhadra is also reflected later on the Amriteśvara temple at Amritāpura (dated A.D. 1196), a Hoysala monument built in southern Karnataka (pl. 89).

In contrast to Caudadāmpur, the Someśvara temple at Gadag, a twelfth-century monument near Lakkuṇḍī, uses a combination of elements from both the Hāverī and Kuruvatti idioms to more directly represent Hoysala style (pl. 91). Gadag relates to Hāverī in such elements as the bold separation of the walls from its superstructure, the alignment of sculpturesque awnings of the walls' architectural motifs, and the configuration of the superstructure with paired nāsīs facing the madhyaśālā. Shrines framed by triangular makara toraṇas facing the adhiṣṭhāna moldings at Gadag recall Kuruvatti.

Gadag's features are made to fit a Hoysala mold. Although its walls seem horizontally prolonged, as in Hāverī, its configuration is closer to a Hoysala wall. The offsets themselves are tall. Their pavilions have short towers raised high to provide space at the bottom for figural panels. These panels directly recall a Hoysala format of a stele. Also, while the bhadra niche itself is low, as is characteristic of Hāverī, an additional tower and awning above its original awning raises it to align with other towers on the wall.[38] Finally, wide decorative bands for adhiṣṭhāna directly recall Hoysala moldings (pl. 92); the lowest bhiṭṭa scroll suggests an affinity with Caudadāmpur.

The Rāmeśvara temple, built in the twelfth century near its contemporary Someśvara at Gadag, refines our understanding of local style (pl. 90). It combines aesthetics of Hāverī and Kuruvatti but shows no response to the Hoysala aesthetics. The walls of this small temple suggest grandeur in tall cantoning pilasters for its tripartite division, made even more emphatic by an expression of sheer masonry. Even the pratikaṇṭha rafters above the base are removed, as the temple rises ponderously on thin basement moldings that closely compare with Kuruvatti. The superstructure mostly shows features from the Hāverī type, especially seen in the closely packed rafter moldings for karṇakūṭas, the square dormers facing the kūṭa's dome as well as in the recesses on the hāra, and more emphatically in Hāverī's variant of vertical pairing of nāsīs above the central projection. This last feature shows stepped vertical panels with figures instead of the mahānāsī alternating with an arch-shaped pediment with broad decorative band around it facing the rafter moldings. For the first hāra level above the wall's bhadra, however, the circular pediment is enlarged and rendered as a looped lace treating the Hāverī-like detail in a Kuruvatti-like fashion.

Caudadāmpur and Gadag are examples of "local style" created in northern Karnataka in the twelfth century in an interaction between idioms of the Tuṅgabhadrā region and Hoysala (international) style. As northern Karnataka came increasingly under the Hoysala rule, these monuments showed an absorption of stylistic concept along the lines of political movement from southern to northern Karnataka, as in Winter's Near Eastern example. The monuments, however, also suggest that "local style" can go two ways in such a context of interaction: one toward emphasizing its regional roots while transforming the "emulated" ideas, the other toward transforming these regional roots to express affiliation with the style it absorbs. This two-sidedness of "local style" conveyed by Caudadāmpur and Gadag argues for the complexity of receptivity, which the idea of "emulation" only partially explains. The Rāmeśvara temple at Gadag, furthermore, shows no trace of Hoysala, indicating that local styles could develop in a period of political hegemony only in an interaction of local idioms, so that emulation of international style may not even be a precondition.

Hirehaḍagali

The Kaṭṭeśvara at Hirehaḍagali also tests Winter's characterization of "local style" based on such models of political domination. While Caudadāmpur and Someśvara at Gadag seem to directly emulate Hoysala ideas during Hoysala occupation of the area, Hirehaḍagali does not. It reflects the "southern" aesthetic when the Hoysala ruler Viṣṇuvardhana was still a Chālukya feudatory, as the two inscriptions discussed subsequently show. The temple is located on the southeastern side of the Tuṅgabhadrā River, not far from Kuruvatti and Huvināhaḍagali. In contrast to both those monuments, as well as Hāverī, this temple is richly decorated (pl. 93).[39]

The flamboyance of wall surface at Hirehaḍagali can be associated with the Hoysala heartland in southern Karnataka. The monument is laden with sculpturesque motifs that obscure their structural base. The pilasters framing the wall off-

Plate 93. Hirehaḍagali, Kaṭṭeśvara temple, north, ca. A.D. 1100

Plate 94. Hirehaḍagali, Kaṭṭeśvara temple, north wall, detail

sets are transformed by a vegetal imagery. Their bases are decorative roots connected to bulbs. Short branches sprouting from these bulbs also support small shrines filling upabhadra spaces. Above, the cantoning pilasters also have candelabra-like stands possibly for figural brackets (pl. 94).

Hirehaḍagali, however, combines this Hoysala surface with features that are recognizably that of northern Karnataka, particularly the idioms of the Tuṅgabhadrā region, where it itself is located. The adhiṣṭhāna of this temple is a type common in the northern, Chālukya territory (pl. 95). Unlike the southern, Hoysala versions, in which these base moldings are usually obscured by carved bands, the configuration here clearly shows a jagatī sharp karṇikā, and a shallow kapotapālī having bosses carved with dormer motifs. The adhiṣṭhāna may also be compared in its proportions to the Mallikārjuna temple at Kuruvatti.

Of importance is that the Hirehaḍagali temple is marked by a strongly individual character. Base moldings are faced at the bhadra and karṇas by toraṇas, as in Lakkuṇḍī's Kāśīviśveśvara and Sūrya temples, but their configuration is unusual. These toraṇas are freestanding, placed on stepped, projecting pedestals. Their loops are held above by a tiny kīrttimukha carved under the temple's vedikā. A much larger mask dominates the frame, holding a dormer or tubular, jagged vegetal roundels, with Dikpāla figures in them. Dikpālas on base moldings are unusual both in northern Karnataka as well as southern Karnataka, and may suggest a local practice.

Through a thick encrustation of florid motifs, one can discern the basic composition of the wall only into a wide projecting bhadra and karṇas. The offsets have wide and deep niches placed high on the walls and must have had figures in them (pl. 93).[40] Niches on karṇas are unusual in both northern Karnataka and southern Karnataka. These niches are shaded by narrow but deep eaves. The eaves are laced by a pendant and chain motif, which became common on Hoysala temples but originated in the Tuṅgabhadrā region. The architectural motifs on Hirehaḍagali are fanciful Vesara examples—some circular, others having a stellate shape popular in the Hoysala territory. However, these are all framed by triangular makara scrolls reminiscent of the motif on the bhadra of the Mallikārjuna temple at Kuruvatti.

The wall is separated from the superstructure by an eaves that is also embroidered with tassels. The carving of large lotus petals on the eaves is unusual and indicates a local treatment of the feature. The moldings of the hāra above have an additional kapota under the vedikā platform showing miniature kūṭas on the corner of every indentation. This added molding is an idiosyncrasy that gives weight and grandeur to the whole string course. The hāra moldings of each story are marked at the bhadra and karṇas with toraṇa motifs similar to ones facing the adhiṣṭhāna. Makara toraṇa at the superstructural level—instead of a nāsī—is also seen in the Bhimeśvara temple at Nīlagunda, a twelfth-century temple not far from Hirehaḍagali. Toraṇas for karṇakūṭas, however, are unusual.

The three-storied superstructure is surmounted by a square śikhara and a kalaśa bordered by lacework and placed above a spiked lotus base. The diminished barrel-vaulted backs of the madhyaśālā of the second and third stories are carved with candraśālā roundels with figures, unusual features that distort the curvature of the śālā back but are true to the spirit of decoration that characterizes Hoysala architecture.

Two inscriptions, dated A.D. 1057 and 1107, set on a slab in front of what the inscription calls the "Bhīmeśvara-Demeśvara" temple at Hirehaḍagali, seem to give us a date for the Kaṭṭeśvara temple.[41] The A.D. 1057 text gives the genealogy of the Chālukyas and states that Vikramāditya VI was a prince *(kumāra)* at the time, that Demarasa, a *mahāmātya* (prime minister), built a temple, set up lord Demeśvara in it, and granted land for the service of that god to the mahājanas of Posavaḍagile. The A.D. 1107 text further explains the circumstances, particularly that Udayāditya caused the temple to be built under the orders of Demarasa, and adds that Vire Viṣṇu Tirbhuvana Poysa-

Plate 95. Hirehaḍagali, Kaṭṭeśvara temple, south, basement

ladeva (Hoysala), among others, made grants to this temple.

The compound name of the temple in the Hirehaḍagali inscription must refer to the Kaṭṭeśvara temple along with a smaller shrine facing it. The two parts of the inscription give the temple a time frame. The older inscription of A.D. 1057, however, gives a date that is stylistically too early for the temple. In all likelihood, the temple was built by the end of the eleventh century.

The inscriptions also suggest an overlap of patronage. The 1107 text recounts the time that passed after its building, in which it especially mentions Vira Viṣṇuvardhana Hoysala among those people who made grants. The monument was, hence, already built before the time of the Hoysala king. Viṣṇuvardhana, whose presence in the region is recorded since ca. A.D. 1079–80 and who is known to be a feudatory of Vikramāditya in several inscriptions,[42] could have made his grant to the Hirehaḍagali temple in this period of his career. The political hierarchy between Chālukya Vikramāditya and this ruler is suggested by the mere mention of this Hoysala king among other donors in contrast to the detailed genealogy given for the Chālukya emperor. The inscriptions thus suggest that it was built while the Chālukyas were still sovereign and the Hoysala king a feudatory.

The decorative surface of Hirehaḍagali suggests a localized expression of Hoysala style. If, however, the inscriptions suggest that the temple was built under Chālukya rather than Hoysala patronage, the absorption of Hoysala aesthetic hardly can be explained on the basis of "local needs" to "emulate" the Hoysalas. This absorption will have to be explained on the basis other than the political motive. Perhaps it is purely aesthetic.

Hirehaḍagali, however, also leaves an issue of anachronism unresolved. While visually it demonstrates close ties with the south, the majority of those southern temples, with which we identify the "style," were built in the twelfth century.[43] The ambiguity allows us to argue that the impulse toward a decorative surface, as in the case of motifs, might also have originated in the Tuṅgabha-

Plate 96. Lakṣmeśvara, Someśvara temple, southwest, wall detail, twelfth century

Plate 97. Lakkuṇḍī, Lakṣmī Nārāyaṇa temple, east, twelfth century

drā region. The Hāverī temple, for example, tends to provide many occasions for figural imagery even while emphasizing architecture.

Hirehaḍagali may have elaborated upon this local tendency in a period of political transition. Its wall surface is in many ways distinguished from the Hoysala norm. Instead of the well-stratified composition of mature Hoysala monuments, Hirehaḍagali is built up by small clumps of decorative motifs—miniaturized shrines at various levels, rootlike forms gathered at the base of each architectural element, branches sprouting from pilasters, and florid candraśālā bosses strewn on kapotapālīs. These busy, firecracker-like eruptions on the surface, in addition to idiosyncratic motifs themselves, might characterize Hirehaḍagali's flamboyant "idiom." This idiom is reflected in such monuments in the Chālukyan heartland as the Someśvara temple at Lakṣmeśvara and may also have contributed to the spirit of decoration that characterizes Hoysala style in the south (pl. 96).

While monuments in the Tuṅgabhadrā region in ca. A.D. 1100 provide many examples to demonstrate Winter's "feedback model," by which northern ideas are absorbed into the dominant, Hoysala style, the flow of ideas themselves seems to be determined more on the strength of artistic traditions. Also, while some artistic ideas might ride on political streams, run parallel to material exchange, and be subjected to political expansion, others might not.[44] Hirehaḍagali proves that monuments with strong individuality can be built in a period of political instability. Its sculpturesque surface, embroidered with tassels and toraṇas, even forecasts Hoysala aesthetic. On the other hand, such a proper Hoysala monument built in northern Karnataka as the Lakṣmī Nārāyaṇa temple at Lakkuṇḍī stands out as a "graft" with seemingly no influence on the local tradition of building (pl. 97). The differences among the many monuments discussed in this chapter suggest that local craftsmen exercise judgment rather than regarding just any intrusion worthy of emulation.

Winter's sample tends more toward similarities between "local style" and "international" style than the differences between them. These similarities explain a local need to reach out and absorb the dominant style. While Winter's emphasis on "emulation" as an "active gesture on the part of the receiving culture" is an important shift from the idea of "influence,"[45] the "need" for that local outreaching gesture is determined by relations of political power; local patrons emulate to raise their esteem in relation to the dominant culture, presumably to reduce the gap between center and periphery. This mode of bridging the gap through a need to be similar seems ironically to only reinforce an agreement with the superpower about one's own peripheral and dependent status.[46]

Such an irony arises in Winter because the idiomatic base in the locality of her "local style" is not clearly defined, or missing. Meister defines the interaction of idiom and style by emphasizing the way local traditions define themselves through time in a context of shifting political sway over the region. Idioms for him "represent local traditions rooted in the work of local artisans, traditions which endure even as political authority shifts or declines. . . . Although idioms may absorb general characteristics of a style they remain essentially cumulative and self-defining. I see idiom and style as independent rather than dependent variables, however much they may interact."[47] The example of Vesara in Karnataka might differ from the interaction both scholars define, in that the centers and networks of its artistic geography are primarily generated and characterized by idioms of ca. A.D. 1100.

For Winter, the homogeneity of "Interaction Sphere" can result in a lessening of the gap between the local and international styles. Applying Winter's conclusions to India, Meister concludes that "[i]n India, the political definition of style was possible, but not given, and greater homogeneity, rather than differentiation, within India's diverse society was often the result."[48] For Meister, interacting idioms produce stylistic homogeneity. Karnataka monuments demonstrate that an interaction of idioms produces what Winter calls "local style," but idioms prevent stylistic homogeneity from occurring. An increase in the "Interaction Sphere" creates a tension between idiom and style, resulting in a heterogeneity of exchanges and a proliferation of diverse local styles.

7

So What? The Expressive Content of Vesara

THIS CHAPTER EXPLORES THE LOGICAL FRAMEWORK of Vesara as architects themselves may have understood it, using the foregoing documentation to offer a perspective on the possible motive for Vesara's regional experiment in the eleventh century. The framework and the motive are embedded in the process of making, and hence the preceding chapters were devoted to a detailed archaeology of monuments by the end of the eleventh century. Vesara architects reaffirmed their regional roots in the temple form they created, using regional eclecticism as a means, and Drāviḍa's Kūṭina, or "hut"-based, morphology as a significant asset. By the end of the eleventh century, idioms of Vesara emerged as time-tested options. Within them, as well as in many non-standard monuments of the period, the modification of regional conventions as well as the exploration of meaning continued. An elaborate iconography of shrine models on temple walls, Nāgara references within a Drāviḍa format, as well as the bhadra cluster for various unprecedented architectural effects, demonstrate how Vesara architects required a rethinking of Drāviḍa architecture. As architects searched for new meanings, a distinction between the outer shell and inner content blurred, and Karnataka's Kūṭina temples gained quite a different resonance.

CLUE FROM THE INSCRIPTION

A closer look at the inscription from the Koṭiśvara temple at Kuppatur discussed in chapter 1 suggests key components of the constitutive framework in Vesara as they were valued by Vesara architect themselves. The passage reads:

> (Kaiḷāsā)driya Viśvakarmaṇe bhavaṅga end-oldu sad-bhaktiyoḷ bhadradiṃ kaṇḍarisiṭṭan-embineg-aneka Drāviḍaṃ Bhūmijaṃ piriduṃ Nāgaraṃ-emba bahuvidhada bhadrōpetadiṃ kaṅge varadiṟe Koṭīśa-bhavālayaṃ su-lalitaṃ saumayaṃ karaṃ sausṭhavaṃ

> (Within this village of Kuppatur) was built, as if by Viśvakarma himself, out of sublime devotion for the Lord of the Kailāsa mountain, the elegant, equipoise and shapely temple of Koṭīśa-Bhava, freely ornamented with Drāviḍa, Bhūmija and Nāgara, and, with bhadra-offsets manipulated in many ways.[1]

The boastful declaration of the architect as divine Viśvakarman is in part stereotypical. The presumption of a divine status, however, is related to particular architectural challenges that the architect had to meet, giving the universalizing cliché a local value. It is precisely the architect's way of attending to specific features on the temple that suggests their importance in his estimation.

This inscription has been used by M. A. Dhaky to investigate the various temple forms to which architects referred in using the terms Drāviḍa, Bhūmija, and Nāgara. By the early thirteenth century, when this inscription would have been written, the play with regional shrine models was clearly taken in a competitive spirit by every architect who considered himself worth the epithet of Viśvakarman.[2] However, the Kuppatur inscription also boasts that the architect has manipulated the bhadra as part of his creation, an aspect that does not concern Dhaky but is important for my analysis. It suggests that the elegance and balance of the temple intended for the Lord of the Kailāsa mountain in Kuppatur was to depend on how bhadra was used to project expressive architectural models. In other words, the two aspects of the architectural enterprise that the inscription addresses are intimately related in the minds of the local Karnataka architect qualifying as Viśvakarman. Manipulating the bhadra, architects develop an elaborate scheme to interrelate shrines on their Vesara walls. Kuppatur's statement, considered as a whole, suggests the architect's own estimation of the challenges involved.

The Bhadra in a Vesara Temple

Karnataka architects used "bhadra" to mean the central, projecting offset. Evidence of numerous temples also suggests that these architects intend the bhadra projection to include the intermediary offsets flanking it (what in North India would be called pratirathas). The manipulation of this projecting cluster of offsets between the karṇa piers suggests that Vesara architects intended to explore this "bhadra" as a device to give the temple its focus, its centrality.[3]

The central emphasis seems a common and consistent feature of Karnataka's Drāviḍa architecture, absorbed in part from the Nāgara temples also built in the region. In early Drāviḍa temples, the offset was usually articulated as if it were a pillared pavilion against a wall that itself only had cantoning pilasters on corners (pl. 5). The hāra above this central projection had a madhyaśālā, the domed śikhara above had a cardinal *nāsī*. Such a configuration was based on the logic of enclosures and lookout points along the walls of a divine mansion, pierced by windows or provided openings for the appearance of a figurative divinity. Vesara provides a new intellectual aspect to this Drāviḍa vocabulary. Within the Drāviḍa matrix, Vesara's originality requires a conceptual shift.

The wide projecting bhadra of the Kalleśvara temple at Kukkanūr, separated from corners by deep recesses, suggests that conceptual shift (pl. 99). Unlike the narrow, porchlike pavilion that had evolved in early, mainstream Drāviḍa temples, Kukkanūr's central projecting offset is a wide section of the wall itself, separated from corner buttresses by deep, narrow recesses and indented into three steps marked by thin, cantoning pilasters. Partly, this widening of the offset can be related to developments in Drāviḍa temples at Aihole (see chapter 3), but Kukkanūr's immense, projecting wall section also equals the width of the inner sanctum, suggesting an outward, organic expansion of its space (fig. 2). The architectural motif of a "blind pavilion" marks the central face of this bhadra as well as the corner piers. As the wall below presses forward in multiple projections, the nesting śālās and the crowning śikhara also break into planes of minor offsets.

The wide, multiplying, projecting offset bhadra of the Kalleśvara temple at Kukkanūr cannot be described merely as an elaboration of a Drāviḍa form. The alignment of this bhadra with the internal cell signals both a conceptual move and a reorientation within Drāviḍa. The oblong śālā shrine placed on this bhadra wall pinpoints the projection of the bhadra; as a miniaturized version of the wide bhadra and the crowning śālā, it becomes an icon of the sanctum itself. This reorientation of the wall so that the bhadra represents the sanctum space creates a basis for Vesara explorations after the Kalleśvara temple at Kukkanūr.

Vesara temples after Kukkanūr develop a rich and varied architectural vocabulary to explore the mystery and power of the sanctum on their exterior walls. The various ways of manipulating the bhadra referred to in the Kuppatur inscription implies the architectural vocabulary that must have been fully developed by the early thirteenth century in order to achieve the sanctum's expressive focus. Kuppatur's bhadra parallels the verbosity of the inscription; using a double awning instead of a single awning for the central shrine niche, it only uses a formula common in southern Karnataka temples (pl. 100). But in pressing the importance of manipulating the central feature, the inscription refers to a tradition of practice, to which its architect must be heir, where indeed the bhadra was developed into a flexible framework for Vesara's formal experiments.

Like Kukkanūr, in the Rāmaliṅgeśvara temple at Guḍur the bhadra and recesses together combine to measure the sanctum's interior space, the recesses marking the inner edges of the sanctum, while the karṇas represent the thickness of the enclosing wall (pl. 40). The offsets and recesses are each faced by an architectural model. Notably, the recesses are more conspicuously orna-

Plate 98. Aihole, Ambigerguḍi, west

Plate 99. Kukkanūr, Kalleśvara temple, west wall

Plate 100. Kuppatur, Koṭiśvara temple, southwest, wall detail, ca. A.D. 1235

mented than the projecting bays. Each is filled by a North Indian, Nāgara tower placed on a single column. This Nāgara kūṭastambha motif is then framed by an elaborate, cusped toraṇa spewing from a kīrttimukha mask.

This enrichment of the recess framing the bhadra is a major step in the definition of Vesara architecture. Before the Nāgara motif was introduced in it, by the end of the tenth century the Iśvaraguḍi at Ron had already hinted at the prominence of recesses in a Drāviḍa temple (pl. 101). The plain, pilastered walls of this temple resemble the monotony of its contemporary, Ambigerguḍi at Aihole (pl. 98), except for the decorative architectural motifs in recesses between the central and corner wall sections. Sculptured out of the stone cubicle, and seen against bare details of the remnant offsets, the recess evokes a vision of the inner sanctum expressed in the exterior recesses, as it were, through the walls' crevice and on the walls' thinnest, most transparent layer. Guḍur is the first temple to use a Nāgara kūṭastambha with a toraṇa surround to indicate the shrine's embedded content on this deep layer of the wall, introducing a pattern for Vesara temples built soon thereafter, where kūṭastambhas dramatized the recess by the exuberance of their makaras and framing arches. Their decorative energy animates the recess and communicates in it the mystery and the generative power of the hidden sanctum.

Plate 101. Ron, Iśvaraguḍi near Anantaśāyiguḍi, south, late tenth century (courtesy: American Institute of Indian Studies)

The Function of Northern References

The use of a Nāgara kūṭastambha is part of a conscious, reflective use of contemporary North Indian motifs that seems to have begun in Karnataka in the late tenth century. For example, at the bottom of the corner piers of Ambigerguḍi in Aihole is another folksy representation of a North Indian motif (pl. 98). The detail represents in an abbreviated form the ornate pediment enclosures used for images, called rathikās, that had become a common decorative detail in superstructures of North Indian monuments by the tenth century. The intrusive motif gives a clue that the architect of this temple might have had northern temples in mind.

I can explain the function of this detail on Ambigerguḍī using "index," a term from the triad of signs in Charles Sanders Peirce's semiotics.[4] Peirce identifies index as a sign that gains its meaning by being contiguous to the object it represents. Aihole's wall graffiti points at contemporary North India. The indexical sign gives the barest hint of an early exploration in Karnataka for parallel terms from other contemporary architectural contexts.

In Aihole's contemporaneous shrines, the more usual motif used on the walls was a Drāviḍa kūṭa pavilion, with which Ambigerguḍi's northern graffiti were matched (pl. 33). The kūṭa motif refers to the Kuṭina morphology of the Drāviḍa shrine itself, which I have defined in chapter 2 as a formal system of hut-shaped sheltering units on which a mansionlike shape of the typical southern temple fully develops. The kūṭa pavilion representing a unit of shelter on Aihole's walls is an

Plate 102. Huli, Kāśīviśvanātha temple, west, detail, twelfth century

Plate 103. Niralgi, Siddharāmeśvara temple, northeast, twelfth century

Plate 104. Gadag, Sūrya shrine in Trikūṭeśvara group, north *bhadra,* detail of shrine model

irreducible icon of the mansionlike temple itself. The North Indian rathikā, commonly used as a framed shelter for deities on North Indian walls, is only used as a northern equivalent.

Notice that Ambigerguḍi's rathikā in fact functions as a double sign, indexically referring to the northern regions as well as providing a northern parallel to the kūṭa pavilion common in tenth-century temples at Aihole. In Peircean terms, the graffiti rathikā is absorbed within Drāviḍa's Kuṭina morphology as an "icon." Peirce defines icon as a sign that refers to its object by analogy. The dual function of the northern motif also allows it to remain an interesting novelty, a sport in Karnataka, without achieving the formal breakthrough required for Vesara.

The rathikā motif is never repeated in any other Karnataka temple. Nevertheless, by the mid-eleventh century, Vesara temples give full play to such direct pointers of regional typologies in accurate depiction of contemporary northern temple forms such as Bhūmija and Śekhari in the Joḍa Kalaśa in Sūḍi or Lakkuṇḍī. The most complex of such novelty is an architectural model depicted on the Sūrya shrine in the Trikūṭeśvara temple complex at Gadag (pl. 104). Dhaky has classified the Gadag example under "composite representations," showing within the outlines of a curvilinear Nāgara tower a Bhūmija as well as a Drāviḍa shrine.[5]

Such a playful use of northern motifs does not constitute Vesara, but it records a moment in the history of Indian monuments when regional eclecticism was explored more creatively and self-consciously than in any other period. Such a moment of deliberate reflection seems to have begun in tenth-century Aihole shrines, extending for about hundred years, in which some foreign motifs are entertained and discarded, others incorporated within the framework of Vesara.

Nāgara Kūṭastambha

Unlike Aihole's graffiti rathikā, the Nāgara kūṭastambha takes root in the region. Having a single column supporting a conical North Indian, Nāgara temple tower, it could have been first introduced as part of an indexical play around A.D. 1025 in the Kalleśvara temple at Kukkanūr. The motif appears inconsistently there: on the north wall of the sanctum, crowding the recess between the sanctum and the closed hall preceding it, and in a few other places on the hall preceding the sanctum (pls. 38, 39). If Aihole's motif is a failed irregularity, I will show that Kukkanūr's develops into a logical anomaly, altering the conceptual frame of the Drāviḍa type in Karnataka.

The Nāgara kūṭastambha at Kukkanūr functions as a significantly different motif from a northern rathikā. On Aihole's Ambigerguḍi, the rathikā may have sportfully recalled a northern parallel for the typical southern kūṭa pavilion motifs. A kūṭastambha is not a visual abbreviation of a sacred shelter. The Nāgara kūṭastambha suggests the Vesara architect's grasp of the ritual meaning embedded in the Nāgara temple, beyond merely a knowledge of its formal type. A tapering North Indian tower placed on a single column refers to a Nāgara logic by which sacred structures developed as architectural embodiments of sacred altars for fire sacrifice; the tall form of a Nāgara temple represents a stone casing for the column of smoke and fire rising above the temple's symbolic altar platform (pl. 4).[6] As a concrete, irreducible embodiment of this northern imagery, the Nāgara kūṭastambha adjacent to a Drāviḍa kūṭa pavilion does not adequately serve as a North Indian equivalent of a Drāviḍa kūṭa pavilion. Unlike the northern rathikās, it is made to exist in tension with the Drāviḍa motifs. Pointing indexically to its exotic status, the kūṭastambha is also used as an icon of a Nāgara temple, challenging the normative relationship between the wall's earlier ideographs for "shelter" and the temple's sheltering form that had prevailed thus far in the Drāviḍa context.

By Guḍur in the early eleventh century, the irregular motif first introduced in Kukkanūr is given a consistent place within the decorative scheme of the temple. Occupying the recesses, I suggest, it refers to the Nāgara-like mystery now recreated in the Drāviḍa sanctum. The most obvious expression of the northern motif's iconic function in Karnataka is given in the Kāśīviśvanātha temple at Huli, an unfinished temple belonging perhaps to the early twelfth century, when Nāgara motifs had generally ceased to appear on sanctum walls (pl. 102). The temple has in the center of its staggered bhadra projection a large, circular column carrying a Nāgara tower, shown prominently against the hāra.[7] The Huli temple is unusual and revealing in the blatant directness with which its central motif brings the northern conception to the interpretation of its dark sanctum. Flanked by small Vesara kūṭastambhas (as if by attendants), the Nāgara motif spans the height of the sanctum and is repeated also on the upper story. Huli's exceptional use of the Nāgara *stambha* icon extends the motif's symbology to the whole Vesara temple.

The Bhadra-cluster Format

Since Sūḍī, Nāgara kūṭastambhas are used as a means to define a basic tripartite composition for a Vesara temple while the walls themselves increase the actual number of projecting offsets. The bhadra and flanking pratirathas are treated as a cluster distinguished from the corner piers. This group has been called in this book a bhadra cluster to indicate the conceptual link between this clustering and the bhadra projection of Vesara temples such as Kukkanūr, indicating the sanctum within, and the manner in which its essential mass is developed into an elaborate Vesara framework.

The use of Nāgara kūṭastambhas as markers for the bhadra cluster is a Vesara invention. Inflected by these markers, the wall becomes strikingly different from the composition of bays and recesses sheltering major and minor divinities in previous Drāviḍa architecture. The Nāgara kūṭastambha itself was discontinued in ca. A.D. 1075, except for the brief, unsubtle revival at Huli. The tripartite clustering of the wall, however, was firmly established.

Standardized Vesara monuments built in ca. A.D. 1100, using only a Vesara kūṭastambha in their recesses, do not clearly articulate the bhadra cluster as earlier temples did. Three examples from that period, a Vesara shrine model on the eastern bhadra of the Siddheśvara temple at Hāverī, the Kāśīviśvanātha temple at Huli, and the Siddharāmeśvara temple at Niralgī, however, provide evidence of the continuation of this Vesara conceptualization even in this period. The shrine model at Hāverī shows a wall composed of karṇa offsets, a two-stepped bhadra, and pratirathas shown as thick pilasters (pl. 70). This five-part division continues from the base moldings up to the finial. A thin extra pilaster appears beyond the pratiratha half-pillars, however, as if to bind the offsets to which the pratirathas were applied. The superstructure reflects this offset by marking it by the vertical end panels of a śālā, as if the stepped madhyaśālā stretched to encompass the pratiratha kūṭas as well. Thus, although the shrine has a five-part wall, the decorative elements in the superstructure help to group the bhadra and pratirathas together as components of a single, central wall unit.

The twelfth-century Kāśīviśvanātha temple at Huli has a very wide bhadra cluster, with flanking recesses that show Vesara kūṭastambhas (pl. 102). The three-staged bhadra displays at the center the Nāgara kūṭastambha already discussed. The corners of the pratiratha offsets framing the bhadra are marked by clearly distinguished offset pilasters. This frame for the bhadra cluster is perhaps even more emphatic than on Hāverī's shrine model. Both Hāverī and Huli emphasize the bhadra cluster without needing to use the Nāgara kūṭastambha.

The Siddharāmeśvara temple at Niralgī, ca. A.D. 1100, uses both shrine models and pilasters to focus the bhadra cluster (pl. 103). Its bhadra offset is framed by pratirathas marked by offset pilasters with bell-shaped upper sections. These ghaṇṭās on pratiratha may suggest a condensation of the motif on the pratiratha half-pillar of the Kāśīviśveśvara temple at Lakkuṇḍī (pl. 54). The bhadra has a bold niche with awning and shrine model above, and the karṇas have pavilion motifs with a Vesara tower. Each recess shows a Vesara kūṭastambha, except only those that frame the bhadra cluster have distinguishing toraṇa frames, as at Guḍur.

Vesara Logic

Such expressions of the wall suggest the conceptual logic of Vesara. The wide bhadra cluster provides a visual format for an exploration of the symbolic potentialities of the sanctum. The Kāśīviśveśvara and Sūrya temples at Lakkuṇḍī represent a high point in this exploration (pls. 51, 56). Perhaps the archaeologist Henry Cousens had these Lakkuṇḍī temples in mind when he wrote that in "Chālukya" temples "the vigorous and purposeful lines of [Drāviḍa temples] were broken up and whittled away . . . until they became, with the addition of much overloaded ornament, rather a jumble of details all jostling one another in apparently aimless confusion."[8] Cousens failed to see the systematic organization of the Vesara wall. The projections of the Kāśīviśveśvara show a variety of Indian temple forms (Latina, Śekharī, Bhūmija, Drāviḍa) making the temple's compositeness one of its most compelling characteristics.

Such combination of features has deep roots in Karnataka, as can be seen even in the earliest examples of monumental architecture. Miniature shrine models carved in the latter part of the century mix Nāgara, Drāviḍa, and other forms into what Dhaky has called a "composite representation."[9] Such a combination is not "confusion," nor does it define Vesara. Vesara should properly be understood in the organization of its architectural elements, not their apparent disarray.

The faceted appearance of the Sūrya shrine and the way various elements on the Kāśīviśveśvara temple are staggered help reveal the conceptual logic of their design. The bhadra cluster in Lakkuṇḍī was used for the first time to frame a deeply sunk niche that would have contained an image of the inner deity. On the Kāśīviśveśvara, the bold superstructure of this niche is a Nāgara tower, itself framed in a cavelike toraṇa against the superstructure of the temple. The architectural form emerging through the ornamented cavity absorbs an ideational structure of North Indian, Nāgara temples.

While all Indian temples represent a "monument of manifestation,"[10] framing divinity as a living germ appearing in the sanctum, the North Indian, Nāgara temple fully absorbed this cosmogony into the architectural logic of its form. The temple is considered not only the house but also the organic body in which the divine manifestation is enacted. Its exterior walls represent an outward expression of the sanctum, called the garbhagṛha (womb house), its central projection (bhadra) revealing the germ as a fully formed deity appearing in a niche as if it were emerging from the temple's body. At Lakkuṇḍī, the decorative frame of the bhadra opens up the madhyaśālā as well, fully absorbing the cosmogonic logic of a Nāgara temple, only that it conveys a realistic Nāgara shrine through this opening as if it were the manifesting unit, not merely a frame.

In Peircean terminology, the Kāśīviśveśvara temple embodies a "symbolic" sign, referring to the generic logic of Nāgara in a manipulation of Drāviḍa vocabulary. A symbol, according to Peirce, "is a sign which refers to the Object that it denotes by virtue of a law, usually an association of general ideas, which operates to cause the symbol to be interpreted as referring to that Object."[11] As has been pointed out in chapter 5, the specific language used in Lakkuṇḍī is an archaized version of Drāviḍa, expressed by a Drāviḍa madhyaśālā, visible over the bhadra in contrast to the nested variation normally seen in Vesara architecture by the time the temple was made. The archaized language in which the symbolic reference to Nāgara is recreated, combined with an unprecedented range of indexical models referring to various regions of India with realistic accuracy, makes the Lakkuṇḍī temple the best expression of Vesara's conscious, conceitful intelligence.

Manipulation of the bhadra cluster as a signage for the inner sanctum gains other expressions in Vesara architecture. One of the most daring of such manipulations is documented in the angled pratiratha half-pillars framing the bhadra cluster of the Sūrya temple at Lakkuṇḍī. Scholars of North Indian architecture have shown that turning these offsets relates to experiments in which the sacred square diagram ritually embedded in the sanctum is rotated to generate prismatic ground plans on which the temple's sanctum is plotted. Michael Meister has pointed out that such rotated ground plans geometrically fortify the temple by creating protective corners for its vulnerable garbhagṛha.[12] Reinventing Drāviḍa vocabulary, turned subsidiary piers of the Sūrya shrine act like watch-towers protecting the sanctum, as in that northern experiment. Unfolding between the interlocking facets of the pratiratha bastions, the manifesting unit on the bhadra represents a typology of excavated architecture fully developed in the Deccan by the fifth century, and is thus comparable to the indexical references to other North Indian types in Kāśīviśveśvara. The close reflection of Deccani caves is unique to the Sūrya temple at Lakkuṇḍī, and never repeated. The turning of subsidiary offsets is unprecedented in all of South India.

The Language and Meaning of Shrine Models

Vesara architects use architectural motifs extensively and with conceptual refinement. As primary wall ornament, these motifs provide a different order of representation than the general proliferation of figurative images on contemporary temples elsewhere in India. The Kāśīviśveśvara temple at Lakkuṇḍī shows Drāviḍa, Bhūmija, and Vesara models on its karṇas and large multi-spired Nāgara on its bhadras (pl. 53). The Siddheśvara temple at Hāverī shows two variations of Vesara on its bhadras plus a Bhūmija model. The Kaṭṭeśvara temple at Hirehaḍagali shows stellate and circular variants of Vesara itself (pl. 94). These shrine models, like *iṣṭadevatās* (personalized deities), are the mythic variants of the manifesting divinity. They occupy locations precisely where one would expect images of such divinities.

Vesara temples are not completely devoid of figural images, but when figures do appear their conceptualization in relation to the whole structure is greatly different from that in both Nāgara and Drāviḍa. On the Yallamā temple at Badāmī, for example, the walls are crowded by tall, empty Drāviḍa pavilions (pl. 65). Only the mahānāsīs in the superstructure above each bhadra contain divine figures (pl. 66; photograph shows Narasiṃha). Niches in all Vesara monuments would also have had a figural divinity within. Tiny figures also appear at the base of the elaborately ornamented offsets (pl. 14). The Kāśīviśveśvara and the Sūrya temples at Lakkuṇḍī add narrative panels and tiny figures in the wall's recesses (pl. 56). In all these cases, figures are tiny in size if not in importance.

If the iconographical programming of a temple were structured in layers, I would suggest that figural imagery only occupied a minor layer on a Vesara temple, fulfilling at best a specific ritualistic need of a localized community. The architectural forms that are used as decoration visually overlap and dominate this layer of imagery. Since Lakkuṇḍī, shrine motifs are often graded in a hierarchy starting from the central niche, which houses a figure. Karṇas bear architectural pavilions with tiny figures inserted at the base seemingly as afterthoughts.[13] Pratiratha piers bind the bhadra cluster, acting like enlarged kūṭastambhas. Small kūṭastambhas fill the recesses. Also, shrine forms create a gradation of types; the Yallamā temple at Badāmī creates a delicate hierarchy of size and complexity of only Drāviḍa kūṭas, with no figural images. While the architectural gradation is clear on all Vesara monuments, the iconographical order of the figural images on the bases is much harder to decipher.

The use of architectural motifs in Vesara architecture, cannot be dismissed as simply decorative; it suggests an attentiveness to their potential meaning. The language of shrine models carries nuances that parallel contemporary Nāgara and Drāviḍa conventions. As in all Indian architecture, Vesara's bhadra shrines convey the manifesting divinity into the worshiper's space. But in the Kāśīviśveśvara at Lakkuṇḍī, the shrine itself is expressed as a manifesting unit. The architectural motifs are framed and projected with great semantic complexity by Vesara architects. A "composite representation"[14] superimposing Bhūmija, and Drāviḍa forms within a Nāgara outline, when placed deep in a crevice on the bhadra, and framed by a cusped arch enlivened by monkeys, lotus buds, and vegetation, seems to show these different shrine forms as sequential, iconic emanations from a fluid sanctum (pl. 104). Other architectural motifs, placed on the other "opaque" offsets of the wall, are graded toward this "perforated" center.

Unlike the typical Nāgara or Drāviḍa temple, in which structural parts form only the frame for anthropomorphic images, in Vesara temples the overall encasement—the shrine model—becomes the expressive figure. The deeply hollowed-out shrines on later Vesara temples are in direct relation to the blank pavilions marking the bhadra cluster of Vesara temples early in the eleventh century. These swelling forms, as in the fully developed shapes of the Lakkuṇḍī or Gadag temples, or the use of a Nāgara stambha on the bhadra at Huli, are all meant as consistent, visible embodiments of the manifesting divine substance within the garbhagṛha.[15]

At the end of his monograph, *Temple Forms,* Dhaky asked why the Karnataka architects had so indulged in depicting models. The question was not intended to probe the nature or significance of their presence on Vesara temples. Dhaky explains them in terms of the pride Karnataka architects may have felt in their ability to command a wide range of forms. This "healthy curiosity concerning knowing about architectural forms other than their native" was, for Dhaky, a regional characteristic, one he perceives as well in the classical music of Karnataka today.[16] Why such architectural forms became such a primary mode of representation on these temples, however, did not concern him.

These shrine models are key to understanding the distinctness of Vesara. Absorption of Nāgara ideas by itself did not make Drāviḍa into Vesara. This is not to underestimate the significance of Nāgara logic to Vesara. Resultant features such as the offsetting of the wall, the sunken niche on the projecting bhadra, and the vertical emphasis at the center carried up to the finial are essential to Vesara's final form. Yet to point only to such features is to beg the real question of Vesara.

Dhaky groped with this issue of Vesara's distinctness, but his mode of questioning led him to suggest that Vesara could have become Nāgara if only its Kūṭina references disappeared.[17] This line of reasoning cannot sufficiently explain Vesara. The Kūṭina morphology of Vesara is not a hin-

Plate 105. Kuruvatti, Mallikārjuna temple, south *bahdra*

drance but an asset to Vesara's morphology. Insisting on the kūṭa within the frame of its bhadra cluster, the delicate changes Vesara brought about in Nāgara's manner of manifestation and the resultant transformation of the underlying Drāviḍa matrix together made Vesara an original architecture.

Vesara architects made the arrangement of shrine motifs comparable to the use of figurative imagery in temples from other traditions of India. While figures can represent the multiplicity of cosmic manifestation in all traditions, the cosmos as composed of units of measured space can best be embodied by shrine models. These models in Vesara are differentiated as pan-Indian forms (Lakkuṇḍī) or characterized as graded reproductions of the temple's own form (Iṭṭagi and Hāverī). In either case, the iconic unit is the *garbha,* not its figural image. The pavilion, kūṭastambha, and cell become iconographically potent. They embody the garbha's sacredness. Thus, while this vocabulary of the kūṭa (sheltering form, the "container" for the divinity) evolved from a Kūṭina matrix, its transformation into the semiological "content" (divinity itself) is brought about in Vesara architecture by means of a self-conscious interaction not with Nāgara forms but with Nāgara ideology.

The sophistication of this overall iconic transformation can perhaps best be exemplified by the Mallikārjuna temple at Kuruvatti (pl. 105). Its realistic bhadra shrine has its own tiny bhadra crowned by a multistoried tower that is framed by a makara toraṇa similar to the bhadra shrine's own frame. A series of architectural forms shown on the central spine of this miniature shrine model suggests space folding into more and more minute enclosures. The Kuruvatti temple represents the cosmos as an endless serialization of measured boundaries.

Vesara architects explored many ways to represent the garbha as a measure of the potentiality of cosmic space. They defined the temple by manipulating the central cluster in new and original ways and by their extensive use of shrine models. From elaborate unfolding to condensed emblem, Kuruvatti and Huli also indicate the range of ways in which shrine motifs define a distinct type of iconography on these Vesara temples.

Puruṣa as Measure

Vesara's formal experiments as well as their use of architectural motifs as wall ornament cannot be understood solely in aesthetic or egotistical terms; they define an approach to divinity and are part of a conscious creation of meaning in architectural form. Built ca. A.D. 1100, the Doḍḍa Bassapā temple at Ḍambhal represents a fruition of Vesara's experimentation (pl. 106).[18] How this well-known stellate temple embodies Vesara's expressive intent in the totality of its form will be analyzed in this section. On plan, its sanctum is derived by turning six squares whose corners provide the twenty-four points of its stellate shape; the preceding gūḍhamaṇḍapa is created by rotating eight squares (fig. 6).[19] The two stellate shapes overlap. The juncture between the two walls is adjusted by a slender, turned half-pillar facing the antarāla wall (pl. 107). The antarāla is surmounted by a superstructure comprising three stories faced by a large, handsome kīrttimukha with leaping makara heads on either side.

Since the Joḍa Kalaśa at Sūḍī, Vesara monuments have shown a fascination with North Indian experiments of turning offsets. Unlike Ḍambhal, however, the turned offsets on those monuments do not show an overall manipulation of the ground plan, only an articulation of the pier. The eastern shrine of Joḍa Kalaśa shows a turned subhadra against a bhadra that is preserved within the orthogonal plan (pl. 46). This turned configuration is reproduced on the antarāla wall, where the subhadra's pier is even more clearly shown as a thick half-pillar.

The turned half-pillars find their most effective use on the wall connecting the sanctum to the hall in front. This intermediary space (antarāla) was given prominence in Deccan-Drāviḍa architecture by a śukanāsa crown.[20] Inside, Ḍambhal and other high Vesara temples mark this transitory space between the sanctum and the closed hall by an ornate threshold and a lavish makara toraṇa. On the exterior, they also distinguish this intermediary crossover between the worshiper and the worshiped divinity by a solid, and often turned, half-pillar. In the massive antarāla half-pillar of the Kāśīviśveśvara temple at Lakkuṇḍī, the convention of turning piers as knuckles between the sanctum and the preceding hall is fully consolidated (pl. 52). Just as the turned pratiratha framing the bhadra cluster in the Sūrya temple at Lakkuṇḍī also provides a knuckle between the karṇa and the bhadra, so does the half-pillar on the antarāla wall tie the sanctum firmly to the *gūḍhamaṇḍapa,* and is also compared to the sanctum itself, as at Sūḍī. Thus the turned antar-

Plate 106. Ḍambhal, Doḍḍa Bassapā temple, southwest, ca. A.D. 1100

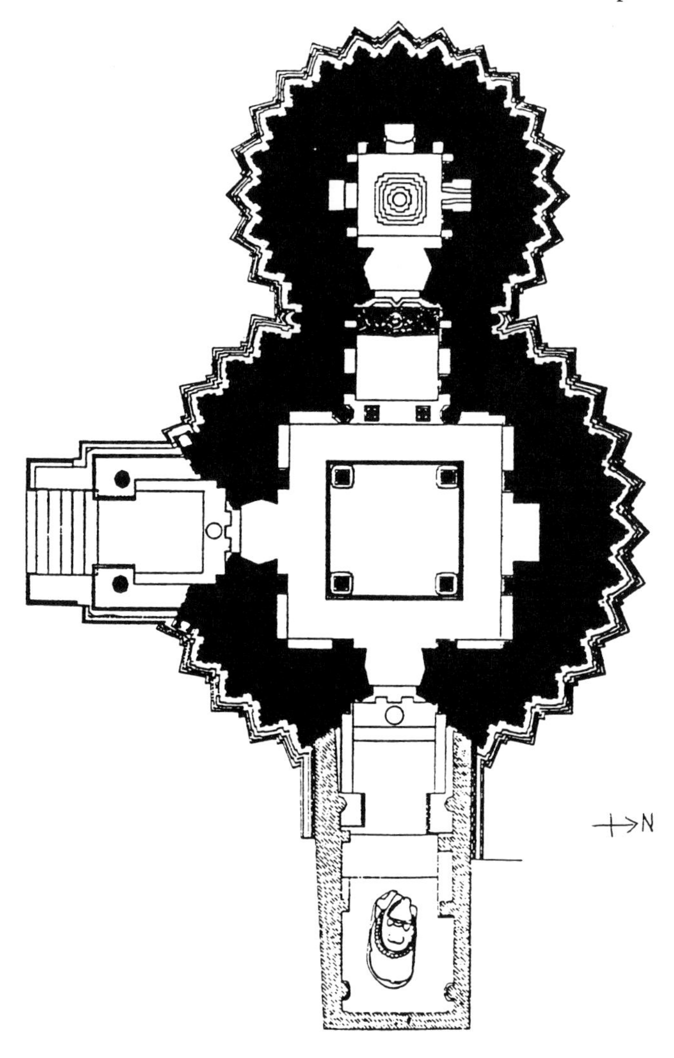

Figure 6. Ḍambhal, Doḍḍa, Bassapā temple, plan (Cousens, Plate CXXV)

āla half-pillar and its equivalent features on the sanctum wall adapt the North Indian motif to a local use. The mimicry of these piers is different from the transformation of ground plan at Ḍambhal.

One precedent for the stellate plan of Ḍambhal is the Brahmadeva temple at Savaḍī, discussed in chapter 4 (pl. 48). As at Savaḍī, the principal offsets of the Ḍambhal temple are created by the corners of squares rotated to accomplish the temple's stellate plan (pl. 108). On elevation, these gradually turning offsets are treated like karṇa piers, surmounted by square kūṭas. The two visible faces of these offsets show tall kūṭa pavilions recalling the Yallamā temple at Badāmī (pl. 63).[21] Recesses are filled by Vesara kūṭastambhas framed by narrow, looped makara toraṇas.

The Ḍambhal temple shows another wall portion projecting between the karṇa piers, rotating and alternating with them (pl. 109). Unlike Savaḍī, the pointed corner of this wall portion projects beyond the boundaries of the rotated square. At the base, it is angled and fits the intersection of the karṇa piers, appearing like small additional points in the star-shaped plan. Above, it is isolated from the karṇas by the recesses.

This wall portion is architecturally ambiguous, unlike the karṇas. The inverted bell laśuna and other moldings that crown it make it appear like half-pillars that are commonly used for pratirathas as well as for antarāla walls. The remaining "shaft," however, is not articulated into features such as the prominent bell and molded bands that typically defined those half-pillars. I suggest that this projecting wall condenses the bhadra cluster in its very ambiguity. At one level, it resembles a pratiratha half-pillar crowned by a kūṭa at the hāra level. At another, it is treated as if it were bhadra that has been folded in, showing only the masonry of its offset sides.[22] This wall is identified as bhadra further by a makara toraṇa crossing it at midregion, recalling frames for the bhadra subshrines of such monuments as the Kāśīviśveśvara at Lakkuṇḍī, Mahādeva at Iṭṭagi, and the Mallikārjuna at Kuruvatti.

At the superstructural level, the crowning members for all offsets—the karṇas as well as the adjacent "column"—are archetypal square Drāviḍa kūṭa that, as karṇakūṭas, maintained the Drāviḍa appearance of all Vesara temples.[23] Except for the final śikhara, the seven diminishing stories of the superstructure of Ḍambhal seem archaic for A.D. 1100. The śikhara stands over a shoulder molding, a deep recess faced with dancing musicians, a fillet raised over a curved *cippikā,* and a virtually flattened dome above. Reminiscent of a Bhūmija *āmalasāraka,* this flattened, layered finial is the closest Vesara approximation of a northern element.

The Ḍambhal temple evokes a comparison with northern temples, particularly the Bhūmija (pl. 55). The attraction of Bhūmija in Vesara is noted since the Kāśīviśveśvara temple at Lakkuṇḍī, in which a shrine model accurately portrays a Central Indian variant, and also from its overuse at Savaḍī. Also in Bhūmija, the experiment with stellate plan in North India finds its final fruition,[24] of which Ḍambhal and Savaḍī could be considered Vesara counterparts. In Bhūmija, however, the bhadra projection is emphasized as the temple's central spine, boldly projecting

Plate 107. Ḍambhal, Doḍḍa Bassapā temple, wall span from sanctum to preceding hall

against a ground of diminished offsets, while the karṇas are only stepped back and reduced to one such offset. Neither Savaḍī nor Ḍambhal articulate the bhadra projection on the sanctum wall.[25] Their stellate appearance, on the other hand, emphasizes the karṇas.

While the bhadra in a Bhūmija temple folds out, Ḍambhal folds it back in. The columnlike condensation of the bhadra cluster barely marks the potentiality of the sanctum on the rotated exterior, where it is contained by multiplying karṇa buttresses. The twenty-four re-entrant karṇa angles for the sanctum (and thirty-two for the gūḍhamanḍapa on the basis of the same geometric principle) suggest that the play of measuring, extending, and framing the potentiality of the sanctum can continue.

Stella Kramrisch provides a basis for understanding this play of measure in her definition of Puruṣa.[26] In answer to the question "Who is Puruṣa?" Kramrisch says, "Puruṣa is Man, but Man is here a term of reference, the nearest at hand, if we experience, feel and think allusively in referring to something which is beyond form."[27] Beyond this reference, however, Puruṣa is "the impulse towards manifestation." Once this creative impulse is felt and conceived, it "is immediately productive or procreative. From Him was born Virāj. Virāj is cosmic intelligence ordering the process of manifestation; and from that cosmic ordering intelligence once more that very impulse in a self-generating way is born."[28]

In these opening passages of her short essay, Kramrisch has quickly articulated the metaphysical process of creation in India. Puruṣa is impulse or urge to take form; Virāj is the intellectual technique that gives shape to the urge. Unless Puruṣa is in its productive aspect, unless it stirs, it cannot be conceived. The ordering intelligence gives Puruṣa a framework in which to become manifest again and again, and the interaction of the two goes on endlessly. Kramrisch explains that "matter itself is measured out. Whatever is material has its measure, its limit, its order. This order in

Plate 108. Ḍambhal, Doḍḍa Bassapā temple, wall detail, west

Plate 109. Ḍambhal, Doḍḍa Bassapā temple, wall and superstructure, close-up from south (courtesy: American Institute of Indian Studies)

the cosmos is reflected in the temple, the work of man, which to his own satisfaction he creates as he assumes the creator to have created the cosmos."[29]

Kramrisch's explanation of Puruṣa and the continuing act of its containment give me a context to understand Vesara's specific ideology. In the Indian temple, the container and its content—space and its material form—are ambiguous entities, and Kramrisch explains both to be condensations *(mūrtis)* of divinity. The development of Nāgara and Drāviḍa temples into large and complex structures by the eleventh century can be seen as a simultaneous and interrelated elaboration of both. The essential ambiguity of the container and the contained expressed in those temples is pan-Indian, shared also by Vesara.

Vesara architects of the eleventh century, however, created an elaborate iconography of measure itself. In their monuments, pratirathas frame bhadra, and karṇas frame the bhadra cluster, creating a basis for a play of measure and boundary. The bhadra cluster projects the sanctum's spatial potency into many representational schemes on the exterior (a control of which was a mark of Viśvakarman, according to the architect of the Kuppatur temple, as I have suggested). The architectural motifs with no enclosure in earliest Vesara monuments, such as Kukkanūr, are the primary icons of measure. By A.D. 1100, Kuruvatti revealed the sanctum's potentiality in serialized boundaries created out of its own Vesara form. In framing and revealing the garbha by rotating and multiplying karṇas around "infolded" bhadra clusters, Ḍambhal also represents the cosmogonic enactment of Puruṣa. While all Viśvakarman-like architects create an ordered cosmos in measuring the square space of the temple sanctum, Vesara architects experimented with the temple's overall form and with shrine models in order to transform the act of measure itself into a mūrti (condensation, embodiment) for Puruṣa, ordering and extending space in order to display the cosmos.

8

Conclusion: Makers and Making of Indian Temple Architecture

Architects as givers of particular form and meaning to sacred buildings barely exist in the history of Indian temple architecture. It is generally assumed that the making of sacred art, as much as its use, is determined by the enduring norms of India's age-old religious traditions or the ambition of kings. While the role of patrons, priests, and worshipers cannot be underestimated, the book has worked against the line of thought that formal and conceptual problems of temples are raised and solved by agencies outside the actual architectural practice and before individual monuments are built. Making and use of shrines are closely linked, but it must be recognized that it is the designers who synthesize the two in the visible form of the temple.

The book has paid close attention to the architectural activity in Karnataka in an attempt to give the designers of temples a visibility commonly denied to them in the historiography of Indian art and architecture. The invisibility of designers in traditional literature owes partly to a lack of adequate record and partly to the influence of Western definitions of individuality and originality on non-Western fields.[1] Karnataka temples have challenged this scholarly knowledge. Vesara's many inventions have shown that sacred structures evolve and change because their designers intellectually engage with the formal and conceptual challenges of their traditions.[2] The study of architectural practice and the emphasis on makers of Vesara question the relationship between religion and religious architecture in current scholarly literature and refine the existing notion of artistic originality in a non-Western culture.

Among recent works on architectural practice, an ambitious publication by Adam Hardy, an architect scholar in England, explores the designing of temples as I have. In a detailed analysis of the visual evidence from Karnataka, Hardy defines what he has called the "Karṇāṭa-Drāviḍa tradition" of architecture, borrowing a phrase M. A. Dhaky had earlier coined for Karnataka temples of a pre-Vesara phase. Hardy claims that his project is distinguished from previous accounts in that "the intention here is to reach an understanding of the tradition as a whole."[3] He covers seven hundred years of architecture between the seventh and the thirteenth centuries, following the archaeologist Henry Cousens's long historical scope, to which he adds Hoysala monuments of southern Karnataka. Thus also extending Dhaky's original use of Karṇāṭa-Drāviḍa to include Vesara buildings, Hardy has created a single, unbroken tradition of Drāviḍa architecture, in contrast to the problematizing of "Vesara" in my book.

Hardy brings to his analysis of forms an architect's detailed understanding of architectural morphology, explained by an exemplary series of sketch drawings of ground plans, elevations, architectural features, and decorative motifs. The sequence of drawings well demonstrates Hardy's central thesis that architecture in his single Karṇāṭa-Drāviḍa tradition expresses a dynamic line of evolution moving toward an expression of one idea—cosmic proliferation in its visual form, or, as Stella Kramrisch has expressed it, the temple as a "monument of manifestation."[4]

I differ from Hardy in seeing a conscious transformation of Karṇāṭa-Drāviḍa in the eleventh century. It is not I, but the Karnataka architects themselves, who "problematized" what has come to be called Vesara architecture. A closer view of tenth- and eleventh-century, north Karnataka temples shows many interruptions within the single, sweeping momentum of Hardy's analysis of seven hundred years. Vesara architecture emerges in the eleventh century when architects apply conceptual and formal changes to the formal matrix of South Indian architecture of Karnataka.

Hardy represents formal complexity as a logic of "manifestation." For him, Indian temples demonstrate manifestation as the working of general formal principles leading them from their simple architectural units toward increasing proliferation and fragmentation. As the formal logic unfolds through the history of monuments in various Indian traditions, Hardy is able to predict the particular regional developments of Karnataka by applying those principles.[5] I disagree with Hardy, in whose account no single monument ever challenges or checks the momentum of evolutionary progress. The seven hundred years of Karnataka monuments are serialized as continuous multiplication and fragmentation of moldings, offsets, and architectural motifs that constitute them. For me, Vesara is not simply a matter of applying general, pan-Indian principles to regional monuments nor that of continuing Drāviḍa's local evolution. Vesara is a matter of explaining the history of a new architectural creation in the eleventh century. The active role played by architects in Vesara's formal as well as conceptual definition is of fundamental importance. The intellectual trends controlling the choices made by designers in the eleventh century constitute what I have called Vesara's process of origination.

This book has analyzed key monuments of the eleventh century not simply as a historical sequence but as examples of the creative experimentation on the part of architects, who consciously made a new and modern form for architecture within a consistent system of use and meaning. Vesara's later history was shaped by these eleventh-century monuments, so close to their Drāviḍa roots and yet so radically different in their results. The interruptions and deviations within the Drāviḍa form as early as the tenth century suggest the extent of their makers' critical self-reflection within the indigenous tradition. In the eleventh century, Vesara monuments show many new and varied interpretations of the Drāviḍa vocabulary.

The book has also explored the numerous ways in which Vesara architects attempted to incorporate a North Indian, Nāgara ideology, not simply as a source of new forms but as a means to strengthen and extend the temple's meaning. Vesara's originality lies in the way it has creatively absorbed and redefined both forms and ideas from Nāgara and Drāviḍa architecture. Karnataka has had its separate geographical identity from an early period, which has provided the soil for the creative intellection demonstrated in her eleventh-century monuments. In breaking away from the Drāviḍa tradition and bringing about a conceptual shift in its basic framework, Vesara architects searched beyond regional hybridization to give their sacred structures a modern form and a new architectural iconography.

My analysis of Vesara's experiments shares with recent scholars of South Asian art and architecture a need to understand artistic practice in ancient and medieval India against the burden of normative, sacred texts.[6] Those studies, however, seek models to define ancient practice in an ethnography of living, folk-art traditions. Art making thus becomes an issue of adapting old skills to new requirements.

Such an approach to making art is well reasoned only if making is understood as performance, whereby the modulation of skills for new needs will mean an enactment of the entire body of knowledge and training for the particular context of use and pleasure. From puppeteers in Indian village fairs to acrobats on the pavements of modern Indian cities such as Bombay and Delhi, performers contextualize their skills depending on the humor of their particular spectators—village, urban, Western tourist. Classical Indian musicians accustomed to long, nightly concerts for connoisseurs in India adjust to popular taste in Europe and America, or to limited airtime on television. While driven by economic change, the way artists generate meaning in relation to their particular audience in each performance has not been sufficiently addressed by the advocates of adaptation theory. On the contrary, attempts to understand ancient practice by extrapolating from an area whose major concern has been the survival of traditional crafts in a modern market economy has biased the issue toward the artists' tenacity to sustain under economic pressures rather than their capacity to create a living tradition, a coherent body of knowledge and practice.

The makers of religious art in India claim a lot more initiative for its form and meaning than we have been willing to grant them so far. In more recent approaches to the meaning of images, the role of makers has been underplayed by an emphasis on audience and contexts of use, influenced partly by anthropology and partly by literary criticism's deconstruction of the author and a treatment of written text as a social performance.

Thus, in a stimulating and challenging series of essays, Richard H. Davis has proposed the viewers and users of Indian images as the primary agents for their meaning.[7] In particular, Davis applies a theory of reader's response by literary critic Stanley Fish to explore visual images in various contexts through which they circulate. He analyzes the physical sites where sacred images would be seen once they were installed. He discusses cultural and epistemic frames that demonstrate, for instance, the difference in meaning when Hindu images are seen in an Indian temple as opposed to an American museum, or when an image from a kingdom in the Hindu world is taken away as a war trophy by a king of another kingdom. Davis explores the destruction of Hindu images by Muslim invaders, the memory of destroyed images by Hindu nationalists, and the transformation of Indian images into icons of British colonial power. He evocatively calls these explorations the "biographies" or "lives" of Indian images.

I agree with Davis that a full historical study of works of art "ought to consider all the responses they have evoked during their long lives and all the significances that audiences have given them over time."[8] Davis's biographies highlight what is missing from the period of Vesara architecture, namely, the active cultural response of contemporary viewers, barely evident in an eleventh-century inscription I use in chapter 4. But his treatment of ancient Indian sculpture and architecture on the analogy of literary texts, acquiring their meaning in their readings within "interpretative communities" also shifts the burden of meaning away from their original makers.[9]

In Davis's metaphoric "lives," the original making of images is reduced to "birth,"[10] which suggests the emergence of bare flesh that gains interest only when it is socialized in the world of adult meanings. For me, an important part of the social life of temples has been its designing, which deserves a critical reading like other biographies by Davis. I have described Vesara's century-long formation as one such life, with its own meanings and meaning-making agencies I have called the architects. I partly share Davis's framework by describing the formation of Vesara architecture as a record of the way their architects respond to past architecture as well as to visual and intellectual traditions beyond Karnataka, giving to their regional monuments a new iconographic meaning. Although Vesara's contemporary audience cannot be clearly discerned, the continuous renewal and change in eleventh-century monuments suggests to me the challenges of their viewers and users, which the architects meet.

Stone temples are not literary texts in Fish's sense, with their meaning only hovering in the social arena of subsequent readings.[11] True, Vesara's modern interpretation has a history of more than a hundred years, and its premodern interpretation is traced to the first use of the term Vesara in twelfth-century texts. But these temples are, first, a trace of the moment of their making; fundamental to my study of them is the recognition of this indexical role of archaeological remains.[12] As concrete evidence of facture, stone remains exceed and resist the community of viewers even as they yield different meanings. They play referee in a game of shifting interpretations and multiple agencies unlike the literary text, whose identity blends with interpretative narratives. While my claim to Vesara's intellectual identity adds to the interpretative literature, I recognize the basic archaeological reality of monuments, which leads me, like footprints or handprints, to the people to whom they may belong.

The fundamental question of Vesara architecture in this book has been the creative process rather than the formal sequence, although formal consequences become my primary evidence. Separating facture from interpretation, I have explored a particular moment of thinking and making usually overlooked in traditional accounts of India's sacred art.[13] I have searched in Karnataka's monuments for the "mentality" that began to make a difference in Karnataka's Drāviḍa tradition, led to the transformation of Drāviḍa to Vesara, and created new meanings in the region's architectural form. While historian Fernand Braudel provided tools to describe Vesara's multileveled history in the eleventh century and to conceptualize the transitions and discontinuities in the material evidence, Michael Baxandall, Charles S. Peirce, and Stella Kramrisch have provided models to probe the issue of intentionality. By focusing on Vesara's play between a Nāgara conceptual logic and a Drāviḍa morphology—as a means by which architects could explore how meaning and form are related—I hope to have made Vesara's complexity and distinctness accessible to a contemporary audience as well as to have brought us closer to the architects themselves.

Notes

Preface and Acknowledgments

1. Michael W. Meister, "Categories of Utility," in Michael W. Meister (ed.), *Cooking For the Gods: The Art of Home Ritual in Bengal* (Newark: Newark Museum, 1995), 16.
2. Ibid., 15.

Chapter 1. An Architectural Mule

Unnumbered headnote. Ludwig Wittgenstein, *Culture and Value,* ed. G. H. von Wright in collaboration with Heikki Nyman, trans. Peter Winch (Chicago: University of Chicago Press, 1980), 36e.

1. Vesara is traditionally considered part of a triadic classification of temple architecture in India. N. V. Mallaya, "Nāgara, Drāviḍa and Vesara," *Journal of the Indian Society of Oriental Art* 9 (1941): 94 suggests that the term Vesara "in its primary, significatory capacity denotes a 'mule' which is an animal produced by the union of horse and ass." This idea of "heterogeneous parents" is borrowed by Kramrisch to describe Vesara as a "mixed style." Stella Kramrisch, *The Hindu Temple* (Calcutta: University of Calcutta Press, 1946), 1:291.
2. Ajay J. Sinha, "The Construction of 'Mule' in Indian Temple Architecture," *Journal of Arts and Ideas* 30–31 (December 1997): 33–62 explains a canonization of Vesara in scholarly literature through a "discursive hardening" of historical narratives, using the phrase from James Clifford, "On Orientalism," in *The Predicament of Culture: Twentieth Century Ethnography, Literature, and Art* (Cambridge, Mass.: Harvard University Press, 1988), 264.
3. The triadic classification of Indian temple styles (note 1) is based, arguably, on the geographical distribution of monuments in medieval India: Drāviḍa suggests a style dominating South India; Nāgara, North India; and Vesara, Karnataka. See M. A. Dhaky, *The Indian Temple Forms in Karnāta Inscriptions and Architecture* (New Delhi: Abhinava Publications, 1977), 29–34, for a good summary of extensive debates over such a classification. Emphasizing geography, Kramrisch (*The Hindu Temple,* 291) explains Vesara's hybridization in Karnataka as "natural in a region betwixt two powerful schools of which Nāgara, the first and foremost is centered in Madhyadeśa . . . and Drāviḍa in South India." The notion of Vesara as an intermediary style is reflected in many subsequent studies as well as standard surveys.
4. Probably the first modern scholar to resolve the three traditional styles of Indian temple architecture into "essentially" two, the Nāgara and the Drāviḍa, was S. K. Saraswati, who dismissed Vesara from the triad on the basis of its hybrid nature. S. K. Saraswati, "Origin of Medieval Temple Styles," *Indian Culture (Journal of the Indian Research Institute)* 8, no. 2–3 (1941–1942): 184.
5. E. H. Gombrich, "Norm and Form: The Stylistic Categories of Art History and their Origins in Renaissance Ideals," in *Norm and Form: Studies in the Art of the Renaissance* (London: Phaidon, 1966), 88–89.
6. Dhaky, *Temple Forms,* 28.
7. James Fergusson, *History of Indian and Eastern Architecture,* rev. ed. with additions by James Burgess (London: John Murray, 1910), 1:420. For Fergusson this name simply signified the region's architecture. Two dynasties having the name Chalukya with unclear linkage between them ruled Karnataka first in the seventh–eighth centuries and then from late-tenth until the twelfth (the latter sometimes distinguished as Chālukya, with a long first syllable). Monuments representing the height of Fergusson's Chalukya style, interestingly, were patronized by the Hoysala rulers of southern Karnataka, who dominate Karnataka from the twelfth century onwards. See chapter 2 for more discussion.
8. Fergusson called the three styles "northern or Indo-Aryan; Dravidian; and Chalukyan." Fergusson's classification of three styles matches the triad of Nāgara, Drāviḍa and Vesara in a parallel, text-oriented, scholarship. See n. 1.
9. Henry Cousens, *The Chālukyan Architecture of the Kanarese Districts,* Archaeological Survey of India, vol. 42, New Imperial Series (Calcutta: Government of India, Central Publication Branch, 1926), 17.
10. Susan L. Huntington, *The Art of Ancient India* (New York and Tokyo: Weatherhill, 1985), 540.
11. The image might be called a hidden metaphor, by which I mean an image that may not necessarily relate to the topic at hand but inspires the initial excitement in it or partly guides it and is justified as an appropriate analogy when the study itself takes a coherent form. For a defense of such a "matrix" of hidden analogies against empiricism, see W. J. T. Mitchell, *Iconology: Image, Text, Ideology* (Chicago: University of Chicago Press, 1986), 15–19.
12. In defending hidden metaphors, Mitchell makes a dis-

tinction between "illegitimate analogies" and "functional symbols . . . in the same logical space." While questioning the biological metaphor pervading earlier works on Vesara, this chapter is intended to describe the "logical space" of my own analysis.

13. George Kubler has called this separation "the bristling ugliness of 'material culture.' " See *The Shape of Time: Remarks on the History of Things* (New Haven and London: Yale University Press, 1962), 9. He uses the phrase "the history of things" in his essay as a euphemism particularly to counter this emphasis on material as separate from "mental culture" by anthropologists and instead to define all material remains as tools or expressions "worked by human hands under the guidance of connected ideas developed in temporal sequence."

14. Kubler (*The Shape of Time,* 8) writes:

> "Purpose has no place in biology, but history has no meaning without it. Because modes of biological description cannot be made to account for purpose, the historian working with biological ideas avoided the principal aim of history, which usually has been to identify and reconstruct the particular problem to which any action or thing must correspond as a solution."

15. M. A. Dhaky, *Temple Forms.*

16. Dhaky, *Temple Forms,* 27.

17. The documentation of Karnataka monuments, conducted mainly (but not exclusively) by regional scholars, has included detailed study of many subregions of Vesara. See a Cousenslike mapping of Vesara monuments in Eswar N. Katkar, "Art and Architecture of the Chālukyas of Kalyana," (Ph.D. diss., Karnataka University, Dharwar, 1982). For "Hemāḍpanti" temples at the northernmost tip of Vesara's geographical boundary, see O. P. Verma, *A Survey of Hemāḍpanti Temples in Maharashtra,* Temples of the Vidarbha Region, vol. 2, (Nagpur: 1973). Among extensive documentation of Hoysala monuments in southern Karnataka, see Robert J. Del Bonta, "The Hoysala Style: Architectural Development and Artists, Twelfth and Thirteenth Centuries A.D.," (Ph.D. diss., University of Michigan, 1978); S. Settar, *The Hoysala Temples,* 2 vols., (Bangalore: Kala Yatra Publications, 1992); and Gerard Foekema, *Hoysala Architecture: Medieval Temples of Southern Karnataka Built During the Hoysala Rule* (New Delhi: Books and Books, 1994). C. S. Patil has focused more pointedly on monuments in the modern Raichur district of northern Karnataka. See his "Portrait Sculpture in Mahādeva Temple at Iṭṭagi" in M. S. Nagaraja Rao, ed., *Kusumāñjali: New Interpretation of Indian Art and Culture* (Delhi: 1987), 311–14, as well as Ph.D. dissertation, Karnatak University, Dharwar. Regional scholarship in Karnataka is especially significant because it incorporates vast amounts of epigraphic information.

18. An early exploration of alternative models to visualize time in art history, rejecting linear time, is George Kubler's study. Kubler viewed historical time as a stem of many separate, intertwined, artistic ideas, each having a different evolutionary movement, so that each archaeological monument becomes a visible cross section of that complex stem of time. See George Kubler, *The Shape of Time,* 33–39 and passim.

19. Fernand Braudel, "History and the Social Sciences," The *Longue Durée",* in Braudel, *On History* (Chicago: University of Chicago Press, 1980), 25–54.

20. Ibid., 37. The spatial overlap of the two maps has been used to document the economic history of peasants in South India in David Ludden's *Peasant History in South India* (Princeton: Princeton University Press, 1985).

21. For ethnography of a modern craft workshop applied to an understanding of the micro level of making sacred art in India, see John F. Mosteller, "Texts and Craftsmen at Work," in *Making of Things in South Asia: The Role of Artist and Craftsman,* ed. Michael W. Meister (Philadelphia: Department of South Asian Regional Studies, 1988), 24–33, and Joanna Williams, "From the Fifth to the Twentieth Century and Back," *Art Journal* 49 (winter 1990): 363–69.

22. See Bernard C. Cohn and McKim Marriott, "Networks and Centers in the Integration of Indian Civilization," *Journal of Social Research* 1 (1958): 1–9 for a notion of India's historical region based on centers and networks of production, viewed especially against fixed boundaries of colonial British and modern Indian administrative units in the nineteenth and twentieth centuries.

23. See *The Encyclopaedia of Indian Temple Architecture,* ed. M. A. Dhaky and Michael W. Meister, an ongoing, multivolume series of the American Institute of Indian Studies, published since 1983.

24. For an example of this approach, see Michael W. Meister, "Bīṭhū: Individuality and Idiom," *Ars Orientalis* 13 (1983): 169–86. On p. 173 Meister writes, "Change in art occurs at the micro level of craftsmen working on specific monuments. We can rarely approach that level in our analysis of Indian architecture."

25. See George Kubler, *The Shape of Time,* 12–13, for the distinction between "duration" and "time" in art historical investigation.

26. For substyle, see M. A. Dhaky, "Coḷa Sculpture," in *Chhavi, Golden Jubilee Volume,* ed. Ananda Krishna (Varanasi: 1971), 263–89, and the overall conceptual structure of the *Encyclopaedia of Indian Temple Architecture.* For local style, see Irene J. Winter, "Perspective on the "Local Style" of Hasanlu IV B: A Study in Receptivity," in *Mountains and Lowlands: Essays in the Archaeology of Greater Mesopotamia,* ed. L. D. Lavine and T. C. Young Jr. (Malibu: Undena Publications 1977), 371–86. For another rich argument against a diffusionist model for understanding local styles in relation to centers and peripheries, see Michelle I. Marcus, "Center, *Province* and Periphery: A New Paradigm from Iron-Age Iran," *Art History* 3.2 (June 1990): 129–150. For idiom, see Meister, "Bīṭhū: Individuality and Idiom," *Ars Orientalis* 13 (1983): 169–86, and Meister's "Style and Idiom in the Art of Uparamāla," *Muqarnas: An Annual on Islamic Art and Architecture* 10 (1993): 344–53.

27. Mitchell, *Iconology: Image, Text, Ideology,* 3–4, has offered me a lucid understanding of the "doubleness" of the concept of ideology, as an object and as a tool, as a structure in itself but one that also has a critical purpose.

28. Mieke Bal and Norman Bryson begin their essay "Semiotics and Art History" (*Art Bulletin* [June 1991]: 174) by stating that a rigorous denial of any reality outside the "permanent process of sign making" is the basic tenet of semiotics. My comments below explore the application of this recent, antirealist trend of semiotics in a non-Western area.

29. For the phrase and a full use of this theory of reception in art history, see Mieke Bal, *Reading "Rembrandt"* (Cambridge, England: Cambridge University Press, 1991). The quotation in the next sentence below is taken from Bal, p. 3. Bal has focused her semiotic approach elsewhere against what she has called disparagingly the theoretically weary "art history police." Bal, "Signs in Painting" under "Art History and Its Theories," *Art Bulletin* 78 (March 1996): 7.

30. Mieke Bal, "Signs of Painting," 6, resolves the prob-

lem of subjectivism arising from the blurring of distinction between the historical subject matter and the modern viewer under "reception" by urging historians to take "the subjective nature of seeing or 'reading' images into account: as objective fact, that is."

31. Carol A. Breckenridge and Peter van der Veer, ed., *Orientalism and Post-Colonial Predicaments: Perspectives on South Asia,* (Philadelphia: University of Pennsylvania Press, 1993).

32. Martin Kemp, "The Taking and Use of Evidence; with a Botticellian Case Study," *Art Journal* (fall 1984): 207–15.

33. For this and other paintings of Sheikh, see Ajay J. Sinha, "Envisioning the Seventies and Eighties," *Contemporary Art in Baroda,* ed. Gulammohammed Sheikh, (New Delhi: Tulika Press, 1997), 145–210, especially 162–6.

34. *Epigraphia Carnatica,* 8, Sorab no. 275, ed. B. L. Rice. Dhaky's translation. *Temple Forms,* 3.

35. For a structuralist position, see Louis Dumont, "Individual as an Impediment to Sociological Comparison and Indian History," in *Social and Economic Change (Essays in Honor of Professor D. P. Mukherjee),* ed. Baljit Singh and V. B. Singh (Bombay and New York: Allied Publishers, 1967), 226–48, also Gunter-Dietz Sontheimer, *Pastoral Deities in Western India* (New York and Oxford: Oxford University Press, 1989). Where agency is examined, it is confined to the question of patronage. See *The Powers of Art: Patronage in Indian Culture,* ed. Barbara Stoler Miller (Delhi and New York: Oxford University Press, 1992).

36. Lionel D. Barnett, "Inscriptions of Sūdī," *Epigraphia Indica* 15 (1919–20): 85–90, especially verse 16.

37. Sūḍi is known in inscriptions as a "Rājadhānī," meaning at least a local political and cultural center.

38. The literature on Indian Urbanism is extensive. See Howard Spodek and Doris Meth Srinivasan ed., *Urban Form and Meaning in South Asia: The Shaping of Cities from Prehistoric to Precolonial Times,* Studies in the History of Art 31 (Washington, D.C.: National Gallery of Art, 1993). For studies on Karnataka's urban centers, see George Michell, *Architecture and Art of South India: Vijayanagara and the Successor States* (Cambridge, England, and New York: Cambridge University Press, 1995); Burton Stein, *Vijayanagara* (Cambridge, England: Cambridge University Press, 1989); Om Prakash Prasad, *Decay and Revival of Urban Centres in Medieval South India: c. A.D. 600–1200,* (New Delhi: Commonwealth Publishers, 1989); Anna Libera Dallapiccola, ed., *Vijayanagara, City and Empire: New and Current Research* (Stuttgart; Steiner, 1985); John M. Fritz, George Michell, and M.S. Nagaraja Rao, *Where Kings and Gods Meet, the Royal Centre of Vijayanagara, India* (Tucson: University of Arizona Press, 1984).

39. For this somewhat "passive" sense of intention from Franz Brentano ("A direction toward an object"), as it is used within phenomenology, and later developed as an aspect of cognitive science, see Francisco J. Varela, Evan Thompson, and Eleanor Rosch, *The Embodied Mind: Cognitive Science and Human Experience* (Cambridge: Mass.: MIT Press, 1991), 15–16. Also Bimal Krishna Matilal, *Perception: An Essay on Classical Indian Theories of Knowledge* (Oxford: Clarendon Press, 1986), 114, on intentionality in the view of Brentano, Husserl, and the Buddhists.

40. Tracing the intentions of a work of art to the world outside itself amounts to functionalism. As opposed to this clearly reductive procedure, my approach is closer to methods of including intentions within the distinctive qualities of the act itself, or within what E. H. Gombrich has defined as "style" in his classic essay. See Gombrich, "Style," in *International Encyclopaedia of the Social Sciences,* ed. David L. Sill, 18 vols. (New York: Macmillan, 1968–79), 15, 352–61.

41. Michael Baxandall, *Patterns of Intentions: On the Historical Explanation of Pictures* (New Haven: Yale University Press, 1985), 42. Baxandall has explained that the question of intention is a matter of defining "a relation between object and its circumstance," not that of reconstituting a historical state of mind.

42. Oleg Grabar, *The Formation of Islamic Art,* rev. and enl. (New Haven and London: Yale University Press, 1987), 5–6 and passim.

43. Grabar, *Formation,* 21.

44. Dhaky, *Temple Forms,* 28.

45. See a summary and critique of this standard archaeological definition of style in Svetlana Alpers, "Style is What You Make It: The Visual Arts Once Again," in *The Concept of Style* (1979), ed. Berel Lang (Ithaca and London: Cornell University Press, 1987), 137–62.

46. Michael W. Meister, "Uparāmala," 344–54. Also Meister's "Biṭhū: Individuality and Idiom," 169–86.

47. Philip B. Wagoner, "Mode and Meaning in the Architecture of Early Medieval Telangana (c. 1000–1300)," (Ph.D. diss., University of Wisconsin, 1986) for a distinction of architectural mode in terms of social or religious function.

48. Most useful is Meister's example of early Islamic art in India, where he has analyzed remains from Hindu temples as well as local Indian craftsmanship as they were adapted to the formulation of a new structural type, the mosque, when Islam was first introduced in India. "Uparāmala" and Michael W. Meister, "The Two-and-a-half Mosque," *Oriental Art* n.s., 18 (1972): 57–63, and also his "Indian Islam's Lotus Throne: Kaman and Khatu Kalan," *Proceedings of the International Seminar on Regional Varieties of Islam in South Asia* (in press).

49. Alpers, "Style Is What You Make It: The Visual Arts Once Again," 141 and passim.

Chapter 2. Regional Theory in the Definition of Hybrid

1. Thus, temples built under a major Karnataka dynasty in the seventh and eighth centuries named Calukya but located in the adjacent region within modern Andhra Pradesh—a Calukya territory in that period—are overlooked by Karnataka scholars and recorded separately by archaeologists in that state. See, thus, M. Rama Rao, *Early Cālukyan Temples of Andhra Desa,* Andhra Pradesh Government Archaeological Series, no. 20 (Hyderabad: Government of Andhra Pradesh, 1965). George Michell, *Early Western Chalukyan Architecture,* 1975.

2. See Rao, *Andhra Desa.* Also, Carol Radcliffe Bolon, "Evidence of Artists of the Early Calukya Period," in *Making Things in South Asia: The Role of Artist and Craftsman,* ed. Michael W. Meister (Philadelphia: Department of South Asia Regional Studies, University of Pennsylvania, 1988), 52–66, for interaction across the modern boundaries described through exchange of carvers as well as a knowledge of carving stone images for temples during the seventh and eighth centuries.

3. Joseph Schwartzberg, "Prolegomena to the Study of South Asian Regions and Regionalism," in *Regions and Regionalism in South Asian Studies: An Exploratory Study*

(Duke University Program in Comparative Studies in South Asia, monograph no. 5, Durham, N.C., 1967), 93.

4. Bernard S. Cohn has called this region "subjective" as opposed to the "objective" region of the developers. See Bernard Cohn, "Regions Subjective and Objective: Their Relation to the Study of Modern Indian History (1967)," reprinted in *Anthropologist Among Historians* (Delhi and New York: Oxford University Press, 1987).

5. Bharat L. Bhatt, "India and Indian Regions: A Critical Overview," in *An Exploration of India: Geographical Perspectives on Society and Culture*, ed. David E. Sopher (Ithaca: Cornell University Press, 1980), 35–61, addresses "folk region" to reflect a phenomenological stance in geographical studies since the late 1970s.

6. Bernard S. Cohn and McKim Marriott, "Networks and Centers in the Integration of Indian Civilization," *Journal of Social Research* 1 (1958): 1–9.

7. B. L. Rice, ed., *Epigraphia Carnatica*, Sorab no. 275. M. A. Dhaky's translation, *Temple Forms*, 3.

8. See discussion on such inscriptions in the earlier period in Bolon, "Evidence of Artists of the Early Calukya Period", 61. For more evidence from Karnataka and Eastern India, refer also to Mary F. Linda, "The Architect/Artist: Agents of Change" (paper presented at the College Art Association meetings, Boston, February 1996).

9. The term Vesara as it is applied to architecture appears commonly in sections on architecture in South Indian *āgamas*, or ritual texts, datable to about the eleventh and later centuries. In these southern texts, most probably from Tamilnadu, Vesara is described as a circular or elliptical building distinguished from Nāgara, a square, and Drāviḍa, an octagonal temple. See Dhaky *(Temple Forms)*, who points out that the reference to "shapes" of structures applies only to a southern, specifically Tamil, temple. The Kāmikāgama is an exception to this body of southern texts. The emphasis on shape seems to have a larger, looser use, in that Vesara also refers to a circular or elliptical nose ring in the history of Indian ornaments. Dr. B. N. Goswamy, conversation with author, summer 1996.

10. Stella Kramrisch, *The Hindu Temple*, 1:291.

11. N. V. Mallaya quotes Hemachandra and Magha as the oldest writers known to have used Vesara to designate a cross between a horse and an ass. See "Nāgara, Drāviḍa, and Vesara," 94.

12. Kramrisch, *The Hindu Temple*, 291.

13. M. A. Dhaky, *Temple Forms*, 28.

14. Ibid., endnotes 2, 3.

15. Ibid., 25. Bhūmija is a preferred form of temple in Central and Western India. See Krishna Deva, "Bhūmija Temples," in *Studies in Indian Temple Architecture*, ed. Pramod Chandra (New Delhi: 1975), 90–113. The form is distinguished by a curved superstructure with spirelets above single pilasters arranged vertically to look like chains of beads on either side of a central band. The fact that this form does not appear on the walls of the Kuppatur temple, although the inscription mentions the term Bhūmija, may support the theory of possible confusion between Bhūmija and Vesara.

16. See F. H. Gravely and T. N. Ramachandran, "The Three Main Styles of Temple Architecture Recognized by the Śilpa-Śāstras," *Bulletin of the Madras Government Museum*, n.s., 3, pt. 1 (1934): 6–7 and 10–20. The basis for this argument is that the Tamil region of South India was the heartland for the production of all these texts. For a usage of the southern vocabulary in Karnataka, see also K. V. Sounder Rajan, *Early Temple Architecture in Karnataka and its Ramification*, (Dharwar: Kannada Research Institute, 1969). Kramrisch, on the other hand, writes, "[T]he classification Nāgara, Drāviḍa, Vesara of the South Indian Vāstuśāstras is an expression of the exuberance of the builders. They call their types and patterns after the various schools, and after the main regions of India, giving in this way a universal value to their work. Nāgara, therefore heads the list; it is square, for the square is the perfect shape." *The Hindu Temple*, 294. The application of these southern Vāstu texts is restricted to temples in the Tamilnadu. As Dhaky has argued, the strictly Tamil definition of Vesara as a circular (and by extension an apsidal) temple does not match the knowledge of Vesara in the Karnataka region. Dhaky, *Temple Forms*, 24.

17. Gravely and Ramachandran, "Three Main Styles," 4 and 23, have argued that the North Indian temples modern scholars have called Nāgara are more properly Vesara. An extension of this in survey books is Benjamin Rowland's *The Art and Architecture of India, Buddhist Hindu Jain* (1953; reprint, Harmondsworth and London, 1984), 276, in which Vesara is designated as barrel-vaulted buildings (meaning apsidal temples?) that derive from the old Buddhist type of chaitya halls.

18. Kramrisch, *The Hindu Temple*, 291.

19. Michael W. Meister, M. A. Dhaky, and Krishna Deva, ed., *Encyclopaedia of Indian Temple Architecture: North India, Foundations of North Indian Style, c. 250* B.C.–A.D. 1000 (Princeton: Princeton University Press), 1988. Compare chapter 20 on temples in Karnataka especially with chapter 21, in which a group of Nāgara temples under the same Calukya dynasty but built in Andhra Pradesh indeed make a deliberate reference to Central India. Borrowing from neighboring regions seems less a matter of natural contiguity and more a matter of conscious choice.

20. Michael W. Meister, "Reading Monuments and Seeing Texts," in *Shasric Traditions in Indian Arts*, ed. Anna Libera Dallapiccola et al. (Stuttgart: Steiner Verlag Wiesbaden, 1989): 169.

21. M. A. Dhaky, "The 'Gothic' in Indian Temple Architecture," *East and West* n.s., 24, no. 1–2 (1974): 137.

22. I have used an 1899 reprint of these volumes, published posthumously in New York, as representative of Fergusson's initial ideas. In 1910, James Burgess revised and edited Fergusson's volumes, enlarging Fergusson's framework and adding new material.

23. Henry Cousens, *The Chālukyan Architecture of the Kanarese Districts*. See a continuation of Cousens's framework in Percy Brown, *Indian Architecture (Buddhist and Hindu)*, published in the 1940s and printed in at least three more editions.

24. Emphasis mine, to indicate Cousens's sensitivity to the flexible relationship between patronage and artist, and a separation of style from dynasty.

25. Relating the eleventh century chronologically to earlier Karnataka monuments, Cousens gave "Chālukyan" architecture a regional base. In such a regional history of architecture, Cousens paralleled the first summation of the political history of Karnataka, created by J. F. Fleet with available epigraphic information. John Faithfull Fleet, *The Dynasties of the Kanarese Districts of the Bombay Presidency from the Earliest Historical Times to the Musalman*

Conquest of A.D. *1318* (Bombay: Governmental Central Press, 1896). Cousens did with archaeology what Fleet did with inscriptions.

26. Cousens, *The Chālukyan Architecture of the Kanarese Districts,* 17.

27. *The Encyclopaedia of Indian Temple Architecture,* vol. 1, discussing Drāviḍa architecture of the Upper and the Lower Drāviḍadeśa in two separate parts, clearly makes a case for this regional distinction.

28. Temples such as Bāṇantiguḍi, Upper Śivālaya, Mahākūṭeśvara, Lower Śivālaya, Mallikārjuna at Mahākūṭa, and Malegitti Śivālaya, in their chronology, illustrate the point. For dates and individual description of these seventh and eighth century temples, see Michael W. Meister and M. A. Dhaky, *The Encyclopaedia of Indian Temple Architecture: Upper Drāviḍadeśa* (Philadelphia: University of Pennsylvania Press, 1986).

29. One example of such a cell is seen embedded in the excavated halls of the great sixth-century cave at Elephanta.

30. Among formal peculiarities distinguishing all Karnataka monuments, one must note a barrel-vaulted fronton *(śukanāsa)* over the vestibule *(antarāla)* connecting the sanctum to the hall preceding it, a feature not seen in Tamil temples. See B. R. Prasad, "Śukanāsa in Dravidian Architecture," *Journal of the Oriental Institute* 20 (September 1970): 62–69.

31. Fergusson, *History of Indian and Eastern Architecture* (1910 edition), 422.

32. He concluded, "[A]ll that is wild in human faith or warm in human feeling is found portrayed on these walls; but of pure intellect there is little—less than there is of human feeling in the Parthenon." Ibid., 448–49.

33. Henry Cousens, "Chālukyan Temples," *The Journal of Indian Art and Industry* 2 (1887–88), 1. The passage is repeated almost verbatim in his monograph, 17.

34. Cousens, *The Chālukyan Architecture of the Kanarese Districts,* 58.

35. See chapters 4 and 5.

36. Cousens, *The Chālukyan Architecture of the Kanarese Districts,* 17. Adam Hardy, *Indian Temple Architecture: Form and Transformation, The Karṇāṭa Drāviḍa Tradition, Seventh to Thirteenth Centuries* (New Delhi: Indira Gandhi National Centre for the Arts and Abhinava Publications, 1995).

37. Hardy, *Form and Transformation,* 9, 296–304.

38. Dhaky, *Temple Forms,* 276.

39. On the other hand, as I will point out in chapters 4 and 5, this corner pier plays an essential role in conceptually defining Vesara architecture.

40. Past scholarship is abundant with such views. S. K. Saraswati, for example, writes, "The style seems to have emerged under the rule of the Later Chālukyas who dominated the politics of the Deccan for a little over two hundred years beginning from the later part of the tenth century A.D. It is known to have reached its ripest expression in the Mysore territory under the Hoysaḷas of Dvārasamudra." "Architecture" in *The Struggle for Empire: The History and Culture of the Indian People,* 2d ed., vol. 5 (Bombay: Bharatiya Vidya Bhavan, 1957), 628.

41. The Belūr temple has undergone a series of changes since its dedication in A.D. 1117 and some of its characteristics can be attributed to later additions. Robert J. Del Bonta, "The *Madanakais* at Belūr," in *Kalādarśana: American Studies in the Art of India,* ed. Joanna G. Williams (New Delhi and Oxford: IBH Publishing Co. and American Institute of Indian Studies, 1981), 29, however, suggests on the basis of epigraphic evidence that the sumptuous bracket figures for which Belūr is well known do not date much later than the first dedication of the temple.

Chapter 3. Drifts in Southern Architecture

1. George Kubler, *The Shape of Time,* 60.

2. For those early Nāgara and Drāviḍa monuments in Aihole, see Michael W. Meister and M. A. Dhaky, ed., *Encyclopaedia of Indian Temple Architecture,* vol. 1, part 2 (1986) chapters 1 and 2 and vol. 2, pt. 1 (1988) chapter 20.

3. For a discussion of the famous Aiyyāvoḷe (Aihole) guild of merchants, see Meera Abraham, "A Medieval Merchant Guild of South India," *Studies in History* 4, no. 1 (January–June 1982), 1–26. For reference to their spread in other parts of South India, see R. Champakalakshmi, "The Urban Configurations of Toṇḍaimaṇḍalam: The Kāñcīpuram Region, c. A.D. 600–1300," in *Urban Form and Meaning in South Asia: The Shaping of Cities from Prehistoric to the Precolonial Times,* ed. Howard Spodek and Doris Meth Srinivasan (Washington, D.C.: National Gallery of Art, Studies in the History of Art 31, 1993), 194.

4. Meister and Dhaky, *Encyclopaedia,* vol. 1, part 2, chapter 24.

5. Only the west-facing single Jaina shrine opposite the Gaurīguḍi (Virupākṣa temple) has a plank molding (pratikaṇṭha) and a vedī platform above the base moldings.

6. Comparing the plain Aihole temples with mortuary *chatrīs* in many sites in North India, Mate and Gokhale have suggested that Aihole might be a mortuary site. M. S. Mate and Shobhana Gokhale, "Aihole: An Interpretation," in *Studies in Indian History and Culture,* P. B. Desai felicitation volume, ed. Shrinivas Ritti and B. R. Gopal (Dharwar: Karnatak University, 1971), 501–504. The formal characteristics of these small Drāviḍa monuments are shared by many types of monuments through various centuries at Aihole, making an argument about a persistent formal preoccupation at the site against a specific social function. It is also possible to dismiss a lack of funds as an explanation sometimes given for the rudeness of these temples. Inscriptions about the Aihole guild of merchants throughout this period suggest that funds may not be at issue in a consideration of such austere tendency of these shrines.

7. See chapter 2 for such regional distinctions of a Drāviḍa temple.

8. For a basement, it has only a jagatī and a kapotapālī whose heaviness is comparable to its contemporary eastern shrine at Rāciguḍi.

9. Fragments of the finial surviving on top of the shrine near the Huccimalliguḍi indicates that it had a Drāviḍa *śikhara* (domed crown). See also Temple nos. 37 and 38 in Cousens, *Chālukyan Architecture,* Plate 25, for similar evidence of a southern śikhara rather than a northern āmalaka (ribbed stone). Because they do not have a *ghaṇṭā* above, these temples may not be strictly Phāṃsanā in spite of a trim pyramidal superstructure.

10. Michael W. Meister, "Forest and Cave: Temples at

Candrabhāgā and Kansuāñ," *Archives of Asian Art* 34 (1981), 56–73, for the basic observation.

11. Meister and Dhaky, *Encyclopedia,* 146. These figures are, alternately, Bahubali and Pārśvanātha.

12. The pañjara pavilion raised on split pilaster, borrowed from Tamil temples, in Temple no. 52 is an exception.

13. See chapter 2 for Deccano-Drāviḍa morphology as opposed to the Tamil variant of Drāviḍa. The point was made there that a Deccano-Drāviḍa temple is conceptualized as a kūṭa cell that grows from within toward increasing differentiation, whereas an elaborate Tamil temple is conceived as a unit created out of a gathering of separate kūṭas.

14. Michael W. Meister's idea of a "systemic wobble" accounts for a change of thinking embodied by a linguistic change much more than Kubler. Michael W. Meister, "De- and Re-constructing the Indian Temple," *Art Journal* 49 (winter 1990); 399. However, in Meister's formulation—and in spite of an implied "parturition"—he seems more urgently concerned with a loss of thinking rather than an acquisition of one. North Indian temples in the sixteenth century, thus, represent for him a "systemic wobble" in the way an older "system's own particular time" . . . "had become weakened by either loss of memory or misuse." In moments of historical transition, Kubler cherishes the "parturition" more than Meister.

15. Milton Singer, "Signs of the Self: An Exploration in Semiotic Anthropology," *American Anthropologist* 82.3 (September 1980): 485–507, quotation from 485. Singer explains that Peirce's self is anti-Cartesian, opposed to an innate, intuitive character given to it in Cartesian subjectivity.

16. The use of such a motif itself can be traced in Karnataka at least since the eighth century, as, for instance, a backing for Naṭarāja in the cavity of the śukanāsa of the Virupākṣa temple at Paṭṭadakal. In the Jaina temple at Paṭṭadakal, it is seen within the attic window of the dome, in which a figure would have been shown. A blank pavilion motif, however, fills the recess of the third-story wall, becoming perhaps the closest antecedent to Rāciguḍi.

17. The emphasis such figures give the outer edges of the śālā is seen also when uprights are carved with floral bands or when side panels themselves are replaced by square ornate blocks, as in the Kalleśvara temple at Huvināhaḍagali, and, from then on, in a number of Hoysala temples such as the Amriteśvara temple at Amritāpura and the Lakṣmī Nārāyaṇa temple at Lakkuṇḍi.

Chapter 4. The Vesara Moment

1. Lionel D. Barnett, "Inscriptions of Sūḍī," *Epigraphia Indica* 15 (1919–20): 85–94, especially lines 29–30. The inscription is discussed more fully later.

2. Although the temple, located in a coconut grove near the main temple compound at Mahākūṭa, is called Nāganātha in the American Institute of Indian Studies photo archive, suggesting M. A. Dhaky's designation, some scholars also call it the Aḍakeśvara, the lord of betel-nuts, a name that has some local relevance although most pilgrims will not recognize either of the two names. (S. Rajashekhar, conversation with author, Dharwar, India, 1989.) I prefer Aḍakeśvara because the other misleads visiting scholars to the Nāganātha temple at Nāgaral, a well-known eighth-century temple near Mahākūṭa.

3. For other early Drāviḍa temples, see K. V. Soundara Rajan, "Calukyas of Bādāmi," in *Encyclopaedia of Indian Temple Architecture, Upper Drāviḍadeśa, Early Phase,* ed. Michael W. Meister and M. A. Dhaky (Philadelphia: University of Pennsylvania Press, 1986).

4. Dhaky, *Temple Forms,* 27.

5. Ibid.

6. Ibid. For those proto-Nāgara temples, see Krishna Deva, "Pāṇḍuvaṁśīs of Śripura and Nalas," in *Encyclopaedia of Indian Temple Architecture, North India: Foundations of North Indian Style,* ed. Michael W. Meister and M. A. Dhaky (Princeton: Princeton University Press, 1988). Also see Michael W. Meister, "Śiva's Forts in Central India: Temples in Dakṣiṇa Kośala and Their 'Daemonic' Plans," in *Discourses on Śiva: Proceedings of a Symposium on the Nature of Religious Imagery,* ed. Michael W. Meister (Philadelphia: University of Pennsylvania Press, 1984), 119–42.

7. Dhaky, *Temple Forms,* has fully explored the representation of various regional types of contemporary shrine models on Vesara monuments as evidence of architectural knowledge in eleventh and twelfth-century Karnataka.

8. Krishna Deva, "Bhūmija Temples," 90–113.

9. I borrow here from Michael W. Meister, who has shown that, while all temples in India represent a shelter for the enshrined divinity, the North Indian, Nāgara form overlays this architectural reference with a symbolic surface that represents a sacred altar, where ancient Indian fire rituals embodied the process of cosmic creation. Michael W. Meister, "On the Development of a Morphology for a Symbolic Architecture: India," *Res* 12 (autumn 1986): 38–39. The conceptual distinction between Drāviḍa and Nāgara forms has earlier been made more succinctly in his "Altars and Shelters in India," *AARP: Art and Archaeology Research Papers* 16 (1979): 39.

10. The date is borne out by an inscription dated 1054 A.D. in the temple that mentions it as Akkeśvara and records rules for its funding. Barnett, "Inscriptions of Sūḍī," 80–83. The temple could have been built prior to the inscription.

11. Barnett, "Inscriptions of Sūḍī," verse 16.

12. Michael W. Meister, "Maṇḍala and Practice in Nāgara Architecture in North India," *Journal of American Oriental Society* 99.2 (April–June 1979): 204–19, makes a similar point in relation to the sacred diagram underlying the square plan of a typical Hindu temple.

13. The switch from Nāgara to Vesara kūṭastambha ornament occurs first in the Siddheśvara temple at Haverī of ca. A.D. 1100 and is consistently maintained thereafter. See chapter 6.

14. For reproductions of these seventh-century Drāviḍa temples named, see *Encyclopaedia of Indian Temple Architecture,* ed. Michael W. Meister and M. A. Dhaky, vol. 1 (South India), pts. 1 and 2, 1983, 1986.

15. A short wall between the Eastern shrine and the connecting open hall of the Joḍa Kalaśa is rendered in the manner of the shrine's bhadra, except that the offset with cantoning pilasters is replaced by a thick pier and the kūṭastambhas facing the angular walls are without their ornamental frame.

16. One of these lions survives on the motif on the south wall.

17. Barnett, "Inscriptions of Sūḍī," verse 16.

18. Barnett, "Inscriptions of Sūḍī," 93.

19. R. S. Pathak, *Vakrokti and Stylistic Concepts* (New Delhi: Bahri Publications, 1988).

20. For this eighth-century temple, see Deva and Meister in note 6.

21. A. Sundara dates Savaḍi on the basis of an inscription dated A.D. 1083 (*South Indian Inscription* 15: no. 246, 304–5) that mentions a land grant. A. Sundara, "Some Temples of North Dharwar District and the Hoysala Architecture," *Journal of Karnataka University* 9 (1973): 107. The Doḍḍa Bassapā temple at Ḍambhal of ca. 1100 A.D., discussed in chapter 7, is the most well-known monument in northern Karnataka using a stellate formula, which is also commonly reproduced from the twelfth century onward in southern Karnataka.

22. Dhaky, *Temple Forms,* 25.

23. Michael W. Meister has observed that precisely such a substitution and alteration had separated Nāgara architecture in about the seventh century from previous temples in North India that had shared with the more evolved, multistoried Drāviḍa temple of South India a formal basis in hut-shaped sheltering units. See Meister, "Prāsada as Palace: Kūṭina Origins of the Nāgara Temple," *Artibus Asiae* 49 (1988–89): 254–80. The creation of Vesara differs from such a process of substitution.

24. Based on such formal similarities, some scholars have suggested that Vesara is merely a late expression of Drāviḍa architecture. The view was held originally by archaeologists in the nineteenth century. See Henry Cousens, *The Chālukyan Architecture of the Kanarese Districts.* More recently, Adam Hardy has specifically argued for the treatment of the eleventh-century Karnataka monuments only as part of a continuous development of Drāviḍa architecture. See his "Pattern of Thought and Form in Hindu Temple Architecture," *Architecture and Design* (November–December 1986), 51. The argument is fully detailed in "The Karṇāṭa-Drāviḍa Tradition: Development of Indian Temple Architecture in Karnataka, Seventh to Thirteenth Centuries," (Ph.D. diss., Birmingham Polytechnic, U.K., 1991) and more recently in a book based on the dissertation. See Hardy, *Form and Transformation.*

25. The impact of these eleventh-century experiments is evident by the spread of Vesara architecture in all areas of Karnataka and neighboring regions for more than two hundred years.

Chapter 5. Individuality and Agency in Vesara Architecture

1. Twelfth-century inscriptions describe "Lokkiguṇḍi" as a "city" with its own mint and a strong community of mahājanas, and it is a popular convention in the area today to hold that the city once had 101 temples and 101 wells.

2. M. A. Dhaky, *Temple Forms,* 26. Lakkuṇḍi's western Indian plinth is recognized by its tall *bhiṭṭa,* a *jāḍyakumbha* with bold lotus petals carved on its slopes, a cushioned karṇikā with a sharp edge, and a plank supported by shallow ūrdhvacippikā having a row of elephants (and a few human figures) above.

3. The difference in stone may not represent chronology, as it had for archaeologists such as Henry Cousens, but indicate the geology of local quarries. Cousens connected a shift from sandstone temples to the grey soapstone as a marker of the change from the earlier, Drāviḍa temples to the "later Chālukyan" style. The majority of earlier temples are centered around the area of Badāmī, north of Lakkuṇḍī, while the majority of the centers of building activity from the eleventh century onward are located around Lakkuṇḍī and farther south, where the soapstone is more readily available. The confusion of geology with chronology led Cousens to describe such major Vesara temples in sandstone as the Kalleśvara at Kukkanūr a Drāviḍa temple and even dismiss the Yallamā temple at Badāmī simply as a ruined temple.

4. The play with vedībandha sequence is seen also in the Virupākṣa temple at Lakkuṇḍī. Although the adhiṣṭhāna of all these temples is properly below the floor level of the sanctum, the formal "confusion" between the two is raised into an art form in the Virupākṣa temple, where the adhiṣṭhāna shows different forms under different wall offsets—the southern tripaṭṭa kumuda and dhārānvita kumuda and so forth on some are mingled with details of the North Indian vedībandha form on others, including khura-kumbha, kalaśa and kapotapālī. For the interaction of adhiṣṭhāna and vedībandha in Karnataka, see Michael W. Meister, "Reading Monuments."

5. To backtrack a bit, when the thick pier was introduced on the pratirathas of the sandstone group, as on the twin temples at Sūḍī, the type contributed to the temple's mass in a way that was not achieved by the simple pratiratha offsets with cantoned pilasters. The bold, assertive appearance of the broad half-pillar is a characteristic that continues later as well. The treatment of this half-pillar on the Kāśīviśveśvara temple so that it loses its mass is unusual in this context.

6. The pyramidal superstructure made of horizontal kapotas, as in Orissa, is probably the type recognized in Karnataka as Kaliṅga. See Dhaky (*Temple Forms,* 36) on this temple type in Karnataka.

7. Aṇṇigeri, Hāverī, and Iṭṭagi temples are some of these examples.

8. Soundara Rajan discusses the Rāvaṇa themes in relation to an eleventh- or twelfth-century text, the *Rāmāyana campu Kāvya* by Bhoja, and compares the Gajāntaka to the version in the *Kūrmapuraīna.* K. V. Soundara Rajan, "A Unique Rāvaṇa-Theme Sculpture from Lakkuṇḍī," in *Glimpses of Indian Culture: Architecture, Art and Religion* (Delhi: Sandeep Prakashan, 1981), 182–84. Soundara Rajan, however, misconstrued the Gajāntaka and the Rāvaṇa shaking Mount Kailāsa as being on either side of the west wall niche, but went on to discuss the "didactic" message in this arrangement of the two "*Gajamardana* themes" on the same wall as that of producing a contrast between the "ephemeral" conquest of a "mortal," "egocentric" "*dikgaja*" and the "gracious and protective" gesture of the divine. The Gajāntaka image, however, is on the north wall. In the latter image, Soundara Rajan thinks that the figure with peacock, Skanda in my view, is "probably Brahmā."

9. For conceptual difference as well as regional choice between references to wooden and stone construction on the decorative surface of Indian temples, see Michael W. Meister, "Forest and Cave: Temples at Candrabhāgā and Kansuāñ," 56–73; Meister, "Symbol and Surface: Masonic and Pillared Wall-Structure in North India," *Artibus Asiae* 46.1–2 (1985): 129–48.

10. As, for instance, in the eastern shrine of Rāciguḍi and other mid-tenth-century temples at Aihole.

11. Phrase from Stella Kramrisch, *The Hindu Temple,* 165.

12. Michael W. Meister, "On the Development of a Morphology," 33–50.

13. For Kośala experiments, see Michael W. Meister, "Śiva's Forts in Central India," 119–42; Donald M. Stadtner, "Ancient Kośala and Stellate Plan," in *Kalādarśana, American Studies in the Art of India,* ed Joanna G. Williams (New

Dehli and Oxford: IBH Publishing Co. and American Institute of Indian Studies, 1981), 137–45; also his "The Siddheśvara Temple at Palārī," *Ars Orientalis* 12 (1981): 49–56. For an analysis of other North Indian temples, see Meister, "Muṅdeśvarī: Ambiguity and Certainty in the Analysis of a Temple Plan," in *Kalādarśana,* 77–90; "Analysis of Temple Plans: Indor," *Artibus Asiae* 63 (1982): 302–20; and "The Udayeśvara Temple-Plan," in *Śrīnidhih, Perspectives in Indian Archaeology, Art and Culture, Shri K. R. Srinivasan Festschrift* (Madras: 1983), 85–93. The symbolic intent of these experiments will be taken up in chapter 8.

14. B. R. Prasad, "Śukanāsa in Dravidian Architecture," 62–69.

15. Kramrisch, *The Hindu Temple,* 1:218. Krishna Deva writes, "In fact the Latina provides the framework, while the Kūṭina lends to the Bhūmija its decorative charm and character in the form of the storied composition of the kūṭastambhas." See "Bhūmija Temples," 113. The Śiva temple at Ambaranātha in modern Bombay, dated A.D. 1060, uses flattened domed forms resembling a Drāviḍa crown, not a Nāgara spirelet, for its kūṭastambha motifs.

16. For example, the Śiva temple at Ambaranātha.

17. For Bhūmija shrine models on Karnataka temples, see Dhaky, *Temple Form,* 18, figs. 26–33. The Vesara temple that can arguably be seen as influenced by a Bhūmija temple is the Someśvara temple at Lakṣmeśvara, whose bhadra is accentuated into a pulled-out cavernous mouth against a receding offsets treated like kūṭastambhas. On the superstructure of the Lakṣmeśvara temple, the receding kūṭas on stambhas are not distinguished as in the Sūrya temple at Lakkuṇḍī. The central projection has superimposed shrines like the *urahśṛṅgas* on the Sūrya temple at Jhalrapatan, a Bhūmija temple (Krishna Deva, "Bhūmija Temple," 44).

18. The Sūdī inscription dated A.D. 1060 stated that the daṇḍanāyaka Nāgadeva was a "Garuḍa to the serpent of Bhoja, a suppressor of the Gurjaras' pride, a destroyer of the Seguṇas," etc. Lionel D. Barnett, "Inscriptions of Sūḍī," 91. B. R. Gopal, *The Chālukyas of Kalyāna and the Kalachuris* (Dharwad and Prasarang: Karnatak University, 1981), 155–298, provides a good description of the reign of Someśvara I and Vikramāditya VI with extensive use of epigraphic references. Schwartzberg's *Historical Atlas of South Asia* remarks that the northern contact of the Karnataka rulers in this period shifts in its orientation from central and western India to eastern India even so that "the Senas of Bengal and local dynasties in Mithilā claimed to be Karṇāṭa-Kṣatrīyas, and they may indicate the extent of Cālukyan campaigns that are otherwise difficult to corroborate, much less plot on a map." Joseph E. Schwartzberg, ed., *Historical Atlas of South Asia* (New York and Oxford: Oxford University Press, 1992), 190. Refer also to Vasudev Vishnu Mirashi, *Inscriptions of the Kalachuri-Chedi Era (Corpus Inscriptionum Indicarum)* 4, (Ootacamund: Government of India, 1955) for the intensity of traffic with the Kalachuris, a dynasty of eastern India that also overthrew the Cālukyas in the second half of the twelfth century.

19. Dhaky (*Temple Forms,* 28) asks if Vesara architects might have desired a Nāgara temple. Beginning by suggesting that Vesara's Drāviḍa heritage is a hindrance to achieving Nāgara, he finally answers, if merely rhetorically, that Vesara architects did not wish to make a Nāgara temple. Dhaky's answer is proved to be correct by Lakkuṇḍī, but his line of reasoning is also questioned. Far from hindering, Vesara's Drāviḍa base is essential for Lakkuṇḍī's conceit to work.

20. John Faithfull Fleet. "Sanskrit and Old Kanarese Inscriptions," *Indian Antiquary* 6 (May 1877): 139. Cousens, *The Chālukyan Architecture of the Kanarese Districts,* 58. See also a dismissive reference to the temple in the *Annual Reports of the Mysore Archaeological Department,* 1920, 14. This major Vesara temple goes unmentioned in most general surveys of Indian architecture.

21. Dhaky, *Temple Forms,* 6, 28.

22. Adam Hardy accepts Dhaky's date in his "Patterns of Thought and Form in Hindu Temple Architecture," *Architecture and Design* (November–December 1986): 51. More recently, Hardy dates the temple ca. A.D. 1100. See his "The Hindu Temple: A Dynamic Microcosm," in *Sacred Architecture in Traditions of India, China, Judaism and Islam,* ed. Emily Lyle (Edinburgh: 1992), 41–57.

23. Dhaky, *Temple Forms,* 6.

24. Ibid., 28.

25. Ibid. Dhaky suggests these as gene characters of Vesara.

26. The Yallamā temple may be slightly later even than the Lakkuṇḍī temples, as a comparison with the Siddheśvara temple at Hāverī will show. It is noteworthy that Dhaky's relative placement of the Yallamā *after* the Kāśīviśveśvara tem ple at Lakkuṇḍī, which he assigns to ca. A.D. 1010, matches mine.

27. This alignment is formed into continuous eaves in Hoysala architecture, and in northern Karnataka relates to the Siddheśvara temple at Hāverī, datable to the last quarter of the eleventh century. See chapter 6.

28. Dhaky, *Temple Forms,* 27.

29. Michael W. Meister, "Kūṭina Origins," for these northern temples.

30. Although Dhaky is cautious enough *not* to make a conclusion that Vesara architects intended to create Nāgara, his framework can easily mislead one. The coalescing of mahānāsīs on the central spine of the Vesara, for example, reminds him:

> of a stage, which, centuries before, the Nāgara form in its throes passed through, much before it achieved its fuller integrated and articulate form. Had it not been for the persistence of the wagon-vault roof of the *śālās* and the square cupola of the *karṇakūṭas*, just as the *vyālamālā* at each floor, the Nāgara form could have once again leaped out of such a structural matrix and what happened earlier in [the] North would have been repeated in [the] South five centuries hence. But this did not happen. . . . The totality of form here in Karṇāṭa has been arrested, in terms of evolution, between the late Dravidian and the proto-Nāgara; it could not move to Nāgara because it failed to wholly repeat the process which created the true Nāgara form; it lacked some of the basic elements and impulses needed for the Nāgara formulation and could not at the same time unburden those very Dravidian that were not needed for Nāgara formal organization. (*Temple Forms,* 27–28).

This framework is only rhetorically dismissed by Dhaky, and thus I find it worth acknowledging here. Also it is in this context that I make my thesis, in relation to the Yallamā temple, that its Drāviḍa form was not just a burden but a necessary component of the Vesara rhetorical play.

31. Lionel D. Barnett, "Inscriptions of Sūḍī," inscription F, verse 16.

32. Ibid. Barnett's translation of vakrokti as "punning phrases," 93, will suffice for now. Vakrokti is more accurately translated as "deviant speech." It is described by poeticians as a linguistic "twist" or "crookedness," distinguishing literary language. Its characteristic is a "misapplication" of literal modes of thought. See Edwin Gerow, *A Glossary of Indian Figuress of Speech* (The Hague: Mouton, 1971); also R. S. Pathak, *Vakrokti and Stylistic Concepts*. Vācaspati, the name of an Advaita philosopher in the tradition of Śaṅkara, may

simply designate an expert, or perhaps a wizard, in the manner of speaking. See V. N. Sheshagiri Rao, *Vācaspati's Contribution to Advaita* (Mysore: Samvit Publishers, 1984).

33. For models of a linguistic interpretation of Indian architecture, see Michael W. Meister, "Juncture and Conjunction: Punning and Temple Architecture," *Artibus Asiae* 61 (1979): 226–228; Devangana Desai, "Puns and Intentional Language at Khajuraho," in *Kusumāñjali: New Interpretations in Indian Art and Culture,* ed. M. S. Nagaraja Rao, (Delhi; Agam Kala Prakashan, 1987), 2:383–88.

34. Dhaky, *Temple Forms,* 27.

35. Ibid., 24, 28. "We here need the help of an inscriptional notice or a *vāstuśāstra* native to Karṇāṭa country that would clarify the position. This corner is still unlit, and any stipulation on our part must be regarded as a tentative hypothesis" (28). Adam Hardy, in his discussion of the Yallamā temple, expresses reservation about the term Vesara. I take this to be his caution that the term may not have any historical validity, and that its use to designate an eleventh-century temple such as the Yallamā will have to depend on a historian's judgment. See Hardy, "Patterns of Thought and Form," 51. More recently, and hoping to offer a definitive answer within the framework of Dhaky's discussion, M. N. Prabhakar suggests that Dhaky's "Vesara" monuments should in fact be designated "Auttareya Drāviḍa" (Northern Drāviḍa). See Prabhakar, "Classification of Temples—'Auttareya Drāviḍa,'" *The Quarterly Journal of the Mythic Society* 78 (July–December 1987): 52–62. Prabhakar does not clarify whether "Auttareya Drāviḍa" is the same as (or different from) Dhaky's term "Karṇāṭa Drāviḍa," designating the variety of Drāviḍa architecture from which Vesara evolved.

36. Although it is sufficiently clear from Dhaky that the architects understood Drāviḍa as a form distinct from their own (the ambiguity really being between Vesara and Bhūmija), evidence from the eleventh century is still lacking. I share Hardy's reservation about the term Vesara (ibid.) only to the extent of agreeing that labels do not precede but follow practice. I would emphasize that the terminological issue, (particularly of the kind Prabhakar [ibid.] engages) may hardly have had any relevance at the level of architectural practice. I prefer to use the term Vesara for eleventh-century architecture only because it is a convenient way to indicate its difference from the earlier Drāviḍa architecture, the actual nature of which is complex. My intention is to engage with a "difference" that architects consciously created. It is, however, precisely here that I disagree with Hardy's view of the Yallamā and the rationale for his reservation. He writes, "[W]hether or not it is given a separate name, this form is nothing other than the end result of various 'principles of fusion' being applied to Drāviḍa temple, a process which had already begun in the eighth century Paṭṭadakal," "Patterns of Thought and Form," 51.

37. See Michael W. Meister, "Bīṭhū: Individuality and Idiom," 169–186, as well as "Uparamāla," 344–53.

38. See Meister, "Bīṭhū," where individuality is discussed as a function of idiom.

Chapter 6. The Geography of Vesara Architecture: Karnataka in A.D. 1100

1. Dhaky, *Temple Forms,* 25.

2. Michael W. Meister, "Bīthū: Individuality and Idiom," 169.

3. Svetlana Alpers has persuasively separated style as an art historical tool from style as an attribute of artifacts in a period of time. See "Style Is What You Make It: The Visual Arts Once Again," 138–40.

4. See Irene J. Winter, "Perspective on the 'Local Style' of Hasanlu IV B," 371–86, esp. 378. Winter has been used in the field of Indian art by Michael W. Meister in his "Uparamāla," 344–353. I share with both these scholars that style is an averaging of diverse, sometimes loosely related, visual information.

5. Meister, "Uparamāla," 351.

6. George Kubler has somewhat pointedly stated that style is an art historian's construct. "The notion of style has long been the art historian's principal mode of classing works of art. By style he selects and shapes the history of art." Kubler, "Style and the Representation of Historical Time," *Annals of the New York Academy of Sciences* 138 (1967):853. See a critique of style also in Alpers, "Style Is What You Make It," 137–62.

7. To use a term coined and defined by Charles Sanders Peirce in the context of a semiotics of self, Nāgara now formed an "interpretant" in this twist of Drāviḍa forms. I understand Peirce's "interpretant" as a shared common mental image active in the communication of sign, the term that makes exchange of signs a transformative process for the "utterer" and the "interpreter." See Singer, "Signs of the Self," 493–94, for Peirce's elaboration on the interpretants. I understand interpretant as signification that goes on in the minds of the "utterer" and the "interpreter" or a growing sense of meaningfulness of reference points implicit and alive in the communication of signs between the two.

8. Removed from the sanctum after ca. A.D. 1100, Nāgara kūtastambhas become a preferred motif on the balustrade surrounding the porch of the gūḍhamaṇḍapa.

9. This is true of many Hoysala temples as well. The Huvināhaḍagali, Hirehaḍagali, and Caudadāmpur temples discussed in this chapter are some examples of this simplified scheme.

10. An inscription on a slab in the Hāverī temple dated Cālukya-Vikrama year 33, corresponding to A.D. 1109, recording gift of toll collected from trade of betel leaves, etc., suggests that the temple existed at least before this time (*South Indian Inscriptions* 18, no. 108). The town was earlier made into an *agrahāra* in the reign of Āhavamalla, probably in A.D. 1067 (*South Indian Inscriptions* 18, no. 136). Presuming that the temple could have been built only after the town was given to a priestly community, the Hāverī temple can be given a time frame of A.D. 1067–1109, or the last quarter of the eleventh century.

11. This idiosyncrasy is explained in chapter 7 in relation to the idea of "bhadra cluster."

12. Dhaky, *Temple Forms,* 25.

13. Even if scholars looking at such features as the central spine of Vesara's superstructure have suggested that it reflected in Vesara the central band of northern temples, the difference shown in the conception and rendering of this spine on the Vesara and Bhūmija models at Hāverī strikes more points of tension than are allowed in our conception of "influence."

14. The Mukteśvara temple at Caudadāmpur—a temple of the Hāverī type—was built under the Guttas of Guttal, rulers different from those who built the Hāverī temple itself. The Tārakeśvara temple at Hānagal, belonging to the Iṭṭagi type, is a monument built by the Kadambas of Hānagal, while the Mahādeva temple at Iṭṭagi was built by a *daṇḍanāyaka* (general) of the Cālukya king, Vikramāditya VI, himself. A traffic of forms and ideas across political boundaries, which themselves were in constant flux, produced an ongoing interaction between typology and local practices.

15. The term "idiom" is borrowed here from Meister, for whom it signified assimilation of regional styles. For me, idiom belongs to a conceptual category different from that of style. It functions at the level of morphology; in language, idiom is identified as a local production of language itself, sharing its syntactical, grammatical, or structural form. See *Merriam Webster's Collegiate Dictionary* for the basic sense of idiom *as* language with individual peculiarity.

16. These wall subshrines are perhaps the earliest precursors of triple shrines that became so common in the 12th century.

17. The Hāverī temple's arrangement is one solution to the problem of connecting a low and expansive raṅgamaṇḍapa to the sanctum, and perhaps the most successful one. Although awkward in plan, the square raṅgamaṇḍapa's partial overlap with the sanctum creates an inviting *mukhālinda* within the space of the raṅgamaṇḍapa, from where one is led into a cavelike antechamber by the cozy arms of the half-walls. The structural problem of connecting the raṅgamaṇḍapa to the sanctum, however, is never resolved in Vesara architecture. The raṅgamaṇḍapa of the Koṭiśvara temple at Kuppatur is long and rectangular and seems overdrawn as a result, even though the sanctum wall behind it is exaggerated in its height by two tiers of motifs and its superstructure itself is tall. Small side entrances are created at the rear perhaps to avoid the prolonged hall when rituals only relate to the shrine; these entrances lead to the half-walled section similar to that in the Hāverī temple. The Mahādeva temple at Iṭṭagi, the Nagareśvara temple at Bankapur (known as Arvatthu Kambhada, or "temple with sixty pillars" because of its prominent pillared raṅgamaṇḍapa), and the Tārakeśvara temple at Hānagel keep their large, densely pillared raṅgamaṇḍapa separate from the sanctum and its gūḍhamaṇḍapa (fig. 4). The Hoysala monuments in the twelfth century, on the other hand, absorb the raṅga- within the walls or trellis of a gūḍhamaṇḍapa, making the whole enclosure seem ponderous. While these trends in a Vesara raṅgamaṇḍapa aimed generally at emphasizing lofty, spacious, almost monumental effects of a processional access, the Hāverī temple inclined toward exquisiteness.

18. To prevent it from sagging, the awning is propped up by stone uprights today.

19. For example, in the raṅgamaṇḍapa at Iṭṭagi the weight and girth of pillars produce a dense forestlike effect contrary to the sensitiveness the Hāverī temple brings to the elegance of space itself.

20. This middle division of the wall is an aesthetic decision found consistently in the "Hāverī" type of Vesara temples. In Hoysala architecture, this horizontal alignment of motifs at midpoint is conventionalized.

21. On the Kalleśvara temple at Hirehaḍagali, discussed later, the main awning of the temple itself is actually carved with petals.

22. In Lakṣmeśvara, quite literally, the niche is like a mouse hole in relation to the monumental temple.

23. This particular configuration evolves in the late eleventh century in temples such as Hāverī and Huvināhaḍagali, and prevails in the Tuṅgabhadrā belt region.

24. *South Indian Inscriptions* 9, 156, no. 165. This inscription is valuable and asserts Kuruvatti's importance as a religious center. The epigraphic report mentions that the inscription was found in the Kalleśvara temple. As I am not aware of any other temple of the period in Kuruvatti of such importance, I take this to refer to the same Mallikārjuna temple.

25. Name used in an inscription (*South Indian Inscriptions* 9, no. 320). Robert J. del Bonta uses this inscription but the name he gives as Trailokyamalladeva, instead of Āhavamalleśvara, seems to be an error on his part. Del Bonta, "Madanakais," 33, no. 19.

26. Bilhaṇa, a contemporary biographer of Someśvara's son, Vikramāditya VI, quoted in B. R. Gopal, *Chālukyas,* 197, or as an inscription at Balagāmi says, "[H]e performed in Kuruvatti the rite of supreme yoga and in the Tuṅgabhadrā the master of the world, the king Āhavamalla, ascended the heaven . . . thereby increasing his fame." Gopal, *Chālukyas,* 197.

27. See also David N. Lorenzen, *The Kapālikas and Kālāmukhas, Two Lost Śaivite Sects* (Berkeley and Los Angeles: University of California Press, 1972), 155.

28. The Kālāmukha preceptor, Lakulīśvara Paṇḍita, in whose presence the grant dated A.D. 1099 at Kuruvatti was made, is also mentioned in an inscription dated A.D. 1071 at Huvināhaḍagali (*South Indian Inscriptions* 9, no. 135), suggesting a direct, institutional linkage between the two sites.

29. Alexander Rea, *Chālukyan Architecture; Including Examples from Bellāry District, Madras Presidency,* Archaeological Survey of India n.s. 21, 1896; reprint, Delhi: Indological Book House, 1970, 21, ". . . on the east [mistakenly for west] and south are images described as king Urduathandan and Bidchadanar."

30. Iṭṭagi, Kuruvatti and the Doḍḍa Bassapā temple at Ḍambhal share this configuration of the gūḍhamaṇḍapa interior, including the makara toraṇa (supported by a pair of thin, circular pillars) that separates it from the antarāla. At Kuruvatti, the convex volumes of the makara's body, the deep undercuts for the head, and details such as the knife-sharp tongue and the curled ridges of the tail's foliation give it a strong effect of metal repoussé that differs from the ivory-like quality of carving at Hāverī.

31. Since Fergusson, this quality of carving has been noticed on Hoysala monuments but distinguishes Vesara in general. Dhaky uses this "exuberance and love for metallic ornateness" as one of the "gene characters" of Vesara (*Temple Forms,* 28).

32. See Del Bonta, "Madanakais," for these "madanakais."

33. Winter, "Perspective on the 'Local Style' of Hasanulu IV B," 382.

34. Literally "the village of flower boats," as it was called in the time of the Vijayanagara rulers. V. Rangachyra, "A Topographic List of the Inscriptions of the Madras Presidency" (Collected till 1915), (Madras: 1919) vol. 1, inscription no. 182.

35. Ibid., 281.

36. A variant of such a tassel is also seen on the bell of the gūḍhamaṇḍapa pillars of the Mallikārjuna temple at Kuruvatti by ca. A.D. 1100 before it became a common feature in Hoysala.

37. Scholars such as del Bonta and Settar, who have combined epigraphic references to craftsmen with a stylistic analysis of Hoysala sculpture, have suggested a southwardly migration of craftsmen, from the Cālukya territories along the Tuṅgabhadrā River belt or the Shimoga region down to the Hoysala territories. Del Bonta, "Madanakais," 22; S. Settar, "The Hoysala Style of Temple Architecture and Sculpture, Eleventh to Fourteenth Centuries" (Ph.D. dissertation, Cambridge University, 1970), 52, and more recently *The Hoysala Temples.* For a similar discussion on artists as carriers of "Hoysala" style, see Kelleson Collyer, "*The Hoysala Artist: Their Identity and Styles* (Mysore: Directorate of Archaeology and Museums, 1990).

38. This double-storied effect, stretching Hāverī's idio-

matic characteristic to fit the mold of a loftier wall, is also seen on the Koṭiśvara temple at Kuppatur.

39. Dhaky finds in this monument's flamboyancy an Indian counterpart of "High" or "Decorated Gothic" style. See M. A. Dhaky, "The 'Gothic' in Indian Temple Architecture," 137–39.

40. The bhadra's niches also have horses underneath, indicating that the niche images could have been Sūrya. An exquisite image of standing Sūrya is placed in the shrine opposite the main temple.

41. *South Indian Inscriptions* 9.1, no. 118.

42. Gopal, *Chālukyas,* 272.

43. A scarcity of evidence always leaves a possibility for an alternative hypothesis. If the highly evolved Hoysala temples such as Belūr (dated A.D. 1117) and Halebīd (ca. A.D. 1121–60), which are used here as touchstones, are not originators of what may be called Hoysala aesthetic, Hirehaḍagali can still be absorbing a southern aesthetic rather than developing independently.

44. Winter's "Interaction Sphere" does not distinguish between flow of stylistic concepts and that of "finished goods and raw materials." Winter, "Perspective on the 'Local Style' of Hasanulu IV B," 378. Flow of stylistic information can be a kind of exchange among people, but these Karnataka monuments demonstrate that that exchange is flexible and tied only loosely to political interaction in comparison with exchange.

45. Ibid., 382. Compare this criticism of "influence" also to the mind-set of the receiver in Oleg Grabar's idea of "creator/beholder" discussed in the introduction.

46. Although Winter's sample is limited, and conditioned by the circumstance of power in ancient Near East, she explains that "the influence exerted by so-called developed countries upon less-developed countries today is ultimately no different from that of antiquity." The terms of "great style" and "local style" thus continue to maintain their hierarchy. See especially Winter, "Perspective on the 'Local Style' of Hasanulu IV B," 380–81, for the assumed inferior status of the borrower within a sphere of social and economic interaction. "Emulation" in today's terms thus could be seen as a manifestation of colonialism, by which is meant a (mytho)logical transformation of invasion into an internal, local wish to be like the superior other. For a classic discussion of that logic by which the power of the colonizer transforms into local needs, see "Myth Today" in Roland Barthes, *Mythologies* (1957; reprint, London: Paladin Books, 1989), especially 125 ff.

47. Meister, "Bīthū," 169, also "Uparamāla," 350–51.

48. Winter writes, "(a)s a result [of interaction], the homogeniety of the 'Interaction Sphere' is also increased." Winter "Perspective on the 'Local Style' of Hasanulu IV B," 381. Such stylistic homogeniety, for Meister, is not a result of relations of power but interaction among community of craftsmen as they lean and sway with the changing directions of the political winds in the region. Meister, "Uparamāla."

Chapter 7. So What? The Expressive Content of Vesara

1. M. A. Dhaky, *Temple Forms,* 3. Inscription in *Epigraphia Carnatica,* Sorab no. 275. ed. B. L. Rice. Dhaky, n. 11, gives Rice's original translation of the text and notes differences between his own and Rice's: " 'Within the village, vying with Kailāsa, stood the temple of Koṭinātha; built by Viśvakarma and carved with complete devotion, planned in perfect accordance with the many rules of architecture, and freely decorated with *drāviḍa, bhūmija and nāgara.*' Rice adds in a footnote: 'These (i.e. *drāvida, bhūmija and nāgara*) and bhadropeta appear to be technical terms of the śilpa-śāstra or science of architecture.' " See M. N. Prabhakar, "Classification of Temples," 57, for yet another translation. In Prabhakar's interpretation (ibid., n. 1), "bhadropetam" is a position of temple models on the walls or sometimes the models themselves.

2. Dhaky summarizes another late-twefth-century inscription from the Amriteśvara temple at Holal, where the architect again declares himself as a veritable divine architect on the basis of his mastery of the "four classes of temples (namely) Nāgara, Kaliṅga, Drāviḍa, and Vesara." Dhaky, *Temple Forms,* 3.

3. The generic meaning of "bhadra" to indicate centrality holds true both in North Indian and South Indian contexts, even if the term refers to different morphological features. In North India, it is the central projecting offset. In the Tamil region of South India, the term bhadra refers to all projecting offsets, perhaps in acknowledgment of the monument as a gathering and synthesis of bays. K. R. Srinivasan, *Temples of South India,* 3d rev. ed. (New Delhi: National Book Trust, 1985), 90, argues that offset bays of a temple are called "bhadras" in South India and "rathas" in North India. Rathas, "chariots," however, are also single shrines, such as the monolithic temples in Mahābalipuram, so that bhadras and rathas in southern terminology are comparable in that they connote shrine units, which "bays" in temples such as the Kailāsanātha at Kāñci in fact are. Srinivasan's glossary defines bhadra as a central projection as opposed to the karṇa, which is inconsistent with the point he makes by comparing South India and North India but consistent with the intrinsic meaning of a shrine core or "centrality" that underlies the conception of the term. In his description of temples, Srinivasan avoids the ambiguity in terminology by consistently calling temple offsets simply "bays."

4. Charles S. Peirce, "Logic as Semiotic: The Theory of Signs," in *Semiotics: An Introductory Anthology,* ed. Robert E. Innis (Bloomington: Indiana University Press, 1985), 1–23.

5. Dhaky, *Temple Forms,* 37.

6. Michael W. Meister, "Altars and Shelters in India," 39. For a more thorough analysis of this distinction, see his "On the Development of a Morphology," 38–39 and passim.

7. For this and other temples at Huli, see James Burgess, *Reports of the First Season's Operations in the Belgām and Kalādgī Districts, January to May 1874,* Archaeological Survey of Western India, Reports, vol. 1, Archaeological Survey of India, New Imperial Series (London: Indian Museum, 1874).

8. Henry Cousens, *The Chālukyan Architecture of the Kanarese Districts,* 19. In his *The Architectural Antiquities of Western India* (London: The India Society, 1926, 30), he compares these Lakkuṇḍī temples to the Mahādeva temple at Iṭṭagi, writing that the stages of the tower of the Iṭṭagi temple "are not so cut up and masked by decorative details as in the Kāśīviśveśvara and others of the same class."

9. Dhaky, *Temple Forms,* 37.

10. Stella Kramrisch, *The Hindu Temple,* 165.

11. Peirce, "Logic as Semiotic," 8.

12. Meister, "Śiva's Forts," 119–42.

13. In the Mallikārjuna temple at Kuruvatti, tiny figures at the foot of the corner offsets are Dikpālas; this is not so on

this temple. C. S. Patil, "Portrait Sculpture," 311–14, speaks of "female Dikpālas" at the karṇas of the Iṭṭagi temple.

14. Term from Dhaky, *Temple Forms,* 37–38.

15. In the Hoysala territory of southern Karnataka, where Vesara architecture took a markedly different regional tone, the bhadra's model was blown up into a virtually detached shrine with a life-size cell in such temples as the Keśava temple at Belūr.

16. Dhaky, *Temple Forms,* 41.

17. Ibid., 28. It is another matter that he consciously checked this possibility with a rhetorical question "Did [Vesara] ever want to be Nāgara?" followed by an instinctive but not an explanatory reply: "Honestly not." As Meister's studies show, while the origins of both Nāgara as well as Drāviḍa architecture can be located in Kūṭina morphology, what distinguishes Nāgara is a radical shift to another kind of symbolism, relating to ancient rituals of the fire altar instead of one embedded in Kūṭina's sheltering form. See the tension between his two articles, "On the Development of a Morphology of a Symbolic Architecture," 33–50, and "Prāsāda as Palace," 254–80. I fully agree with Dhaky's answer to his own question, which suggests that such a transference of symbolism, and formal consequences that made Nāgara, was not even intended by Vesara architects.

18. A. Sundara dates the temple to A.D. 1126 on the basis of an inscription that, he suggests, is a foundation inscription. A. Sundara, "Some Temples of North Dharwar District" 103, n. 6. Stylistic comparison, however, suggests an earlier date. For instance, the pillar with ridged octagonal base used for its southern porch and in the rubble wall of the Nandimaṇḍapa can be compared to the more elaborate version of the pillar in the southern porch of the Mahādeva temple at Iṭṭagi, dated A.D. 1112, (and an even more elaborated version of it in Iṭṭagi's raṅgamaṇḍapa). The doorway to the southern porch of the gūḍhamaṇḍapa is of a type used also at Iṭṭagi, Kuruvatti and Huvināhaḍagali. The doorjambs, in details such as the vine creeper in the outermost jamb, and the *śākhā* with dancing figures on cloudlike formations, however, are closer to Huvināhaḍagali and Kuruvatti (ca. A.D. 1100) than the elaborate version at Iṭṭagi.

19. See Michael W. Meister, "Reading Monuments," drawing 18, for the means by which the stellate sanctum was achieved.

20. See B. R. Prasad, "Śukanāsa in Dravidian Architecture," 62–69.

21. The pavilions stand on lively elephants that frolic on the temple's vedī platform.

22. I credit Michael W. Meister for the observation of a pratiratha half-pillar as well as the idea of an "infolded" bhadra cluster.

23. In this, the intention of all orthogonal Vesara monuments differs from Savaḍī's overlay of Nāgara elements.

24. Krishna Deva, "Bhūmija Temples," where stellate examples are the Sūrya temple at Rāṇakpur and the Udayeśvara temple at Udayapur. Also Michael W. Meister, "The Udayeśvara Temple Plan," 85–93.

25. Ḍambhal sportively relegates a proper bhadra motif—a niche with a temple tower over it—to either side of the southern porch of the gūḍhamaṇḍapa.

26. Kramrisch, *The Hindu Temple,* and "The Temple as Puruṣa," *Studies In Indian Temple Architecture,* ed. Pramod Chandra (New Delhi: American Institute of Indian Studies, 1975), 40–46.

27. Kramrisch, "The Temple as Puruṣa," 40.

28. Ṛg Veda 10–90, referred in Kramrisch, "The Temple as Puruṣa," 40.

29. Kramrisch, "The Temple as Puruṣa," 41–42.

Chapter 8. Conclusion: Makers and Making of Indian Temple Architecture

1. In the early twentieth century, scholars such as Ananda Coomaraswamy, formulating our traditional scholarly understanding of the role of the makers of sacred monuments in India, explained that "all craftsmen regard their art as a mystery, and look upon its traditions, handed down in pupillary succession, as invested with sacred and scriptural authority." Ananda K. Coomaraswamy, *The Arts and Crafts of India and Ceylon* (1913); reprint, New York: Farrar, Straus, 1964), 34. Coomaraswamy consciously opposed this role of an Indian craftsman to Western individualism.

2. Stella Kramrisch emphasizes the control of scriptures in a way similar to Coomaraswamy by showing the tremendous powers invested in the designing of temples. She points out that the makers of sacred monuments were required to remain strictly "harnessed" by prescribed norms because temple designs have magical powers that impact on social well-being, so that an idiosyncratic design could have disastrous consequences on society. See Kramrisch, "Artists, Patron, and Public in India (1956)," reprinted in *Exploring India's Sacred Art: Selected Writings of Stella Kramrisch,* ed. Barbara Stoller Miller (Philadelphia: University of Pennsylvania Press, 1983), 57–58.

3. Adam Hardy, *Form and Transformation,* 5.

4. Kramrisch, *The Hindu Temple,* 165. A powerful metaphor suggests the parallel Hardy has in mind between the historical evolution of forms and the dynamic structure of the monuments themselves. "To imagine the tradition running through like the speeded-up film of an opening flower is to watch the same blossoming out that is captured in a single shrine." *Form and Transformation,* 27. See also his "Dynamic Microcosm."

5. Hardy, *Form and Transformation,* chapter 2.

6. A recent interest in the makers of sacred monuments is indicated in a set of papers presented at the College Art Association meetings in February 1994 in New York City (see panel titled "Alternate Models: Present-Day Artists Working in the Traditional Modes," chaired by Janice Leoshko, under the auspices of the American Council for South Asian Art). The stated purpose of the panel was to find models for the role and identity of ancient practitioners in an ethnography of modern folk artists. See also Michael W. Meister, ed., *Making Things in South Asia: The Role of Artist and Craftsman* (Philadelphia: Department of South Asian Regional Studies, University of Pennsylvania, 1988) and Joanna Williams, "From the Fifth to the Twentieth Century and Back," *Art Journal* 49 (winter 1990): 363–69. For the tradition scholarly emphasis on "scriptural authority," see n. 1.

7. Richard H. Davis, *Lives of Indian Images* (Princeton, N.J.: Princeton University Press, 1997), especially 4 for the following discussion.

8. Davis, *"Indian Images,"* 11. For an attempt in that direction, see my "The Construction of 'Mule' in Indian Temple Architecture," 33–62.

9. For a model for viewer's response different from Davis in that it is detached from the ontology of the work of art, see

Joanna G. Williams, "Construction of Gender in the Paintings and Graffiti of Sigiriya," *Representing the Body: Gender Issues in Indian Art,* ed. Vidya Dehejia (New Delhi: Kali for Women, 1997), 56–67.

10. Davis, *Indian Images,* 11.

11. This point is more fully made in my "The Construction of 'Mule' in Indian Temple Architecture."

12. David Summers has argued for the importance of the "indexicality" in works of art, i.e., its status as an imprint contiguous with the moment in which it is created, using Charles Peirce's triad of signs. Summers, "On Histories of Artifacts," *Art Bulletin* (December 1994), 590–92. Summers writes, "[A]ny work of art, taken as a whole, before it is regarded formally, aesthetically, or expressively, may also be regarded indexically, that is, in terms of its own *facture,* as the result and record of its having been made" (592). The recognition of stone remains as an imprint of its "facture" leads art historical analysis toward inferences about making and makers, and their motivation. Summers has placed this analytical possibility in art history against a "text centrism," which he describes as one that absorbs index into "symbol," i.e., an arbitrary sign whose meaning is agreed upon by viewers and users, or what Davis has called "interpretive communities."

13. A preliminary proposal to include the makers of India's religious art and architecture was made in my introduction to a panel at the College Art Association annual meeting in Boston in 1996, cochaired with Darielle Mason, titled, "The Nature of Change in the South Asian Temple." See excerpts in my "The Nature of Change in South Asian Temple," *American Council for Southern Asian Art Newsletter,* (spring 1996).

Glossary of Sanskrit Terms

(Source: Michael W. Meister and M. A. Dhaky, ed., *The Encyclopaedia of Indian Temple Architecture,* vol. 1, pts. 1 and 2, and vol. 2, pts. 1 and 2, 1983–.)

adhiṣṭhāna	molded basement
āmalaka	"myrobolan fruit"; crowning ribbed member of Latina Nāgara temples
āmalasāraka	flattened "cogged wheel" stone crowning eleventh-century North Indian temples, such as the Bhūmija variety
anekāṇḍaka	multispired; term used for temple towers
antarāla	covered vestibule set between sanctum and the closed hall. (Note: I have used "antarāla wall" to refer to the wall enclosing this intermediary space. In North Indian context this wall may also be called "kapilī," a term I have used for the same feature when there is no closed hall in front, as in chapter 2.)
bhadra	central projecting offset, a wall division
bhāraputras	weight-bearing dwarfs
bhiṭṭa	plinth course in North Indian temples
bhūmi	"earth" levels, or storeys, of a North Indian tower
Bhūmija	superstructure type, with corner and intermediate vertical bands made up of shrine models above pillarets
bhūmikhaṇḍa	segment supporting the "cogged wheel" marking the stories of a North Indian temple
Bhūmiprāsāda	temple type defined in a North Indian context, comprising a series of horizontal levels
candraśālā	dormer window (decorative pattern)
Dikpālas	guardians of directions in Indian cosmology
Drāviḍa	generic name for South Indian temple type
garbha	"womb," sanctum space
garbhagṛha	"womb-house," sanctum
ghaṇṭā	bell
ghaṭa	vase, pot; cushion-shaped pillar part (above laśuna)
ghaṭapallava	vase and foliage, describing a pillar
gṛhapiṇḍī	wall cube of an upper story
gūḍhamaṇḍapa	closed hall
haṃsa	goose, gander (decorative motif)
hāra	balustrade or cloistered parapet in the superstructure
hārāntara	section between architectural motifs of the hāra
iṣṭadevatā	particular manifestation of divinity
jāḍyakumbha	inverted cyma recta molding, used on pīṭha
jagatī	plinth, platform; basal molding of adhiṣṭhāna
jāla	mesh design
kalaśa	pot; torus molding in a North Indian vedībandha
kaṇṭha	necking; a recess between moldings
kapilī	exterior walls for a vestibule in front of the sanctum
kapota	roll cornice, also overhanging cornice
Kapotabandha	southern basement type
kapotapālī	cyma cornice
karṇa	corner offset in the division of temple wall
karṇakūṭa	corner aedicula of a superstructure
karṇikā	knife-edged arris molding
khura	thin basal molding of vedībandha
kīrttimukha	"face of glory," a decorative mask
koṣṭha	niche
kumbha	"pot"; tall basal molding with curved shoulder
kumuda	torus molding in a South Indian basement
kūṭa	"hut"; square aedicula
kūṭastambha	miniature shrine model placed on pillaret (decorative motif)
Kūṭina	"hut"-based temple mode; (primarily South Indian) temple with superstructure having corner kūṭas as dominant elements
laśuna	tall, vase-shaped pillar part (sometimes ridged or faceted or fluted, occupying the upper part of shaft)
Latina	single-spired North Indian temple form with a curvilinear superstructure distinguished by vertical "creeper" bands
madhyalatā	central band of Latina superstructure
madhyaśālā	central, barrel-vaulted hall type motif on the hāra
mahānāsī	large dormer at the cardinal point of a superstructure
makara	crocodile monster, a decorative motif

makara toraṇa	archform gateway pattern spewed by opposing makaras or formed from their luxurious tails
mālāsthāna	pillar part below the ghaṭa (capital) decorated with pearl and floral festoon
mānasūtra	straight cord; line for measuring
maṇḍapa	hall, generally columnar
mukhamaṇḍapa	front hall; entry hall
mūrti	something formless taking form; usually referring to an image or icon
Nāgara	generic name for North Indian temple type
nāsī	dormer motif
nirandhāra	sanctum with no circumambulatory passage
padma	lotus
Padmabandha	basement type
pañjara	"cage"; fronton-vaulted apsidal shrine (decorative motif)
Phāṃsanā	tiered pyramidal roof type crowned by a ribbed bell
pīṭha	pedestal, small platform; plinth in North Indian temples
prāggrīva	projection in front of sanctum
pratikaṇṭha	recess with plank moldings
pratiratha	wall offset flanking the central projection
Puruṣa	popularly "man," used here in the sense of "measure"
raṅgamaṇḍapa	"dancing hall"; open type of pillared hall
rathikā	framed niche
śālā	rectangular chamber, room, or hall; architectural motif with barrel-vaulted roof
sāndhāra	sanctum having circumambulatory passage
śāstric	belonging to the śāstras, ancient texts
Śekharī	complex, multispired North Indian superstructure type
śikhara	domed finial (the book uses this term in its South Indian sense)
siṃhavyāla	leonine griffin or chimera
śṛṅga	spirelet
stambha	pillar
subhadra	central projecting face of the bhadra
śukanāsa	barrel-vaulted antefix above the antarāla
śūrasena, śūrasenaka	pediment made up of trifoliate dormer patterns
tīrtha	place of ascent (for the worshiper) and descent (for a god); a sacred spot
toraṇa	gateway; archform gateway pattern
tripaṭṭa kumuda	tri-faceted torus molding
upabhadra	minor offset of central wall projection
uṣṇīṣa	coping
Valabhī	temple type with barrel-vaulted superstructure
vedī	altar; wall molding above the basement
vedībandha	basal wall molding in a North Indian temple
vedikā	blind rail enclosure surrounding an open, pillared hall
vyāla	composite fantastic creature; griffin, chimera

Bibliography

SERIALS

Annual Report of Indian Epigraphy

Annual Report of the Mysore Archaeological Department, Bangalore

Annual Report of South Indian Epigraphy (Appendix on Stone Inscriptions for Bombay-Karnataka)

Epigraphia Carnatica

Epigraphia Indica

Indian Antiquary

Journal of the Bombay Branch of the Royal Asiatic Society

South Indian Inscriptions

BOOKS AND ARTICLES

Abraham, Meera. "A Merchant Guild of South India." *Studies in History* 4, no. 1 (January–June 1982): 1–26.

Alpers, Svetlana. "Style Is What You Make It: The Visual Arts Once Again." In *The Concept of Style* (1979). Edited by Berel Lang. Ithaca and London: Cornell University Press, 1987, 137–62.

Bal, Mieke. *Reading "Rembrandt."* Cambridge, England: Cambridge University Press, 1991.

———. "Signs in Painting," *Art Journal* 78.1 (March 1996): 6–9.

Bal, Mieke, and Norman Bryson. "Semiotics and Art History." *Art Bulletin* (June 1991): 174–208.

Barnett, Lionel D. "Inscriptions of Sūḍī." *Epigraphia Indica* 15 (1919–1920: 73–112.

Baxandall, Michael. *Patterns of Intention: On the Historical Explanation of Pictures*. New Haven and London: Yale University Press, 1985.

Bhatt, Bharat L. "India and Indian Regions: A Critical Overview." In *An Exploration of India: Geographical Perspectives on Society and Culture*. Edited by David E. Sopher. Ithaca: Cornell University Press, 1980.

Bhattacharyya, Tarapada. *The Canons of Indian Art or A Study on Vāstuvidyā*. 2d ed. Calcutta; 1963.

Bolon, Carol Radcliffe. "Evidence of Artists of the Early Calukya Period." In *Making Things in South Asia: The Role of Artist and Craftsman*. Edited by Michael W. Meister. Philadelphia: Department of South Asia Regional Studies, University of Pennsylvania, 1988.

Braudel, Fernand. "History and Social Science: *The Long Durée*." In *On History*. Chicago: University of Chicago Press, 1980, 25–54.

Breckenridge, Carol, and Peter van der Veer, ed. *Orientalism and Post-Colonial Predicaments: Perspectives on South Asia*. Philadelphia: University of Pennsylvania Press, 1993.

Brown, Percy. *Indian Architecture (Buddhist and Hindu)*. 4th ed. Bombay: D. B. Taraporevala, Sons, 1965.

Burgess, James. *Reports of the First Season's Operations in the Belgām and Kalādgī Districts, January to May 1874*, Archaeological Survey of Western India, Reports, Vol. 1, Archaeological Survey of India, New Imperial Series. London: Indian Museum, 1874.

Clifford, James. "On Orientalism." In *The Predicament of Culture: Twentieth Century Ethnography, Literature, and Art*. Cambridge, Mass.: Harvard University Press, 1988.

Cohn, Bernard C. "Regions Subjective and Objective: Their Relation to the Study of Modern Indian History." In *An Anthropologist Among the Historians and Other Essays*. Delhi and New York: Oxford University Press, 1987.

Cohn, Bernard C., and McKim Marriott. "Networks and Centers in the Integration of Indian Civilization." *Journal of Social Research* 1 (1958): 1–9.

Collyer, Kelleson. *The Hoysala Artist: Their Identity and Styles*. Mysore: Directorate of Archaeology and Museums, 1990.

Coomaraswamy, Ananda K. *The Arts and Crafts of India and Ceylon*. 1913. Reprint, New York: Farrar, Straus, 1964.

———. *History of Indian and Indonesian Art*. Leipzig: Karl W. Hiersemann, 1927; Reprint, New York: Dover Publications, 1965, 117–18.

Cousens, Henry. *The Architectural Antiquities of Western India*. London: The India Society, 1926.

———. *The Chālukyan Architecture of the Kanarese Districts*. Archaeological Survey of India, New Imperial Series, vol. 42. Calcutta: Government of India, Central Publication Branch, 1926.

———. "Chālukyan Temples." *The Journal of Indian Art and Industry* 2 (1887–88).

———. *Revised List of Antiquarian Remains in the Bombay Presidency*. Archaeological Survey of India, New Imperial Series, vols. 8 and 16.

Davis, Richard H. *Lives of Indian Images*. Princeton: Princeton University Press, 1997.

Deglurkar, G. B. *Temple Architecture and Sculpture of Maharashtra*. Nagpur: Nagpur University, 1974.

Del Bonta, Robert J. "The Hoysala Style: Architectural Development and Artists, Twelfth and Thirteenth Centuries A.D." Ph.D. diss., University of Michigan, 1978.

———. "The *Madanakais* at Belūr." In *Kalādarśana: American Studies in the Arts of India*. Edited by Joanna G. Williams. New Delhi and Oxford: IBH Publishing Co. and American Institute of Indian Studies, 1981, 27–33.

Desai, Devangana. "Puns and Intentional Language at Khajuraho." In *Kusumāñjali: New Interpretations in Indian Art and Culture*. Vol. 2. Edited by M. S. Nagaraja Rao, Delhi: Agam Kala Prakashan, 1987, 383–88.

Deva, Krishna. "Bhūmija Temples." In *Studies in Indian Architecture*. Edited by Pramod Chandra. New Delhi: American Institute of Indian Studies, 1975, 90–113.

Dhaky, M. A. "The 'Gothic' in Indian Temple Architecture." *East and West*, n.s., 24, nos. 1–2 (1974): 137–39.

———. *The Indian Temple Forms in Karnāta Inscriptions and Architecture*. New Delhi: Abhinava Publications, 1977.

———. "The Jaina Temple at Harasūr." In *Kusumāñjali: New Interpretations in Indian Art and Culture*. Vol. 1. Edited by M. S. Nagaraja Rao. Delhi: Agam Kala Prakashan, 1987, 197–200.

———. "Yōganārāyaṇa and Bālamukunda from Huvināhaḍagali." In *Studies in Indian History and Culture*. P. B. Desai felicitation volume. Edited by Shrinivas Ritti and B. R. Gopal. Dharwar: Karnatak University, 1971, 163–66.

———., ed. *The Encyclopaedia of Indian Temple Architecture: Upper Drāviḍadeśa*. New Delhi: American Institute of Indian Studies, 1996.

Dumont, Louis. "The Individual as an Impediment to Sociological Comparison and Indian History." In *Social and Economic Change (Essays in Honor of Professor D.P. Mukherjee)*. Edited by Baljit Singh and V. B. Singh. Bombay and New York: Allied Publishers, 1967, 226–48.

Fergusson, James. *History of Indian and Eastern Architecture* rev. ed. with additions by James Burgess, London: John Murray, 1910.

Filliozat, Vasundhara. *The Temple of Muktesvara at Chaudadampura: Little Known Twelfth-Thirteenth Century Temple in Dharwar District, Karnataka*. New Delhi: Indira Gandhi National Centre for the Arts and Abhinav Publications, 1995.

Fleet, John Faithfull. *The Dynasties of the Kanarese Districts of the Bombay Presidency from the Earliest Historical Times to the Musalman Conquest of A.D. 1318*. Bombay: Government Central Press, 1896.

———. *Pali, Sanskrit and Old Kanarese Inscriptions from the Bombay Presidency and Parts of the Madras Presidency and Maisur*. London: M. H. Stationery Office, 1878.

Foekema, G. M. M. "The Mallikarjuna Temple at Kuruvatti." *Aziatische Kunst*, Amsterdam, (June 1987): 8–16.

Foekema, Gerard. *Hoysala Architecture: Medieval Temples of Southern Karnataka Built During the Hoysala Rule*. New Delhi: Books and Books, 1994.

Gerow, Edwin. *A Glossary of Indian Figures of Speech*. The Hague: Mouton, 1971.

Gombrich, E. H. *Norm and Form: Studies in the Art of the Renaissance*. London: Phaidon 1966.

———. "Style." In *International Encyclopaedia of Social Sciences*. Edited by David L. Sill. New York: Macmillan, 1968–79, 15, 352–61.

Gopal, B. R. *The Chālukyas of Kalyāna and the Kalachuris*. Dharwad and Prasarang: Karnatak University, 1981.

Grabar, Oleg. *The Formation of Islamic Art*. Rev. and enl. New Haven and London: Yale University Press, 1973.

Gravely, F. H., and T. N. Ramachandran. "The Three Main Styles of Temple Architecture Recognized by the Śilpa-Śāstras." *Bulletin of the Madras Government Museum*, n.s., 7, pt. 1, rev. ed. Madras: 1962.

Hardy, Adam. "The Hindu Temple: A Dynamic Microcosm." In *Sacred Architecture in Traditions of India, China, Judaism and Islam*. Edited by Emily Lyle. Edinburgh: Edinburgh University Press, 1992, 41–57.

———. *Indian Temple Architecture: Form and Transformation. The Karṇāṭa Drāviḍa Tradition, Seventh to Thirteenth Centuries*. New Delhi: Indira Gandhi National Centre for the Arts and Abhinava Publications, 1995.

———. "Patterns of Thought and Form in Hindu Temple Architecture." *Architecture and Design* (September–October 1986): 28–38; (November–December 1986): 38–55.

Harle, J. C. *Art and Architecture of the Indian Subcontinent*. Harmondsworth, Middlesex, England, and New York: Penguin Books, 1986.

Huntington, Susan L. *The Art of Ancient India*. New York and Tokyo: Weatherhill, 1985.

Jayaswal, K. P. "Nāgara and Vesara." *Journal of the Indian Society of Oriental Art* 1 (June 1933): 57–58.

Katkar, Eswar N. "Art and Architecture of the Chālukyas of Kalyana." Ph.D. diss., Karnataka University, Dharwar, 1982.

Katti, Madhav N. "Inscriptions of the Hyderabad-Karnataka and Telangana Regions and Their Bearing on Art History." In *Indian Epigraphy and its Bearing of the History of Art*. Edited by Frederick M. Asher and G. S. Gai. New Delhi: American Institute of Indian Studies, 1985, 237–43.

Kemp, Martin. "The Taking and Use of Evidence; with a Botticellian Case Study." *Art Journal* (fall 1984): 207–15.

Kramrisch, Stella. "Artists, Patron, and Public in India." 1956. Reprinted in *Exploring India's Sacred Art: Selected Writings of Stella Kramrisch*. Edited by Barbara Stoler Miller. Philadelphia: University of Pennsylvania Press, 1983.

———. *The Hindu Temple*. 2 vols. Calcutta: University of Calcutta Press, 1946.

———. "The Temple as Puruṣa." In *Studies In Indian Temple Architecture*. Edited by Pramod Chandra. New Delhi: American Institute of Indian Studies, 1975, 40–46.

Kubler, George. *The Shape of Time: Remarks on the History of Things*. New Haven and London: Yale University Press, 1962.

———. "Style and the Representation of Historical Time." *Annals of the New York Academy of Sciences* 138 (1967): 849–855.

Lorenzen, David N. *The Kapālikas and Kālāmukhas, Two Lost Śaivite Sects*. Berkeley and Los Angeles: University of California Press, 1972.

Ludden, David. *Peasant History in South India*. Princeton: Princeton University Press, 1985.

Mallaya, N. V. "Nāgara, Drāviḍa and Vesara." *Journal of the*

Indian Society of Oriental Art 9 (1941): 81–96.

Mate, M. S., and Shobhana Gokhale. "Aihole: An Interpretation." In *Studies in Indian History and Culture*. P. B. Desai felicitation volume. Edited by Shrinivas Ritti and B. R. Gopal. Dharwar: Karnatak University, 1971, 501–4.

Matilal, Bimal Krishna. *Perception: An Essay on Classical Indian Theories of Knowledge*. Oxford: Clarendon Press, 1986.

Meister, Michael W. "Altars and Shelters in India." *AARP: Art and Archaeology Research Papers* 16 (1979): 39.

———. "Bīthū: Individuality and Idiom." *Ars Orientalis* 13 (1983): 169–86.

———. "De- and Re-constructing the Indian Temple." *Art Journal* 49.4 (winter 1990): 395–400.

———. "Forest and Cave: Temples at Candrabhāgā and Kansuāñ." *Archives of Asian Art* 34 (1981): 56–73.

———. "On the Development of a Morphology for a Symbolic Architecture: India." *Res* 12 (autumn 1986): 33–50.

———. "Prāsāda as Palace: Kūṭina Origins of the Nagara Temple." *Artibus Asiae* 59 (1988–89): 254–80.

———. "Reading Monuments and Seeing Texts." In *Shastric Traditions in Indian Arts*. Edited by Anna Libera Dallapiccola, et al. Stuttgart: Steiner Verlag Wiesbaden, 1989, 167–73.

———. "Śiva's Forts in Central India: Temples in Dakṣiṇa Kosala and Their 'Daemonic' Plans." In *Discourses on Śiva: Proceedings of a Symposium on the Nature of Religious Imagery*. Edited by Michael W. Meister. Philadelphia: University of Pennsylvania Press, 1984, 119–42.

———. "Style and Idiom in the Art of Uparamāla." *Muqarnas: An Annual on Islamic Art and Architecture* 10 (1993): 344–53.

———. "Symbol and Surface: Masonic and Pillared Wall-Structure in North India," *Artibus Asiae* 46 (1985): 129–48.

———, ed. *Cooking for the Gods: The Art of Home Ritual in Bengal*. Newark: Newark Museum, 1995.

Meister, Michael W., and M. A. Dhaky, eds. *The Encyclopaedia of Indian Temple Architecture*, 2 vols. to date. (1983–).

Miller, Barbara Stoler, ed. *The Powers of Art: Patronage in Indian Culture*. Delhi and New York: Oxford University Press, 1992.

Mirashi, Vasudev Vishnu. *Inscriptions of the Kalachuri-Chedi Era* (Corpus Inscriptionum Indicarum), 4, 2 vols. Ootacamund: Government of India, 1955.

Mitchell, W. J. T. *Iconology: Image, Text, Ideology*, Chicago: University of Chicago Press, 1986.

Mosteller, John F. "Texts and Craftsmen at Work." In *Making Things in South Asia*. Edited by Michael W. Meister. Philadelphia: Department of South Asian Regional Studies, 1988, 24–33.

Nagaraja Rao, M. S. "Aṣṭamātṛikās from Hāverī." *Bulletin of the Deccan College Research Institute* 23: 78–82.

———. "Sculpture from the Later Cālukyan Temple at Hāverī." *Artibus Asiae* 31, nos. 2, 3 (1969): 167–78.

———., ed. *The Chālukyas of Kalyāṇa: Seminar Papers*. Bangalore: Mythic Society, 1983.

Pathak, R. S. *Vakrokti and Stylistic Concepts*. New Delhi: Bahri Publications, 1988.

Patil, C. S. "Portrait Sculpture in Mahādeva Temple at Iṭṭagi." In *Kusumāñjali: New Interpretations in Indian Art and Culture*. Vol. 2. Edited by M. S. Nagaraja Rao. Delhi: Agam Kala Prakashan, 1987, 311–14.

Peirce. Charles S. "Logic as Semiotic: The Theory of Sign." In *Semiotics: An Introductory Anthology*. Edited by Robert E. Innis. Bloomington, Indiana University Press, 1985.

Pisharoti, K. R. "Nāgara, Drāviḍa and Vesara." *Indian Culture* 6 (1939–40): 23–38.

Prabhakar, M. N. "Classification of Temples—'Auttareya Drāviḍa." *The Quarterly Journal of the Mythic Society* 78, nos. 3–4 (July–December 1987): 52–62.

Prasad, B. R. "Śukanāsa in Dravidian Architecture," *Journal of the Oriental Institute Baroda*. 20 (September 1970): 62–69.

Ramesh, K. V. "Epigraphy and Indian Art and Architecture." In *Indian Epigraphy and its Bearing on the History of Art*. Edited by Frederick M. Asher and G. S. Gai. New Delhi: Oxford IBH Publishing Co. and American Institute of Indian Studies, 1985, 77–82.

Rangacharya, V. *A Topographical List of the Inscriptions of the Madras Presidency* (Collected till 1915). Vol. 1. Madras: for Bellary District, 1919, 255–320.

Rea, Alexander. *Chālukyan Architecture: Including Examples from Bellāry District, Madras Presidency*. Archaeological Survey of India, New Imperial Series, vol. 21. Madras: Superintendent, Government Press, 1896; reprint, Delhi: Indological Book House, 1970.

Saraswati, S. K. "Architecture." In *The Struggle for Empire (History and Culture of the Indian People)*. Vol. 5. Bombay: Bharatiya Vidya Bhavan, 1957, 622–34.

———. "Origin of Mediaeval Temple Styles." *Indian Culture (Journal of the Indian Research Institute)*, 8, no. 2–3 (1941–42): 183–89.

Settar, S. *The Hoysala Temples*, 2 vols. Bangalore: Kala Yatra Publications, 1992.

———. "A Study of Shrines." Review of *The Indian Temple Forms in Karnataka Inscriptions and Architecture*, by M. A. Dhaky. *The Times of India*, 9 July 1978, 10.

Sheshagiri Rao, V. N. *Vācaspati's Contribution to Advaita*. Mysore: Samvit Publishers, 1984.

Singer, Milton. "Signs of the Self: An Exploration in Semiotic Anthropology." *American Anthropologist* 82, no. 3 (September 1980): 485–507.

Sinha, Ajay J. "Architectural Invention in Sacred Structures: The Case of Vesara Temples of Southern India." *The Journal of the Society of Architectural Historians* 55, no. 4 (December 1996): 382–99.

———. "The Construction of 'Mule' in Indian Temple Architecture." *Journal of Arts and Ideas* 30–31 (December 1997): 33–62.

———. "Envisioning the Seventies and Eighties." In *Contemporary Art in Baroda*. Edited by Gulammohammed Sheikh. New Delhi: Tulika Press, 1997, 145–210.

Sontheimer, Gunter-Dietz. *Pastoral Deities in Western India*. New York and Oxford, England: Oxford University Press, 1989.

Spodek, Howard, and Doris Meth Srinivasan, eds. *Urban Form and Meaning in South Asia: The Shaping of Cities from Prehistoric to Precolonial Times*, Studies in the History of Art 31. Washington, D.C.: National Gallery of Art, 1993.

Soundara Rajan, K. V. "The Deccan and South India." *Jaina*

Art and Architecture. Edited by A. Ghosh. New Delhi: Bharatiya Jnanapith 1975.

Srinivasan, K. R. *Temples of South India* 3d rev. ed. New Delhi: National Book Trust, 1985.

Stadtner, Donald M. "Ancient Kośala and Stellate Plan." In *Kalādarśana, American Studies in the Art of India*. Edited by Joanna G. Williams. New Delhi and Oxford: IBH Publishing Co. and American Institute of Indian Studies, 1981, 137–45.

Summers, David. "On Histories of Artifacts." *Art Bulletin* (December 1994): 590–92.

Sundara, A. "Some Temples of North Dharwar District and the Hoysala Architecture." *Journal of Karnatak University* 9 (1973): 102–12.

———. "Traipuruṣa Devālayas in Inscriptions and the Related Temples in the Dharwad-Bijapur Region." In *Indian Epigraphy and its Bearing on the History of Art*. Edited by Frederick M. Asher and G. S. Gai, 203–8. New Delhi: Oxford IBH Publishing Co. and American Institute of Indian Studies, 1985.

Schwartzberg, Joseph E. "Prolegomena to the Study of South Asian Regions and Regionalism." In *Regions and Regionalism in South Asian Studies: An Exploratory Study*. Durham, N.C.: Duke University Program in Comparative Studies in South Asia, monograph no. 5, 1967.

———. (ed.). *Historical Atlas of South Asia*, reprint New York and Oxford: Oxford University Press, 1992.

Taylor, Meadows, and James Fergusson. *Architecture of Dharwar and Mysore*. London: J. Murray, 1866.

Varela Francisco J., Evan Thompson, and Eleanor Rosch. *The Embodied Mind: Cognitive Science and Human Experience*. Cambridge, Mass.: MIT Press, 1991.

Verma, O. P. *A Survey of Hemādpanti Temples in Maharashtra*. Temples of the Vidarbha Region, vol. 2. Nagpur: 1973.

Wagoner, Philip B. "Mode and Meaning in the Architecture of Early Medieval Telangana (c. 1000–1300)." Ph.D. diss., University of Wisconsin, 1986.

Williams, Joanna G. "Construction of Gender in the Paintings and Graffiti of Sigiriya." In *Representing the Body: Gender Issues in Indian Art*. Edited by Vidya Dehejia. New Delhi: Kali for Women, 1997, 56–67.

———. "From the Fifth to the Twentieth Century and Back." *Art Journal* (winter 1990): 363–69.

Winter, Irene J. "Perspective on the 'Local Style' of Hasanlu IV B: A Study in Receptivity." In *Mountains and Lowlands: Essays in the Archaeology of Greater Mesopotamia*. Edited by L. D. Lavine and T. C. Young Jr. Malibu: Undena Publications, 1977, 371–86.

Wittgenstein, Ludwig. *Culture and Value*. Edited by G. H. von Wright in collaboration with Heikki Nyman, translated by Peter Winch. Chicago: University of Chicago Press, 1980.

Workman, Fanny Bullock. "Some Little Known Chālukyan Temples." *The Journal of the Royal Asiatic Society of Great Britain and Ireland* (1904): 419–21.

Index